**W9-AQA-776**

# Faith
# Victorious

# Faith Victorious

An Introduction to Luther's Theology

*By*

LENNART PINOMAA

*Translated by*

WALTER J. KUKKONEN

Fortress Press             Philadelphia

This book is a translation from the Finnish of *Voittava usko*, published in 1959 by Werner Söderström Osakeyhtiö of Porvoo and Helsinki in Finland.

Luther, Martin - theology

Printed in U. S. A.                                        UB 1133

# Author's Preface

When as a young student at the University of Helsinki I listened to lectures in church history, I was irritated by the fact that the professor often interrupted his lectures to talk about Luther. I felt that no individual was that important. Since then I have revised my opinion completely. I now talk more about Luther than did that professor. Luther has become my fate, so to speak. I have revered him ever since Professor Ragnar Bring of Lund directed me during the winter of 1932 into the field of modern Luther study.

The present volume was not born of my own will. It is the result of an invitation I received in 1953 from the Lutheran World Federation to lecture on Luther in the United States. The next year I gave a series of lectures during the summer in the graduate school of the Chicago Lutheran Theological Seminary, in Maywood, Illinois, and in the fall at Luther Theological Seminary, in St. Paul, Minnesota. I lectured on the same subject at the University of Hamburg in Germany in the summer of 1956, and at the Ecumenical Institute in Bossey, Switzerland, in the fall of the same year.

As the substance of these lectures now appears in book form in the country where they were initially delivered, I wish to thank the United Lutheran Church in America and particularly Professor T. A. Kantonen of Hamma Divinity School, Springfield, Ohio, who was instrumental in my receiving the invitation that occasioned their preparation.

The thoughtful reader will understand that, given the abundance of material and Luther's exceedingly rich creative power, the writing of a book on Luther's theology in general is an overwhelming and demanding task. In fact, such an undertaking is possible only because of the efforts of the many scholars who have previously written on various aspects of the Reformer's life and thought. To them too I acknowledge with gratitude my indebtedness.

Not all of the original lectures are included in this volume; one chapter is entirely new, and the others have been extensively revised.

I extend my heartfelt thanks to my translator, Professor Walter J. Kukkonen of Chicago Lutheran Theological Seminary, Maywood, Illinois, for his thorough and painstaking work.

Helsinki, Finland                           LENNART PINOMAA

April, 1962

# Translator's Preface

This book is a translation of Lennart Pinomaa's *Voittava usko*, which was published in Finland in 1959 by Werner Söderström Osakeyhtiö. It has not always been possible to follow American standards in supplying bibliographical information beyond that provided in the original. Documentation may seem inadequate at times. Every attempt has been made to direct the reader to available English translations of Luther's writings as well as to the Weimar edition of his works.

The reading list compiled by the translator is not intended to be exhaustive but simply to suggest additional secondary sources in English beyond those actually quoted in the text itself.

W. J. K.

# Table of Contents

# Introduction

The Reformation is like a skyscraper which inspires awe in the man standing beside it but reveals its full majesty only to him who views it from a distance.

This is how it is with Luther and his life's work. Both have grown with the centuries. This is true of all great men; their influence never ceases. They continue to live with each generation, offering light for the way and courage for the heart.

## MARTIN LUTHER IN THE LIGHT OF HISTORY

Recent decades have seen a genuine Luther renaissance. With his faith and thought Luther has captured a more central place than ever before in Protestant theology. By "Protestant" we do not mean simply "Lutheran," for in this ecumenical era Luther's significance in all Christendom has become more and more manifest.

The reason for this has not been mere historical respect for a great man of the church, but a burning need. When Luther's words are given an unprejudiced hearing their relevance is astonishing.

It is easy to think that Luther invented certain special doctrines and then on their account left the Catholic church and established a church of his own. But he invented nothing. In despair and anguish of soul he simply delved deeper into the sacred Scriptures, deeper than many others had done before him, and there found a precious jewel, the pure gospel, God's unspeakable gift in Jesus Christ, first for himself, a struggling monk in a solitary cell, and then for others.

The newly discovered gospel gradually renewed the whole of Luther's theology. How this happened Luther himself could not explain. It is a problem with which research in the present century has grappled seriously.

Luther never offered his theology in the form of a complete system. Theologians have attempted repeatedly to do this, but the task is unrewarding, if not altogether impossible. Compilation of his "system"[1] is a task whose results depend on what the individual himself sees in Luther's world of thought. It is impossible to write two identical "theologies of Luther," and no man can demand permanent validity for his efforts. In a way the history of the study of Luther reflects the history of theology. In it each generation writes its own history, indicating what it considers theologically important.

Luther was a *lector bibliae,* a professor of biblical interpretation, as we would say. In his work he was compelled again and again to reject the traditional interpretation of his Roman Catholic church. His theology is biblical interpretation which corrects the work of earlier generations. His goal was not a complete theological system but answers to questions asked by life itself. Various concrete situations raised issues that demanded clarification and solution. The extensive literature born in this manner suggests the general features of Luther's theology.

If the thoughts of this present volume differ from those commonly held, it is due to a shift in theological emphasis and viewpoint and also to progress in the textual criticism and analysis of the source material, which represents a permanent and positive achievement of the many Luther scholars.

At the time when Ritschlianism gave way in the 1920's to Barthianism, Protestant theology came to be strongly influenced by a resurgent interest in Luther. The comprehensive polemical works of the Catholic Luther scholars Heinrich S. Denifle and Hartmann Grisar gave the initial impetus to Protestant study of Luther in the early part of our century. Joseph Lortz and Adolf Herte demolished in the 1940's the tradition of polemical Catholic study of Luther by their sympathetic attitude toward the great reformer. But twentieth-century Protestant scholars have found in Luther much more than just ammunition for refuting the Catholic critique. The results of their studies have already greatly enriched both the theology and the proclamation of the church.

At the same time, however, it has become apparent that many who looked to Luther have at crucial points drifted away from Luther. No one would dare or wish to accord him the authoritative position of a Protestant pope. Nevertheless there are many reasons to seek a fuller understanding of his teachings. Luther's purpose was not to found a new church but to restore the church of the apostles by eliminating later unbiblical accretions. When the Reformation failed in contemporary Western Christendom as a whole, conditions forced the creation of a new church. Conscious opposition to the Catholic church then became unavoidable. In his remarkably extensive writings Luther indicates in various ways what he had arisen to oppose and what the new was that he considered absolutely necessary.

Luther represents primitive Christianity a millennium and a half after the primitive Christian era. In speaking of the church he knows that he is representing the true Christian church born on Pentecost, which in the course of the centuries had become invisible because the external form of the church had taken on much that was foreign to its true nature.

Luther's best known and most important book, *The Small Catechism,* is outstandingly catholic or ecumenical. It contains not the slightest reference to the existence of a Lutheran church and not a single one of its central Christian affirmations represents a special Lutheran doctrine. For this reason any church founded on the Bible can equally well accept its chief content. In the explanation to the third article of the Creed we read: ". . . just as he (the Holy Spirit) calls, gathers, enlightens, and sanctifies the whole Christian church on earth and preserves it in union with Jesus Christ in the one true faith." Here we have an ecumenical pattern of thought without any denominational emphasis.

We meet the same broad ecumenicity in the Augsburg Confession, which represents Luther's position although it was not written

by him. Here it is noted that Christ's church is wherever the Word
is taught purely and the sacraments are administered rightly. The
church of Christ is not identified with any particular group or de-
nomination, for the perspective is wider than that. The ecumenical
program engendered and envisioned by the Reformation involves
more than simply denominational organization or ecclesiastical tradition. In the final analysis, faithfulness to the Bible is the sole
norm. To the extent that Christendom desires to build on the basic
message of the New Testament and to live by the gospel, it is
drawn to Luther, whatever the name of the particular church may
be.

Martin Luther also belongs among the great figures of history
for the further reason that his influence is not limited to the church
and theology. As a result of his life's work political maps were
changed. Yet he left the deepest tracks in the area of spiritual culture. A veritable avalanche of Bible translations was started by his
German Bible. The effect of these translations on the place of the
vernacular and on literacy in all of Western Christendom cannot
be overestimated. Culture in the broadest sense was given an in-
valuable impetus. Reform extended to education as a whole. The
reformation of university instruction which Luther accomplished
jointly with Melanchthon gives him a significant place not only
in the history of education but of Western culture at its highest
level.

Luther's influence in the life of various churches is immeasurable. In his own century he was the spiritual father of all Protestantism. The reform movements of Zwingli and Calvin received
their most important influences from him. Even Luther's mother
church, the Roman Catholic, has been compelled in numerous ways
during the centuries since the Reformation but especially in our day
to draw from the inexhaustible springs of this spiritual and intellectual giant from Thuringia.

Luther's influence has continued to grow during the past four
centuries. Today his works are coming out in new editions and
translations as never before. And today his personality and world

of thought are being interpreted more eagerly than at any other time. While the heritage of many a great man is perpetuated in the form of lofty ideas and highly developed systems, Luther's life and writings continue to inspire Protestant Christians in their daily struggle of faith. His heritage is reflected also in the world of external events, such as the continuing spread of Protestantism throughout the world. Seldom if ever has the thought, person, and lifework of one man influenced the lives of following generations in this manner.

## SOURCES

One of the problems of Luther research is the abundance rather than the paucity of source material. The productivity of Luther's fertile mind is hardly equaled in all world literature.

During his lifetime Luther published about 450 books and treatises, lectured for nearly forty years at the universities of Erfurt and Wittenberg, and wrote about 3,000 sermons and about 2,600 letters. The critical Weimar edition of his works, published since 1883, now constitutes 100 large volumes and is not yet complete. It includes of course much that Luther himself did not write but only spoke. It also incorporates thousands of pages of introductory material written by scholars. Furthermore, certain important sources are printed twice, since the published text and the manuscript text differ and scholars need both.

Inasmuch as the greater part of Luther's works have been preserved by the hands of others, a critical edition has proved indispensable. Manifestly the reports of his sermons and table talks by unknown students are not as trustworthy sources as the letters he himself wrote and the works he himself published. Before the Weimar publications such awareness was practically nonexistent, which implies that in many respects earlier studies have become almost meaningless.

Scholarship has reached a new phase also as a result of new discoveries. Particularly the earlier period of Luther's life and thought has been illumined in an entirely new way in our century. Luther's lectures on the Letter to the Romans (1515-1516) were first published in 1908, the first lectures on the Letter to the Galatians (1516) in 1918, the lectures on Hebrews (1517) in two editions in 1929, and some preliminary work on the second lectures on the Psalms (1518) in 1940.

The principles of publication of the critical edition have admittedly changed since 1883, when the great undertaking was initiated. Johann Ficker, Emanuel Hirsch, and Heinrich Rückert among others have helped mark the way for future work with their studies on the sources. The standard is being established that the publication must present all the idiosyncrasies of the manuscript. References to the Bible and the early teachers of the church must be as complete as possible. The Weimar volumes published before 1900 have proved inadequate in this respect, necessitating new editions. A new edition of the first lectures on the Psalms (1513-1516) is already in production.

When we speak of the Weimar edition as a critical edition, we do not imply that all its material is equally trustworthy. On the contrary, a critical edition requires critical use, and only such an edition makes such use possible. The available material can very easily be classified into three groups on the basis of trustworthiness:

1) Works or fragments which Luther himself prepared for publication or whose manuscripts have been preserved.

2) Dependable reports. This group includes primarily the reports of Georg Rörer.

3) Relatively undependable reports. Among them are, generally speaking, all reports except those in group two.

Scholars must base their findings on the sources of the first and second groups. The sources of group three can be used only for further collaboration.

## AREAS OF RESEARCH

Luther's spiritual heritage is studied on such a broad international front that a realistic picture of what is happening cannot be drawn with just a few lines. The best conception can be gained from the bibliographies of the *Luther-Jahrbuch* series.[2] The publications of two international congresses of Luther scholars, *Luther-forschung heute* (1958)[3] and *Luther and Melanchthon* (1961),[4] also give an idea of the extensive and diverse character of the research. The former contains bibliographies from several countries, showing that even in largely Catholic lands much serious study is given to Luther.

In the next few paragraphs attention will be called to the German and Scandinavian studies, since the writer is closest to them.

Studies in Luther have concentrated largely in five areas. The first area is the early phase of Luther's theology. Scholars are still asking about the date and content of the so-called tower experience (*Turmerlebnis*). Heinrich Bornkamm,[5] Wilhelm Link,[6] Axel Gyllenkrok,[7] Uuras Saarnivaara,[8] Carl Stange,[9] Ernst Bizer,[10] Hans Pohlmann,[11] Regin Prenter,[12] and others have discussed this problem during the past decade. The cases for an earlier and a later date have both received strong support. It has become ever clearer that the first lectures on the Psalms (1513-1515) and the lectures on Romans (1515-1516) are deeply permeated by the idea of humility. Justification through faith is not presented as clearly as in later writings. When Bizer therefore places the tower experience in a later period, it is not an easy matter to argue against him. On the other hand, serious objections to his position are bound to be raised, indeed already have been raised by Regin Prenter. Very likely the final word in this difficult issue will never be spoken. An extensive and basic study of these problems of Luther's early theology has recently been provided by Reinhard Schwarz.[13]

The second area has to do with the problem of creation, man, law, and reason. Bengt Hägglund has made a comprehensive analysis of Luther's anthropology in Swedish, and in another work has also shed light upon the relationship between Luther's theology and the Occamistic philosophy.[14] Creation, creative word, and reason have been treated recently by David Löfgren,[15] Aarne Siirala,[16] and Bernhard Lohse.[17] The problem of law has been studied by Wilhelm

Maurer,[18] Wilfried Joest,[19] Lauri Haikola,[20] F. Edward Cranz,[21] and Martin Schloemann.[22]

The third series of problems engaging the attention of Luther scholars involves the doctrine of the sacraments. The ideas of the young Luther on baptism have been discussed by Werner Jetter[23] and Wilfried Joest.[24] Greater attention has been given however to the doctrine of the Lord's Supper; Hans Grass,[25] Erwin Metzke,[26] Ragnar Bring,[27] and Carl Fr. Wisløff[28] deserve special mention here.

The fourth area of research is that centering upon the doctrines of justification and sanctification. Rudolf Hermann has devoted a major part of his significant life's work to these questions.[29] Regin Prenter,[30] Svend Lerfeldt,[31] and Axel Gyllenkrok[32] have also shed much light upon these issues.

The last area is Luther's doctrine of society and the state. Interest was heightened by the argument that Luther's views gave the initial impulse to the movement that produced Hitler. If the earthly government is completely autonomous in matters pertaining to its particular sphere and if its decisions must under all circumstances be taken as the will of God, then, according to the argument, the way is open to any form of despotism or dictatorship. Naturally such charges produced an entire literature in rebuttal. The following scholars deserve mention: Paul Althaus,[33] Ernst Kinder,[34] Gustaf Törnvall,[35] Gerhard Pfeiffer,[36] Johann Heckel,[37] Gunnar Hillerdal,[38] Philip S. Watson,[39] and Franz Lau.[40]

Many important gains have been made in the area of Luther's interpretation of the Bible. Here Heinrich Bornkamm,[41] Gerhard Ebeling,[42] and Walter von Loewenich[43] have made significant contributions. In discussing the development of the principles of biblical hermeneutics from the time of the church fathers to Luther, Ebeling shows how fundamental a change Luther brought about when he replaced allegorical interpretation with a form of interpretation that takes grammar and history seriously. We need to note too that the "theology of the cross" has proved to be a central principle that dominates the whole of Luther's theology. Walter von Loewenich[44] has shown how this principle illumines Luther's relationship to mysticism and how it helps toward a better under-standing of his whole viewpoint. The meaning of the experience of affliction and despair (*Anfechtung*) for all of Luther's theology has also become clear during recent decades. The contributors here have been Nathan Söderblom,[45] Ragnar Bring,[46] Eric Vogelsang,[47] Paul Theophil Buehler,[48] and Horst Beintker.[49]

A good picture of the research in Luther's theology is offered by the large works of the American scholars Roland H. Bainton[50] and E. G. Schwiebert.[51] German scholarship has demonstrated it-self in various areas.[52] Results of Swedish and Finnish research have been reported also in the German language.[53] The best over-all picture of research in various countries can be gained from *Luther-forschung heute* (1958).

## Chapter 1

# The Revelation of God

Luther's understanding of God's revelation is the key to his theology. What is the source of our knowledge of God? How does our knowledge of God grow? Luther gives a succinct yet exhaustive answer to the questions in his Heidelberg Disputation of 1518, in which theses nineteen and twenty read:

> 19. *Non ille digne theologus dicitur, qui invisibilia Dei per ea, quae facta sunt, intellecta conspicit:*
> 20. *Sed qui visibilia et posteriora Dei per passiones et crucem conspecta intelligit.*[1]
> (19. That person does not deserve to be called a theologian who sees the invisible things of God as they are comprehended in things which have been created [Rom. 1:20]:
> 20. He deserves to be called a theologian, however, who comprehends the visible and manifest things of God seen through suffering and the cross.)

Here is plotted the path to knowledge of God. To begin with, there is the created world. In nature we have incontestable evidence of the hidden attributes of God (*invisibilia Dei*), his power, wisdom, righteousness, goodness, and so forth. With the words *per ea, quae facta sunt* ("in things which have been created"), Luther apparently means creation or nature. There is no reason why we should not include also history and the personal life of man.[2] After all, they too are the work of God. And in principle it is immaterial whether modern man seeks to know God through study of the laws of nature or by delving into history or the depths of his own soul. All these things belong to the first article of the Creed and are instruments of what we call general revelation.

Luther does not reject in principle this way to knowledge of God. Obviously one ought to reach knowledge of God by means of

God's works. But in reality this does not happen. Luther accepts fully the factual statement of Romans 1, the appraisal of the situation in which the heathen find themselves with natural revelation: "Claiming to be wise, they become fools" (Rom. 1:22). Beholding the works of creation did not lead the heathen to knowledge of the invisible attributes of God. This way proved false. Any "theology of glory" (*theologia gloriae*) which insists on using this way is thereby passing judgment upon itself. A theology of glory cannot be true theology.

With this Luther takes up the second statement. The true theologian is he "who comprehends the visible and manifest things of God seen through suffering and the cross." The twentieth thesis is written in sharp contrast to the idea of the nineteenth, and lays the foundation for Luther's theological program. While the theologian of glory seeks to reach knowledge of God's invisible attributes by observing visible nature, the true theologian proceeds in the opposite way. Though he observes that which is visible, he does not learn to know God from nature. To him knowledge of God is given by suffering and the cross.[3]

These two theses contain Luther's concept of revelation and his sharp polemic against the theology of the Catholic church. He rejects completely all speculation. One must not meditate upon the majesty of God, for it is beyond reach. Luther has no interest in abstractions. In fact, to him they are dangerous. They are not the way in which God wants us to know him. God turns to us not with his invisible attributes but with the visible. God's revelation directs us not upward but downward, not to abstractions but to events. God has spoken; we can now speak of him. God has shown himself; we can now know where to find him.

The revelation of God is indirect. The term "manifest things of God" (*posteria Dei*) means that like Moses we see God from behind as it were. We cannot look God in the face. We know by inference, faintly.

Nor can we reach knowledge of God through his works (*ex operibus*). The way is "through suffering and the cross" (*per passiones et crucem*). In this connection Luther rejects the works of divine creation as a source of knowledge of God. He does so on the basis of Romans 1, according to which the heathen did not reach knowledge of God by beholding these works. In rejecting all theology of glory Luther exposed the common root of moralism and rationalism. To paraphrase his two theses, man can reach God neither by rational nor moral efforts. There is no ladder from earth to heaven.

This exposure of the common root of rationalism and moralism has been considered by modern theologians as one of Luther's greatest achievements. Religious speculation and work righteousness are but two expressions of the same basic aspiration to immediate, unbroken communion with God. Ethics and thirst for knowledge presuppose one another. But all aspiration to the level of God is "theology of glory."

## THEOLOGY OF THE CROSS

The opposite of such theology is the "theology of the cross." The theologian of the cross learns to know God by way of suffering and the cross. The word *opera* (works) as well the words *crux* (cross) and *passiones* (sufferings) can be interpreted in two ways. We can speak of the cross and sufferings of Christ, and of the cross and sufferings of the Christian. The two belong together, the cross of Christ and the cross of the Christian. Here too Luther follows Paul, who wrote to the Colossians: "Now I rejoice in my sufferings for your sake, and in my flesh I complete what is lacking in Christ's afflictions for the sake of his body, that is, the church" (Col. 1:24). As though the sufferings of Christ alone were not enough to open the way to knowledge of God, it is said that we too must suffer.

To Luther the cross of Christ is more than a historical event, for it demonstrates the fundamental nature of the relationship between God and man. Like a flash of lightning it illumines the life which we live. For this reason there is no relationship to God— in the sense of union with God—outside the reality of the cross of

Christ. But no one can appropriate this reality of the cross simply by trying to understand it. There is no room here for mere spectators. The cross of Christ decides the fate of the spectator. If he wants to enter into this life, he must, so to speak, sink into it with his whole being. For him the counterpart of the cross of Christ is his own cross, the cross of the Christian.

The nature of this participation in life with God also shows the antithesis between a theology of glory and the theology of the cross: the theologian of glory sees God everywhere, while the theologian of the cross sees him in the crucified Christ. True theology and true knowledge of God are in the Crucified One. There is a great difference between the two forms of "seeing." The theologian of glory comes up with flat abstractions. He sees what he wants to see. His God is in the final analysis the creation of his own thoughts, and is therefore anemic, harmless, an unreal figure from fantasy land. The God of the theologian of the cross is the Father of Jesus Christ, the holy God. He is a "consuming fire," uncompromisingly holy in his judgment of and opposition to sin, but also a gracious Father, love that embraces the sinner. This is how God reveals himself to us in Christ.

Yet we need to ask what Luther had in mind in speaking about *visibilia Dei* (the visible things of God). By means of them the theologian of the cross sees God. Luther mentions three such visible attributes: humanity (*humanitas*), weakness (*infirmitas*), and foolishness (*stulticia*).[4] This is astounding, for we look upon humanity, weakness, and foolishness as contradictions of the divine. Luther's explanation is found already in his first lectures on the Psalms. He speaks of the antithesis between divine and human thought. What God condemns, man chooses; and what God chooses, man condemns. This is evident in the cross of Christ.[5]

Man has been given only an indirect approach to knowledge of God. God reveals himself in hiddenness, and he has seen fit to hide himself in humility and the shame of the cross. Even as he reveals himself God remains hidden.

For this reason Luther says of the theologian of glory that he sees what he has comprehended (*intellecta conspicit*) and of the theologian of the cross that he comprehends what he has seen (*conspecta intelligit*). The theologian of glory sees in nature the product of his own mind, but the theologian of the cross looks upon the cross of Christ and from it receives his understanding. He sees the revelation of God as hidden, but grasps it in faith. Theology of the cross is theology of faith: "We live in the hiddenness of God (*in abscondito Dei*), solely in trust in his mercy."[6]

The whole program of the theology of the cross, as Walter von Loewenich points out, rests firmly on Paul, who in Romans 1 rejects the immediate way to knowledge of God and in I Corinthians 1 and 2 outlines the program of the theology of the cross. Paul's appointment was to preach the gospel, but not in words of wisdom lest the cross of Christ be nullified. Among the Corinthians he was determined to know only Jesus Christ and even him as crucified (I Cor. 2:2).

God reveals himself only to him who believes, that is, to him who struggles and suffers, wills and decides. There is no such thing here as the pain-free stance of a spectator.

God in his providence leads man to open himself to the revelation of the cross of Christ. One might think that in this respect the idealist has the advantage over the materialist. But idealism is often allied with a self-centered moralism that has no need for God and blocks the way to the cross. In Jesus' day it was the public sinners who repented and opened themselves to the gospel, while the learned, the good and the eminent did not. The revelation contains an offense. The way to God is equally long for all.

## REVELATION MEDIATED BY CREATION

In the knowledge of Christ and God we must start where Christ himself started, from "the mother's womb," from humanity.[7] Luther left behind completely that theology of Bonaventura and Dionysius the Areopagite, which sought to arrive at the state of ecstasy by way of contemplation and speculation. Concerning Bonaventura he says: "He nearly drove me crazy."[8]

Over against all forms of speculation and ecstasy Luther, as a theologian and preacher of the gospel, wanted to know only Christ, first as man and then as Son of God. But since the Bible alone mediates to us the knowledge of Christ, theology is essentially interpretation of the Bible. Christ lives in the Word and comes to us by means of the Word. But the Bible and "life" must not be set against each other, for the Bible was born in the midst of life. Biblical interpretation is interpretation of life and reality. Here we are confronted by creation. In our attempt to interpret the Word we cannot neglect the richness and diversity of created reality which, as the work of God, declares the wisdom, dominion, and power of the Creator.

The reality of life occupied a prominent place already in the theology of the church fathers. But their understanding of creation differed from that of our scientifically trained generation. Irenaeus taught that the continuous growth of man is the continuing creation of God. He regarded the effective power in physical development not as a biological energy—as it is to our age—but as the ongoing creative activity of God. It was from this standpoint that the early church read I Corinthians 15. There Paul speaks of the grain of wheat to which God gives growth, namely, "a body as he has chosen." The whole biological world grows and develops by the power of God's creative will and not by its own vegetative power.[9]

Basically this is also Luther's view of creation. He understands providence as ongoing creation, for the created world could not exist unless it were constantly renewed by the Creator.[10] The creation is neither self-sufficient nor self-sustaining but depends upon the power of God's Word by which alone it is preserved and sustained. God continues to speak, and by the power of his Word all things exist, live, and function.[11] The Word of God differs from the word of man precisely at the point of effectiveness: "What God says, he does."[12]

Against deistic opinions Luther emphasizes that God has not left his creatures on their own. He provides each creature with its daily needs.[13] Living in this manner from God's hand, the creation also functions as a divine instrument. It serves God in the execution of the judgments of his wrath. The wrath of God then is not really in God but in nature. By his direction and command nature punishes the ungodly.[14] The saying "God helps the strongest" points to this thought of God working through nature. When a ruler is victorious in war, it is God who has used him to put down another. When a wolf eats someone or when some other misfortune occurs, the same thing has happened: the creation has fulfilled God's will.[15] In all this there is unquestionably a trace of the thought that God is actively present in all things, and yet it is not pantheism. The whole of Luther's theology testifies to his constant struggle to cling to a personal God. In this very connection he urges that even the acts of nature, for all that, are not the proper works of God. He cannot be truly known from them, for natural powers are involved in them, so that God's own works cannot demonstrate their proper effect.[16] Creation is not a "pure" instrument in God's hand, and for this reason God cannot use it to perform his proper work. In nature the works of God are veiled. However, because of man's unbelief, this veiling is grace; for the more clearly God reveals himself, the more hardened unbelievers become. The Pharaoh of Egypt is a case in point. God offered him not evil but good. But all the words and works of God had an evil effect.[17] From man's side God's words and works presuppose faith, without which the best gifts of God result only in evil.

The powers of nature, as we know them, are therefore ambiguous. For this reason God cannot be known from creation. To Luther it is self-evident that the Bible does not provide instructions for legislation and governmental functions, since all laws are the product of human wisdom and reason. Thus it is not justice that has given birth to human wisdom; wisdom has its origin in the creative activity of God.[18] Reason says that adultery and murder are improper works. These commandments are written into nature. But so foolish and blind are we that we do not see and know them.[19]

The significance of creation as a reflector of God's will is nevertheless not small at all. In a sense the will of God can be read in nature and human reason. This might lead to consideration of creation as a secondary form of revelation. A deep gulf would then be fixed between the subject matter of the first article of the Creed and that of the second and third articles. Such a possibility was quite remote for Luther and the teachers of the early church. Both Christ and the Holy Spirit participated in creation,[20] with the result that matters pertaining to natural life are sacred. Raising of children, love of wife, and obedience to rulers are fruits of the Spirit. By labeling these matters carnal the papists demonstrated their ignorance about creation.[21] Here is the source of Catholic double morality.

It is not a simple matter to believe that fallen creation is the gift of God.[22] True understanding of creation is, to Luther's way of thinking, the goal and not the starting point of the exercise of faith. Creation as the revealer of God's will therefore does not represent a lower form of revelation. Sarcastically Luther states that people everywhere are finding it a simple thing to believe that God created heaven and earth. Only he himself and a few sinners and fools like Moses, David, Isaiah, and others consider God wonderful and his creation a pure miracle. He himself has barely made a beginning in such faith, and so he must marvel that some of his contemporaries, needing only a whiff of some book, know in no time at all everything that the Holy Spirit knows.[23]

Here Luther touches the most difficult problem of his theology, the problem to which he devoted most of the book which he considered his most important, *The Bondage of the Will.* The God who is active in creation is the same God who comes to us in Christ.[24] Erasmus denied the omnipotence of God and his effective working in all things; he limited the area of God's activity to the inner life of the believers. According to Luther this makes faith unnecessary, and God the product of man's imagination.

Luther sees the possibilities of natural man in terms of this either-or: either he is aware of the law and, being ignorant of God's grace, falls into despair, or he is unaware of the law and becomes proud, despising God's wrath.[25] Natural man therefore either comprehends the lawful order of creation, or considers the punitive righteousness of God as foolishness. In the former instance he takes it as impossible that God should come to man in Christ; in the latter he rejects natural revelation. In both instances he creates for himself an imaginary God. The real mystery of faith, according to Luther, consists in being able to accept both natural revelation and the revelation in Christ.

God preserves his holiness and inviolability in creation by veiling himself as the hidden God. Luther writes:

> It now remains for someone to ask: Why then does God not cease from that movement of omnipotence by which the will of the ungodly is moved to go on being evil, and to grow worse? The answer is: this is to desire that for the sake of the ungodly God should cease to be God; for you are desiring that His power and activity should cease—that is, that he should cease to be good, lest the ungodly should grow worse!
>
> Why then does he not alter those evil wills which he moves? This question touches on the secrets of his Majesty, where "His judgments are past finding out" (cf. Rom. 11:33). It is not for us to inquire into these mysteries, but to adore them. If flesh and blood take offense here, and grumble, well, let them grumble; they will achieve nothing; grumbling will not change God! And however many of the ungodly stumble and depart, the elect will remain (cf. John 6:60 ff.).[26]

Luther does not hold the notion common even among Protestants that the revelation in nature can be understood by reason, and only the revelation in Christ presupposes faith. It is precisely nature that is filled with miracles which reason cannot comprehend. The activity of God in creation provides innumerable opportunities for offense. And yet all mankind has been endowed by nature with reason, to make possible everywhere the establishment of societies, families, and states. The areas of reason and faith are not mutually exclusive in Luther's theology as we sometimes think.

To Luther it is self-evident that the world must be governed and taken care of by reason. The whole of human life is subject to reason, for man differs from the beast precisely because of his mind.[27] In a sense even matters of faith are to be appropriated by reason, since all spiritual appropriation presupposes understanding. On the other hand, however, Luther calls reason *Hure Vernunft* (adulterous reason), because reason seeks to create its own ethos and religion. This happens whenever reason accepts only law, that is, creation and causality, or divorces itself completely from creation and makes God the God only of the inner life and religion. Man then has *einen erdichteten Gott* (an imaginary God), since his knowledge of God does not originate in the reality provided by God.

Luther's theology is solidly anchored in reality. It is throughout an interpretation of reality, reality represented both by creation and by Christ (that is, the Word). These must not be separated into two realities, for Christ was present already in creation, and the same God comes to us both in creation and in Christ. The difference between general and special revelation becomes relative and meaningless, and the touchstone of faith remains trust in the God who is near in various ways.

Luther's conception of God's revelation involves a serious problem which has to do with the role of creation. On the one hand, natural revelation is denied; on the other hand, it is granted considerable significance. Coming from the hand of God, creation bears witness to the Creator. One ought to rely on the knowledge it mediates. But since we know only a fallen creation, our knowledge of God through it is imperfect. It is necessary to distinguish in creation between what is God's will and what is sin. The created world is a reality for which God is responsible; this we must neither ignore nor deny. Our only alternative is to try, in the constant struggle of faith, to distinguish between the will of God and sin.

Reason desires a clear answer to the question of the boundary between the knowledge of God mediated by creation and the knowledge mediated by the Word. The insights of Luther's theology declare such an answer impossible. God reveals and hides himself in creation. But God also reveals and hides himself in Christ's lowliness.

The revelation of God can reach us only within the bounds of our human limitations and imperfections. Luther was able to distinguish between the light of nature, the light of grace, and the light of glory. To him all were God's lights. The light of nature by no means illumines everything, but it was never intended that man should depend wholly upon it. In this life we have also the light of grace, but it too does not clarify all mysteries. Only the light of glory on the other side will provide us with answers to the ultimate questions.[28]

## Chapter 2

# The Concept of God

Interpretation of the Christian concept of God is the central task of theology. The concept of God determines a theologian's understanding of the Christian faith. Luther's concept of God bristles with difficulties, for it is unusually alive and full of tension—though reflecting deep peace—and the book commonly referred to in discussion of it, *The Bondage of the Will,* is intentionally polemical.

Throughout the history of Christendom men with diverse backgrounds have formulated and expressed the Christian idea of God in various ways. In Greek thought God is an absolute, the "unmoved mover" of all that moves. He represents always the same form of being: dispassionate peace. The God of the Old Testament, on the other hand, is angry, punishes, repents, and loves. The teachers of the ancient church faced the task of making these biblical concepts vital in a world dominated by Greek culture. People accustomed to the Greek way of thinking could not accept preaching that endowed "ideas" with erupting emotions. Such proclamation was utter nonsense. The victory of Christianity in this seemingly unequal conflict is an indication of its strength. The destruction of Rome and the establishment of new nations in areas dominated by the ancient culture for thousands of years signaled a change also in thought patterns. But the Renaissance brought back the ancient culture, even as Thomas Aquinas had restored Aristotle to his position of honor. The conflict between Aristotelian logic and the biblical form of thought is still with us. The central concepts of the Bible simply cannot be squeezed into the mold of Aristotelian logic. Hence the conflict between reason and faith. The influence of the fundamental antithesis of our culture, that between Hellenism and Christianity, ancient Greece and Palestine, is felt particularly in the concept of God. The perennial question of doubters and enemies: Since the world is so imperfect can God be both loving and almighty? touches the central nerve of our faith, its deepest feelings.

Luther's concept of God, while tension-filled, is not confused. Emanuel Hirsch is right when he says:

> Luther's concept of God is not only the most vital and most exactly defined but also the clearest and most consistent that Christian theology in general has produced. In the course of history it has come to only partial expression in his church, and that in a weakened form. This is the tragic ailment of our evangelical Christianity to this day.[1]

Hirsch goes on to say:

> When we understand Luther's view of God we understand the whole Luther. This is not so only because piety in general is most powerfully expressed in its concept of God. It is part of Luther's unique greatness that his faith is in a very special measure God-centered.[2]

### THE RELIGION OF GOD—THE RELIGION OF MEN

Broadly speaking, Luther's reformation activity had but one really vital interest. It set the "religion of God" over against the "religion of men." The latter, human religiosity, has existed at all times and among all peoples. Human thoughts and ideas have determined what God demands of men and what forms of worship he approves. Luther recognizes that nature beckons us to call on God for help, and that even the heathen do this much. He insists, however, that such worship leads completely astray from the true God. The incarnation of Christ produced a fundamental change in the realm of religion, upsetting all ancient forms and patterns. Now we are no longer to ask God what we can do, how religious we must become, how humbly we must pray, or what difficult pilgrimages we must undertake. The question is quite different: what has God done for us? Religion, our relationship to God, centers now in God's work—"God was in Christ reconciling the world to himself"

(II Cor. 5:19)—and can even be called God's religion. It was because this was something altogether new that Christ met with such opposition. Even within Christendom attempts have been made to change the act of God in Christ to conform to the ancient forms. The gospel has been reworked into a form of the religion of the law.

The gospel is God's gift in Christ. The righteousness of the law binds the God-relationship to the obedience demanded by the law. When righteousness as a gift and righteousness as a demand are combined, the gospel becomes a duty, and fulfillment of the law a relatively simple matter. The law and gospel, though incompatible, are mixed, with the result that the gospel is lost. At this point Paul and Luther faced the same task. Both had to show the way from the righteousness of the law to the pure gospel, that is, from the religion of men to the religion of God, from human efforts and work to the reception of God's gift.

With his ingenious insights Luther was able to uncover natural religiosity in its many subtly inviting forms. Deeply rooted human pride is unwilling to accept God's gift. Man offers God his own religiosity and worship, his prayers and religious rites. In his conflict with God's religion—that is, with the gospel, God's gift— man finds an ally in reason. Self-sufficient man supposes that with the help of reason he can know what God is like, what he wants, and what his power, goodness, and eternity are like. Such ideas, however, simply reflect the yearnings of the soul and are spiritual idolatry. Man, says Luther, then trusts in "man's god." The rich man who trusts in his riches and the wise man who trusts in his wisdom are both idolaters. Against such idolatry, of which the world is full, stands the first commandment. In stressing faith in God the first commandment speaks of the fountainhead of all faith, humanity, wisdom, and knowledge. It labels all confidence in human ideas as sin. Trust in self is distrust of God. This is unbelief, the fountain and root of all sin. Alongside God's religion man's religion is only sin.

The first commandment, "I am the Lord your God. You shall

have no other gods before me," is to Luther first of all law, for it contains a command. But it is also gospel, for the introductory words are: "I am the Lord your God."

As we study Luther's inner struggle we see how this commandment becomes gospel to him. In the depths of despair no word of comfort was able to help him. His heart argued that the good God was for other people, not for his kind. Man must be better, more perfect than he was. But where the word of comfort failed, the word of law succeeded. The declaration "I am the Lord your God" took on new meaning: "Unless you take me as your God you are a lawbreaker! I command you: put your trust only in me!" It is anguish and affliction (*Anfechtung*) that teach obedience to this commandment.[3]

In delving into the central issues of Luther's theology we deal always with the experience of affliction or torment. Luther was an afflicted and tortured man as few have been in the history of Christendom. He was constantly aware of the living presence of God. This explains his tremendous effectiveness when he speaks of God. It also explains the peculiar power of his decisions and actions. In all things he felt that he was dealing with God and doing his work. For Luther an inexhaustible fountain was concealed in the thought and the constant experience: God sees me, God speaks to me.

Luther's afflictions and torments in the monastery cannot be traced to particular causes, such as a false conception of confession, morbid thoughts concerning predestination, and so forth. In the final analysis they point to one general cause: the ever-present God who judges all sin, the righteous God before whom nothing human can stand. Luther himself says that, standing before God, man would like to flee but knows that he can not. This is the reason for the unending affliction. Thousands upon thousands before and after Luther have been familiar with such affliction, but it is doubtful whether anyone has taken up the struggle with such seriousness and drawn its full implications as Luther did.

## THE ACTIVE GOD

The chief characteristic of this struggle is the activity of God and the passivity of man. The mainspring of this kind of piety is not man's need, but God's. It is God who in his judgment and his grace is seeking man. With the living presence of God as the center of faith, judgment is experienced in a vital and deep sense. Man is led to seek what belongs to God, not what belongs to himself. It is impossible to reject all religious eudaemonism more completely than Luther does.

All the experiences of the human heart spoke to Luther of divine judgment, but in the holy Word he found divine grace. For this reason the objectivity of the Word was to him of supreme importance; it was a necessity of life. The fact that in the Word he found the God of grace explains the rhythm of Luther's life of faith, the rhythm of judgment and grace. Before God Luther stood as a sinner and as a righteous man (*simul iustus et peccator*). His religion had room for nothing besides this twofold understanding of God's work: God judges and God pardons. Judgment is his "strange work" (*opus alienum*), and pardon is his "proper work" (*opus proprium*).[4] Each man has a hell in his conscience, says Luther. And heaven he describes thus: "This is what it means to be blessed, when God rules in us and we are his people."[5]

God's activity was an essential aspect of Luther's concept of God. Comparable was the decisive significance of his view of the glory of God as the chief motive of both faith and prayer. We glorify God when we take him at his word. In his activity God protects his own honor. His activity is the best revelation of the fullness of his grace and power. For this reason the believer must give constant attention to God's works. These works move along two main lines, the line of almighty power and the line of grace which seeks sinners.

Divine omnipotence colors everything that Luther says. To him omnipotence includes the idea that it is God who works all in all. Were it not for God's almighty power everything would collapse into nothing. Even the will of man has its origin in the fact that

God is active and effective everywhere and in everything. Creation can set no bounds for God's activity.

Inasmuch as this divine power that works all in all produces both good and evil, God as the Almighty One is beyond our comprehension; he is the hidden God, *Deus absconditus.* Yet even his hiddenness can lead us to trust in him, for though we fall from heaven and earth and though all creation become as nothing, we would still be in his hands.[6]

## GOD'S HOLINESS AND LOVE

God is omnipotent, but he is also good. In saying this we rely on the revelation of the Word. We cannot learn of God's goodness from nature, or from history, or from our own heart. Luther musters words upon words to describe this goodness of God revealed through the Word. God is holy, righteous, promoter of peace, free, and full of goodness. Two features are dominant: righteousness and truth. God is wholly good. In relationship to creation this goodness appears as holiness, as self-imparting goodness. What God possesses he shares with his creatures. In Christ he gives us his own divine being, which is love.

At this point Luther combines the first and second articles of the Creed. God's holiness and love belong inseparably together, even as creation and redemption. God reveals himself in his awesome holiness and in his attractive love. One of the strongest pillars of Luther's faith was the unchangeableness of God. God's love too is unchangeable. It is eternal and sure (*ewig und fest*). Here evangelical faith clearly departs from the Catholic. According to the latter God is and acts toward us as we are and act toward him; man receives grace only for purposes of response. Luther teaches that God's grace in Christ remains unchanged even though we may depart from it. Grace existed before the world was founded, it is now, and it will continue forever. Human fickleness, transitoriness, and untrustworthiness cannot affect God's attitude.

The all-embracing activity of God forms the basis for everything else. No matter what overtakes man in this life, whether sin or guilt or assaults (*Anfechtungen*) upon his faith, all things are in the good and gracious providence of God. Luther knows nothing of the quiet God of Greek thought. For Luther God is always active, and his activity is basically gracious.

Here we are at the juncture of two main lines in Luther's view of God. God is the free, sovereign Lord, absolutely good in his being; as its creator God rules the world. At the same time God is goodness itself; he loves each of his creatures with everlasting love. The fact that Luther is able to combine these two conflicting lines of thoughts is one of the most magnificent accomplishments of his concept of God.

To Luther the God who justifies is the heart of everything. If as the Lord of the universe God is a distant God, here as the God of justification he must come very close. In the Word he comes so close that we can comprehend him. He opens his heart. A wide gulf indeed remains between what we comprehend of his unsearchable will and what we meet in his Word. In a sense God remains beyond this gulf even in his Word. He is and continues to be outside our realm of experience. The content of the Word goes contrary to our reason, which is always an enemy of faith. In Luther's theology the thought that God is greater than we is fundamental. God judges us. He is the Lord; we are but creatures. Luther never could rid himself of this overwhelming thought.

Albrecht Ritschl and his school were never able to take seriously Luther's talk about God's wrath; to them such talk was virtually medieval superstition. In this respect theology has since made a complete turnabout. God's wrath and judgment now represent a reality that has its own peculiar function. God lets us know how far we are from him. Because of our uncleanness and hardness of heart we are an abomination to him. The judgment of his wrath also demonstrates that power belongs to him and that there is no escape from his hands.

This punitive wrath has a twofold effect. It drives us to despair. We cannot help ourselves, nor can we fulfill the demands of God. In fact, the demands of God multiply our sin. We discover that our will in its innermost being is contrary to God. We hate God, wishing that he and his law would cease to exist. Deep down within us there is something that would destroy God. Having discovered that, we now see the true meaning of God's wrath. He indeed judges us, and we are sinners. Nevertheless this judgment is grace, for in it God comes to us. In experiencing God's wrath man has already received forgiveness of sins, for God has already received the sinner to himself. Feelings of hatred to the contrary, we acknowledge that God is right. We know that his law is holy and good. Our misfortune is that we are not in harmony with what we know to be holy and good. We experience a conflict between what actually rules in us and what ought to rule.

Luther never surrendered the basic thought that God is not a God of wrath and judgment but a God of love. "God is the very beginning and source of pure love." In describing the infinite goodness and mercy of God Luther's rich vocabulary becomes most expressive. God forgives; he receives sinners without any conditions attached. On this forgiveness everything else depends. True, in forgiving God does not forget that we are sinners and therefore unworthy. But in receiving us to himself he simultaneously justifies us. His grace is a grace that sets us aside for him and for his use.

As we trace Luther's concept of God we move from the cosmic starting point to the central areas of justification and sanctification. After all, Luther's concept of God is unified, however much it appears at times to break in two. Some theologians insist that its cosmic aspects point in another direction than its features of grace and love. But it is difficult to understand how Luther could have accomplished his task as a reformer of the faith, if his theology had been involved in inner conflict at such a central point. Would it have been possible for Luther to be the greatest preacher of the gospel since Paul, if the foundation on which he built had been cracked?

## Chapter 3

# The All-Embracing Activity of God

The thought that it is God who works all in all is perhaps the most difficult of Luther's thoughts and involves his whole theology. Luther treated it extensively in his book *The Bondage of the Will* which in his own estimation was one of his two most significant books, the other being the *Catechism*.[1] *The Bondage of the Will* has caused more dissension and given rise to a greater diversity of interpretation than anything else Luther wrote. To understand Luther, particularly his concept of God, we need to understand this book.

The present day reader finds little of immediate interest in *The Bondage of the Will* and for many reasons. Perhaps he dislikes the polemics of the book. Perhaps he cannot agree with Luther on the content of the book and fails to see why Luther held it in such high esteem. In these times of political unrest, however, certain central theological issues have become relevant once more, among them the question of the freedom of the will, the question with which this book is concerned. Before we discuss its treatment of this question, we need to say a word or two about the origin of the book.

The Reformation may have appeared at first to be a by-product of humanism. Luther's attitude toward Rome was quite similar to that of the humanists. Gradually however he showed himself to be far less compromising than the humanists in this regard. In 1524 an actual break occurred between Luther and Erasmus, the leader of the humanists. As early as 1520 Luther had touched on the question of the freedom of the will.[2] Erasmus thus had occasion to write in defense of this freedom. He needed an appropriate topic in order to announce publicly that he had no intention of following Luther on the road away from Rome. Luther felt compelled to answer Erasmus and to discuss the problem once more. The result was *The Bondage of the Will,* which came out in 1525.[3]

In the discussion of this complex problem we must not take sides in advance. It would be an error to suppose that Luther's piety was more genuine and profound than that of Erasmus. In the Reformation movement there was sincere, true piety on all sides. Luther and Erasmus were by nature opposites. Surprisingly, in this particular debate both were out of character. The man of decision and action and readiness to fight argued for the bondage of the will, while the contemplative theoretician, who avoided final decisions and all conflict as much as possible, sought to defend at least a form of "free will."[4]

Erasmus was a typical representative of European culture. He was convinced that true humanism could be reached by way of culture, by means of classical learning, and that it would lead to good will among people and world peace. Erasmus was the great pacifist of his day. His fear was that the religious controversies of the Reformation would disturb the study of classical literature. For other reasons too he looked upon the Reformation as a calamity. It's spirit and inner nature escaped him completely. He had grown up among the Brethren of the Common Life and had been greatly influenced by the Catholic reform movement known as *Devotio Moderna.* He found it difficult to distinguish between early Christianity and ancient culture. Cultivation of the "inner man" was for Erasmus the chief thing in piety. Such cultivation issued in a struggle against the "flesh."[5]

Luther respected Erasmus. He had found the humanists' knowledge of classical literature to be of great help in the linguistic study of the Bible. A reliable knowledge of antiquity aided in understanding the meaning of the biblical word forms and freed one from forced allegorical interpretations. Yet Luther's criticism of Erasmus was decidedly negative. He thought this pioneer of European culture was a superficial man, quite ignorant of the actual content of the Christian faith. Already in 1517 Luther remarked that in reading Erasmus he found his liking for the man decreasing daily, because Erasmus did not give sufficient emphasis to Christ and to the grace of God.[6]

The debate between these two men on the freedom of the will, which shook the entire Reformation movement, had nothing to do with the psychological problem of man and his potentialities. The crucial issue was salvation. Ultimately the issue was the greatness and glory of the Divine Majesty. In this debate Luther's concept of God is set forth in broader and more powerful lines than in any of his other writings.

### THE LORD OF ALL

Without the broad dimensions of the first article of the Creed, without the greatness of creation, our God would be small and powerless. As Creator he is Lord of all. Here faith finds a sure foundation. But here is also the offense of offenses. Is God also the creator of the wickedness that flourishes so abundantly in this world?

In his debate with Erasmus Luther fixed his attention on the biblical statement concerning creation: "And God saw everything that he had made, and behold, it was very good" (Gen. 1:31). Luther says:

> If you want the words "they were very good" to be understood of God's works after the Fall, you will notice that the words were spoken with reference, not to us, but to God. It does not say: "Man saw what God had made, and it was good." Many things seem, and are, very good to God which seem, and are, very bad to us. Thus, afflictions, sorrows, errors, hell, and God's best works are in the world's eyes very bad, and damnable. What is better than Christ and the gospel? But what is there that the world abominates more? How things that are bad for us are good in the sight of God is known only to God and to those who see with God's eyes, that is, who have the Spirit.[7]

Here the door of human understanding is bolted and barred. In matters of God very little credit is given to the wisdom of man. Even more offensive and difficult was the other Bible passage that

Luther introduced into the discussion: "The Lord hardened the heart of Pharaoh" (Exod. 9:12).

When God "hardens the heart," as the Bible puts it, this is indeed an evil thing. Luther felt at this point too that it is best simply to accept the word of the Bible, inasmuch as divine action cannot be expressed in human words. Nevertheless, to please reason and human foolishness, he would be so daft as to try somehow to influence reason with his quivering words.

To begin with, it is clear that the activity of God is all-embracing (I Cor. 12:6). This is true even in regard to Satan and the ungodly. Luther uses the illustration of a horse and rider. The skill of the rider is always the same, but when the horse is badly shod and lame the riding comes off poorly, whereas with a sound horse it comes off well.

> Here you see that when God works in and by evil men, evil deeds result; yet God, though he does evil by means of evil men, cannot act evilly himself, for he is good, and cannot do evil; but he uses evil instruments, which cannot escape the impulse and movement of his power. The fault which accounts for evil being done when God moves to action lies in these instruments, which God does not allow to be idle. In the same way a carpenter would cut badly with a saw-toothed axe.[8]

But why does God not cease driving the wicked into wickedness and thus making them even more wicked? Luther answers:

> This is to desire that for the sake of the ungodly God should cease to be God; for you are desiring that his power and activity should cease— that is, that he should cease to be good, lest the ungodly should grow worse! Why then does he not alter those evil wills which he moves? This question touches on the secrets of his Majesty, where "his judgments are past finding out" (cf. Rom. 11:33).[9]

According to some scholars Luther is here speaking of two Gods.[10] His concept of God, in other words, lacks unity at this point. With good and evil alike having their source in God, the activity of God would be altogether confused and indiscriminate. But if the divine activity were indecisive or ambiguous that would of course preclude all talk about the divine will of love.

One must exercise extreme caution in concluding that Luther's concept of God lacks unity, and that in his innermost being Luther's God is indifferent. If that were true how could we explain Luther as a man of faith, a reformer who made faith central? Would not the Reformation which emphasized faith have meant instead the destruction of faith? In an internationally recognized work Luther's contribution to the history of the Christian idea of love is described as a "Copernican revolution," on the grounds that since the days of the early church no one has carried through the God-centered idea of love so wholly and consistently as Luther.[11]

In Luther's fundamental view it is clear that God cannot sin.[12] God cannot do evil.[13] We cannot argue then that for Luther the activity of God was marked by indifference. Luther's thoughts should be compared with Isaiah 55:9 and Romans 11:33-36. For the sake of God's honor Luther must insist that all human thought and wisdom is inadequate. God's greatness demonstrates its majestic qualities in the midst of human weakness and incompetence. To explain what he means Luther resorts to imagery, giving the illustrations of the lame horse and the dull ax. These images are intended to show that the cause of evil cannot be in God but must be in the "instruments" he uses. Coming from God the action is good, in sinful instruments, however, it becomes evil. But how does it happen that the good action of God produces evil results in some people?

## GOD DOES NOT WORK EVIL

To this question Luther gives a satisfying answer. He says that God offered his word and work to Pharaoh but the evil will of Pharaoh was offended.[14] This is precisely the way God's law works on unrepentant sinners always and everywhere. So universal is this biblical truth with respect to the law that we see nothing strange or offensive in it. The law reveals the evil bent of man's will but cannot alter it.[15] It is in this sense that what is good becomes, under certain circumstances, evil. Like the law, God too works either good or evil. The "strange work" and the "proper work" of God go hand in hand. As the holy God he can only go on offering his word and work, even though man's wicked attitude causes them to bring about a hardening of heart. God's good action is turned into judgment because man's ungodly antagonism toward God remains unchanged, and as such is under God's judgment. The continuing activity of God cannot leave man untouched; unless it achieves its true purpose of repentance, faith, and new life, it inevitably results in further hardening of heart.

The activity of God is therefore not indefinite. It is holy and as such well defined. *The Bondage of the Will* is informed with a strong dualistic-dramatic view of life: God and Satan are engaged in conflict.[16] This conflict is over man's will which, like a "stupid beast" (Ps. 73:22), is ridden either by God or Satan.[17] The human lack of will is but an aspect of Luther's conception of the will. This lack reflects man's dependence upon superior powers.[18] Man is a created being, called to stand in homage before his Creator.

Medieval theology had talked about God's "ordered sovereignty" *(potentia ordinata)*, a concept Luther wanted to reject because of its association with the idea of merit. One of the leading thoughts of *The Bondage of the Will* is that no transaction between man and God is possible within the framework of justice. The idea of merit is a contradiction of God's omnipotence. In regard to man's salvation God has "absolute sovereignty" *(potentia absoluta)*, a sovereignty which manifests itself as pure grace *(sola gratia)*.[19] The power and activity of God which Luther had in mind was neither indefinite nor unknown, but definite and known: God judges and saves. At this point Luther broke away from nominalistic theology.

Luther's pointed statements about God's all-embracing activity are not speculative or theoretical theology; they rise out of a religious concern: man's pride and self-exaltation must be knocked to the ground. Man is nothing and can decide nothing. Luther is not repeating a medieval philosophical notion, neither is he exaggerating when he stresses the universality of God's working. He is pressing a religious truth of first importance. Faith is faith in God's all-powerful and all-embracing activity.[20] Salvation has no other guarantee.

## Chapter 4

# Predestination

The contrast between the true Luther and the traditional Luther is sharpest at the point of the understanding of free will. The issue has to do with the matter of preparation for grace *(dispositio ad gratiam)*. Is there anything man can do to prepare himself to receive God's grace? In answering this question negatively Luther wrote in *Assertio omnium articulorum* (1520), referring to the Pope: "You argue that free will can prepare for the reception of grace, but Christ says contrariwise that such a thing is rejected, increasing the distance between man's possibilities and grace."[1] This same thought is expressed repeatedly in *The Bondage of the Will*. The very opening statement of purpose itself is significant. In the first part of the book Luther quotes Erasmus' definition of free will: "I conceive of 'free will' in this context as a power of the human will by which a man may apply himself to those things that lead to eternal salvation, or turn away from the same."[2] Concerning this definition Luther says:

> Erasmus informs us, that "free will" is a power of the human will which can of itself will and not will the word and work of God, by which it is to be led to those things that exceed its grasp and comprehension. If it can will and not will, it can also love and hate; and if it can love and hate, it can in a measure keep the law and believe the gospel. For, if you can will and not will, it cannot be that you are not able by that will of yours to do some part of a work, even though another should prevent your being able to complete it. Now, since death, the cross, and all the evils of the world, are numbered among the works of God that lead to salvation, the human will will thus be able to will its own death and perdition. Yes, it can will all things when it can will the contents of the word and work of God! What can be anywhere below, above, within or without the word and work of God, except God himself? But what is here left to grace and the Holy Ghost? This is plainly to ascribe divinity to "free will!" For

to will the law and the gospel, not to will sin, and to will death, is possible to divine power alone, as Paul says in more places than one (cf. I Cor. 2:14; II Cor. 3:5).[3]

### FREE WILL DOES NOT MAKE CHILDREN OF GOD

Luther could not agree with Erasmus that free will could make us children of God. Free will limited the all-embracing activity of God and made sinful and enslaved man a being equal and similar to God. Free will was to Luther a reflection of man's most brazen pride, his desire to be "like God." The combination of the words "free" and "will" was to him a horrible thing, representing Satan's kingdom in all mankind.[4] At its best free will is at its worst, because it resists the righteousness of faith.[5] Luther understood the biblical antithesis between flesh and spirit to mean that in the state of false righteousness man is "flesh," that is, confident in his own resources. This righteousness rests upon man's own works, efforts, and strivings. In the very act of trying by the utmost spiritual activity to make himself acceptable to God, man is "flesh." He seeks his own glory as he proffers to God his piety and perfection.

Erasmus too placed free will within the framework of flesh and spirit. For him free will meant freedom of spirit, and any imperfection was due to resistance afforded by the flesh. The English humanist Colet had introduced Italian humanism to Erasmus. In the academy of Florence, Paul was interpreted along the lines of ancient philosophy. Erasmus too began to think of spirit as divine and of body as animal. The spirit aspires upward, but the body hinders its progress. Already Augustine had taught that before the Fall the spirit ruled the body but subsequently the body gained the upper hand and began to dominate the spirit. This domination of the flesh explains the tragic conflict within man. In Erasmus' view reason represents the divine aspect of the soul.

In Luther's view reason is the most characteristically human element in man and therefore reflects most clearly the self-centered state of man. It reveals the "mind of the flesh." Reason signifies man's natural religion in conflict with God's righteousness.[6] Luther writes in *The Bondage of the Will:*

"By the law is the knowledge of sin," says Paul (Rom. 3:20). Here he shows how much and how far the law profits, teaching that "free will" is of itself so blind that it does not even know what sin is, but needs the law to teach it! And what can a man essay to do in order to take away sin, when he does not know what sin is? Surely this: mistake what is sin for what is not sin, and what is not sin for what is sin! Experience informs us clearly enough how the world, in the persons of those whom it accounts its best and most zealous devotees of righteousness and godliness, hates and hounds down the righteousness of God preached in the gospel, and brands it heresy, error, and other opprobrious names, while flaunting and hawking its own works and devices (which are really sin and error) as righteousness and wisdom. By these words, therefore, Paul stops the mouth of "free will," teaching that by the law it is shown sin, as being ignorant of its sin; so far is he from allowing it any power to make endeavors toward good.

And here is the solution of the question which the Diatribe repeats so often all through the book: *"if we can do nothing, what is the purpose of all the laws, precepts, threats and promises?"* Paul here gives the answer: "by the law is the knowledge of sin." His answer to the question is far different from the ideas of man, or of "free will." He does not say that "free will" is proved by the law, nor that it co-operates unto righteousness; for by the law comes, not righteousness, but knowledge of sin. This is the fruit, the work, the office of the law; it is a light to the ignorant and blind, but one that displays disease, sin, evil, death, hell, and the wrath of God. It does not help nor set them free from these things; it is content merely to point them out. When a man discovers the sickness of sin, he is cast down and afflicted; nay, he despairs. The law does not help him; much less can he heal himself. Another light is needed to reveal a remedy. This is the voice of the gospel, which displays Christ as the Deliverer from all these evil things. But neither reason nor "free will" points to him; how could reason point to him, when it is itself darkness and needs the light of the law to show it its own sickness, which by its own light it fails to see, and thinks is sound health?[7]

## THE LAW AND FREE WILL

The commandment of God does not imply that man is able to keep it. Luther writes: "So when Ecclesiasticus says, 'If thou art willing to keep the commandments, and to keep the faith that pleaseth me, they shall preserve thee,' I fail to see how 'free will' can be proved from his words."[8] No more does the admonition, "Choose!" imply that man is able to choose. Luther continues: "Wherefore, my good Erasmus, as often as you confront me with the words of the law, so often shall I confront you with the words of Paul: 'By the law is the knowledge of sin,' not power of will."[9] The alternatives are: Christ or man's free will. If man can do what is required of him, Christ is unnecessary. As Luther sees it, the position of the Bible is clear: "The Scripture sets before us a man who is not only bound, wretched, captive, sick and dead, but who, through the operation of Satan his lord, adds to his other miseries that of blindness, so that he believes himself to be free, happy, possessed of liberty and ability, whole and alive."[10] Luther considered as stupor or daze the notion that the words "turn ye" and "if thou wilt turn" establish the power of free will.[11] He writes:

> Therefore, all that is said against concluding in favor of "free will" from this word "love God," must also be said against concluding in favor of "free will" from any other words of command or requirement. If we suppose that the command to love shows us the tenor of the law and our duty only, but not our power of will or ability (inability, rather), then the same is shown by all other words of demand. . . . The words of the law do not prove the power of "free will," but show us the extent of our duty and our inability.[12]

### MERIT AND GRACE

Luther was well acquainted with the pattern of Erasmus' thought. He quotes Erasmus: "If man does nothing, there is no room for merit, and where there is no room for merit there will be no room for punishment or rewards."[13] But free will cannot be proved on the basis of merit—at least not with the Bible.[14] The whole Bible proclaims that we are saved by grace.

The following quotation represents a key point in Luther's train of thought:

> Now, since reason praises God when he saves the unworthy but finds fault with him when he damns the undeserving, it stands convicted of not praising God as God but as One who serves its own convenience—that is, what it looks for and praises in God is self, and the

things of self, and not God and the things of God. But if a God who crowns the undeserving pleases you, you ought not be displeased when he damns the undeserving! If he is just in the one case, he cannot but be just in the other.[15]

This key passage is a graphic demonstration of what justification of the ungodly looks like within the framework of scholastic Aristotelianism. When philosophy and theology are asked the same questions, it becomes manifest that human reason wants to make even God its servant. This is the intent and purpose of rationalism and idealism: God must behave as we think he ought to behave. Theology must make sense in the same manner as other things make sense. Luther is fully aware of the problem involved:

> Doubtless it gives the greatest possible offense to common sense or natural reason, that God, who is proclaimed as being full of mercy and goodness, and so on, should of his own mere will abandon, harden, and damn men, as though he delighted in the sins and great eternal torments of such poor wretches. It seems an iniquitous, cruel, intolerable thought to think of God; and it is this that has been a stumbling block to so many great men down the ages. And who would not stumble at it? I have stumbled at it myself more than once, down to the deepest pit of despair, so that I wished I had never been made a man. (That was before I knew how health-giving that despair was, and how close to grace.) This is why so much toil and trouble has been devoted to clearing the goodness of God, and throwing the blame on man's will.[16]

Luther was very familiar with the rocks on which reason stumbled. He writes:

> We are nowhere more recklessly irreverent than when we trespass upon and argue about these inscrutable mysteries of judgments. We pretend all the while that we are showing incredible reverence, in that we are searching the Holy Scriptures, which God told us to search (John 5:39). But them we do not search; whereas, in the place where he forbade us to search, there we do nothing but search, with endless audacity, not to say blasphemy![17]

By the words "we do not search" Luther is referring to the fact that men do not want to search the clear passages of Scripture which speak of Christ, but only to investigate and meditate upon

God's unsearchable mysteries which are beyond human comprehension.

## PREDESTINATION NOT FOR INVESTIGATION

Luther expresses his personal attitude toward predestination with the words: it is not for our investigation! We must pay attention to the infinite grace of the gospel right up to the very brink of the precipice where predestination begins, but there we must stop. We must not try to force our way into the mysteries of the Divine Majesty. If we look into the sun with our naked eyes, it will blind us. We must trust God's inscrutable justice and thank him if we are preserved from doubts and despair *(Anfechtung)* associated with predestination. Above all we must cling to the revealed saving will of God.

Luther starts with God's omnipotence, to which the Bible bears witness from beginning to end, and with the Holy Spirit's work, without which no man can believe or be saved. He who proposes to be saved by a faith of his own creation makes himself his own savior, and makes Christ unnecessary.[18] Luther saw the whole problem in the form of the alternative: either self-made faith or Christ. If predestination is simple in meaning—that is, if the term "predestination" always has the same connotation in philosophy and theology—then presumably faith also is simple. We confuse the psychological and theological viewpoints and make repentance and faith into works of man—all in order not to diminish the sense of responsibility! Luther asks:

> Can the endeavors of "free will" lay hold of eternal salvation, when it cannot keep hold of a farthing, or a hair of the head? When we have no power to hold down the creature, can we have power to hold down the Creator? Why are we so crazy?[19]

Reason, flesh, and free will are set over against faith, Spirit, and enslaved will. The former represent man's self-styled divinity and saving activity, the latter represent Christ and the salvation God has prepared in him.

Through the years there have been those who have sought to

extricate themselves from the difficulty involved here by explaining that *The Bondage of the Will* is a departure from Luther's real line of thought. However, if this book is rejected, Luther's main concern is ignored. He himself says that all the rest of his books might be destroyed if only the *Catechism* and *The Bondage of the Will* are preserved, for these are the only worthwhile books he has written.[20]

Luther's dualistic framework is entirely different from that of Erasmus. Erasmus sees everything in the light of the antithesis between God and man. Luther, on the other hand, views life in the light of the antithesis between God and Satan. In Luther's view man is not an independent power alongside God. Man may imagine that his will is free and his reason independent, but in reality he is a captive and slave of Satan. It does not follow, however, that because man's will is enslaved in the matter of his relationship to God, man is helpless in matters of this world. Luther's explanations of the commandments in the *Small Catechism* contain no reference whatsoever to man's impotence or helplessness.

Rejection of reason at this point is not to be interpreted as denial of logic. Luther knew and acknowledged the meaning of logical reasoning. Even though it is inadequate with respect to salvation and knowledge of God, in matters of social ethics it has decisive significance.

Luther's purpose in writing *The Bondage of the Will* was not to stress predestination but to set forth the way of salvation. His concern was to indicate how misinterpretation of passages dealing with predestination can be avoided. Predestination or no predestination, the gospel must be preached! Faced with most serious anxiety in regard to predestination he wanted to cling to saving faith.

We might summarize Luther's thoughts under the following points: 1) These questions are not for investigation or deliberation, since they are beyond human reason. 2) We must cling to faith in the God who has revealed himself in Jesus Christ; we must find refuge in grace and the gospel, that is, in the revealed will of God. 3) While acknowledging that we cannot understand everything, we must yet be assured that God makes no mistakes, regardless of how things may appear to us. 4) Finally, the whole problem is to be viewed in the light of reason, the light of grace, and the light of glory. Since the light of nature or reason and the light of grace fail to illumine all the aspects of the question of God's justice, the light of glory supplies the final answers. Luther puts it this way:

> But the light of glory insists otherwise, and will one day reveal God, to whom alone belongs a judgment whose justice is incomprehensible, as a God whose justice is most righteous and evident—provided only that in the meanwhile we *believe* it, as we are instructed and encouraged to do by the example of the light of grace explaining what was a puzzle of the same order to the light of nature.[21]

Luther sees predestination as the extension or continuation of incomprehensible, infinite grace, and as an acknowledgment of God's majesty and man's impotence. But this extension of the revelation of divine grace, God's judgment upon all human effort, must not be made into a philosophical doctrine. Reason must not plod ahead after faith has called a halt. In matters of faith reason is blind. Luther knew no philosophical predestination. To realize this fact is to have a key to Luther's thought.

## Chapter 5

# The Meaning of History

History has become a matter of life and death. Behind historical problems looms the question of the meaning of human existence as such. Does life have a purpose or is our existence merely a cruel joke? The quest for the answer takes us beyond the bounds of time. Our problem becomes a religious problem. In fact, if we delve deeply enough all problems of human life become religious problems.

The twentieth century especially has seen repeated attempts to delineate Luther's view of history. Already in 1946, the quadricentennial of Luther's death, the German scholar Gerhard Ritter pointed out that we no longer ask "what Luther has done to free the state from the shackles of the Roman hierarchy but what he has to say about the demons of lust for political glory and power, about the moral responsibility of statesmen before God, about the meaning of events that puzzle us more than anything else today, about the sense or nonsense of human history, and about God's ultimate purposes for unfortunate humanity."[1] Each generation must answer its own questions and seek its own way, for historical circumstances change. How can Luther help us in our quest?

### THE VALUE OF STUDYING HISTORY

Luther lived wholeheartedly with his people. Their joys were his joys, their sorrows his sorrows. To him history was alive. All around him he saw signs of the end of time, and evidence of God's wrath in nature, in history, and in the lives of individuals.[2] History was his master teacher.

As early as the summer following the Leipzig debate Luther recommended that rulers study history. He wrote:

It would be most profitable for rulers if from their youth they would read or have read to them the histories in both the sacred and profane books. In them they would find more examples and skill in ruling than in all the books on jurisprudence.[3]

History teaches how God destroys those who despise him and scatters the inheritance of the greedy.

With the years Luther grew in appreciation of the importance of history. In 1538 he wrote that history is a precious thing, providing examples and stories of everything that has to do with outward life, setting the past before our eyes as though we were in the middle of it. If one has eyes to see, history is an indicator, a reminder and sign of God's activity and judgment. It shows how God sustains, governs, chastens, promotes, punishes, and judges the world and especially people as each deserves. Historians are therefore the most useful people and the best teachers and cannot be honored, praised, and thanked too much. True, to write the truth fearlessly one must be an able man with the heart of a lion.[4]

Luther felt that many chroniclers of his day lacked the courage demanded of historians. Moved by fear and the desire for acceptance they falsified history. Like merchants who mixed water with the wine, they falsified God's works.

Luther possessed a deep understanding of history. His genuine sense of reality did not leave him in a quandary even in this area. History provided him with material for theology. And he permitted historical reality to influence him personally. He saw history as the stage upon which God executes his judgments.

## HISTORY AS THE "MASK" OF GOD

Luther saw everything in this world as a "mask" of God. Even history with all that it involved is dependent upon God. Luther found the Old Testament full of illustrations of how God masks himself. When David and his people set out to do battle it is as though God, like a great giant, were sending forth the young and the old as his arrows. God plays with nations of the world as though they are his toys. Luther found this thought in Proverbs

8:31: "Rejoicing in his inhabited world and delighting in the sons of men." Especially Joseph's encounter with his brothers after they had sold him spoke to Luther about divine world government.

Bearing in mind the nature of the circumstances under which Luther had to live once he became a public figure, we find it difficult to comprehend how he could view life and history as God's play. In the course of interpreting a certain Bible passage he writes:

> We must be sure that our misfortunes and trials, our sighs and complaints, even death itself, are merely the delightful and nice game of divine goodness. But how few are they who understand and believe this. . . . But when I know myself as a wretched sinner who is being punished because of his sins, how different things appear. I do not know that God is my Father and that he is good and merciful, but take him to be the devil himself. So you must know that God is almighty and that therefore such a serious game is quite appropriate for him and also quite in accordance with the importance of his majesty. . . . Therefore he gives you his promise, Word and sacraments, as surest signs and testimonies of his grace, namely, that he has adopted you as his child and does not require more of you than that you accept and endure his game, which is so delightful to him and so wholesome for you. . . . Thus God plays a fatherly game with us when he permits epidemics, hard times, sickness, and sorrow to come upon us, or when he permits misfortune to overtake our children or some other calamity to fall upon us, in order that he might melt and purify us. But who can endure all this? Such a Messiah the Jews were not expecting, for they wanted one who would make them kings and lords of the whole world. No, says Malachi, they are mistaken, for he will be stern and will sweep vigorously, as they will see. But no matter how terrible this cleaning, our Savior does not play with us to corrupt us but to heal us. . . . This true wisdom and game of God is for those who groan and weep, for the brokenhearted and downcast, for the flickering candle. To such as feel this way this comfort is offered, that they might not lose heart but remain strong.[5]

God's justice controls the whole process of history. The judgments of God's wrath reside in nature, so that all God needs to do is to withdraw his protective hand and the judgment is in effect.[6] As the Lord of history God is unwilling to share his sovereignty with anyone else. He himself and he alone exalts and puts down nations and kings as he sees fit. He sends one nation against another, the Persians against the Babylonians, the Babylonians and the Romans against the Jews. He gave the Teutonic tribes the task of putting an end to the Romans. Luther felt that in his own day God had called the Turks to threaten the Germans.

God would lose his divinity if something happened in the world without him. Luther says in effect: "There is no war that he does not wage, no peace that he does not conclude, no man whom he does not lead. Even Nineveh is his city, and Satan is God's Satan."[7]

## GOD UNSEARCHABLE IN HISTORY

But if it is true that God simultaneously builds wisely and tears down ruthlessly, grants prosperity and then sends misfortune, where is one to find a norm for the understanding of history? Luther was not unaware of the fact that acknowledgment of God's omnipotence involved some serious repercussions. Yet he rejected the idea expressed in the Old Testament that the righteous must prosper and the ungodly fail. He knew that more often than not the opposite was true: the saints are the ones that must suffer. This did not overthrow Luther's faith in God, however, but confirmed it. After all, what kind of God would he be if man could fully understand him? A fully comprehended God would be no God at all. He would be the product of man's imagination, and hence an idol. The difference between the true God and the god of our imagination is that while the latter is comprehensible the former is not, neither in his judgments nor in his grace, neither in his greatness nor in the care he extends to the least of his creatures. The scale of our thoughts is simply inadequate spacially and temporally, quantitatively and qualitatively, to measure God. All we can do before God is render homage.[8]

Reason cannot fully comprehend God, yet it is not completely devoid of knowledge of God. Natural man knows that there is a God and has some idea about his being. He knows God's greatness but not his will. Luther says:

> He knows that there is a God. But who and what this being with the name of God is he does not know. . . . There is a difference be-

tween knowing that there is a God and knowing what and who God is. The former knowledge is possessed by human nature and written into all men. The latter is taught only by the Holy Spirit.[9]

Natural reason cannot comprehend God in history. Confronted with power, riches, and prosperity it takes them as indisputable evidence of God's goodness, and conversely. From the structure of existing things one deduces the nature of God's will. Luther says that this principle of "analogy of being" *(analogia entis)* is common to all religions. In fact, it is their primary principle. Among all nations the good will of God is read from historical events.[10]

This identification of good fortune and grace stems from a misinterpretation. Good fortune does not reflect God's grace but only God's universal rule *(Weltregiment)*. The heathen too share in the gifts of creation, but these gifts do not reveal the whole of God's will and purpose. History as such is not revelation. Disappointment results therefore from any attempt to read the will of God directly from history. In history as in nature we come face to face with the terrible Divine Majesty.[11]

The real God is found only in Christ. But consider this revelation! In Christ too God is largely hidden. He has veiled himself, for here God reveals himself to a fallen world. This is the reason Christ is powerless on the cross, and yet as the powerless one overcomes sin, death, the world, hell, the devil, and all evil. Luther gives sharp expression to the offense of the cross: "On earth there has never been heard or seen anything so foolish, so impossible or so hopeless as a dying man who is supposed not only to be alive but to be the Lord and giver of life and the one who raises the dead."[12]

This is characteristic of all God's activity. God's "strange work" always precedes his "proper work." He abases in order to exalt. He kills in order to give life.[13] The German theologian Zahrnt has pointed out that when Luther in the Psalms comes across the word *wunderlich* (wonderful) he always gives it the meaning of *widersinnig* (absurd). God acts contrary to man's natural patterns of thought and knowledge. The divine principle is *contrarium* (contrariness). We find this thought quite early in Luther's works. Nothing about the Creator can be deduced directly from creation. Creator and creation do not occupy the same space. From an effect visible in nature we cannot decide concerning the cause behind it. Sense perception does not provide us with a true understanding of God.[14]

God actually reveals himself only in his Word. Faith means turning from works to the Word. Seeing does not help; one must hear. Luther says: "Faith is of such nature that it does not heed or follow that which it sees and feels but that which it hears. It clings to the Word alone, not to visage and appearance."[15]

The attitudes of faith and unbelief are entirely different. The unbeliever views all things a priori. He wants to see things beforehand, face to face as it were. He wants to read the truth directly from events. The believer draws no conclusions while events are still in process. He does not know God in the moment of the event. Yet he does not become exasperated nor give way to unbelief. He waits, that he may understand afterwards. This is the a posteriori approach. Faith is satisfied to see God from behind as it were, without trying to behold his face.[16] Unbelief desires to possess all things now. Faith is willing to wait, knowing that eternal things are the true good, while the temporal last but a moment.

The idea that God is hidden and that in history all things are cloaked in opposites must not be converted into a principle of historical interpretation. The concept of contrariness must not be made into a master key to open all locks. God would then cease to be hidden. With the use of the key of contrariness he could be exposed to anyone and everyone. But God is hidden and prefers to remain that way. He can be known only in his Word, but even the Word does not place into man's hand a key that would open the locks of history. Faith alone understands God's activity in history.

The interpretation of history dictated by faith is in the form of confession: confession of sins and confession of praise *(confessio peccati* and *confessio laudis*). The two are fundamentally the same. In both man gives God the glory. In honor and shame, in prosperity and adversity, in life and death, man acknowledges that God is always in the right.[17] Faith does not provide man with positions of security; on the contrary it drives him from them. Luther describes the believer as a lonely bird sitting on the roof as the people sleep. Between heaven and earth, he is very much alone. He has no human protection or security, only God, to whom he is bound by faith.[18]

The irregular course of history stems from the desire of God to be God. He keeps the reins in his own hands and himself executes his righteousness. This puts the course of history beyond the calculation of man's logic. This irregularity and incalculability of history is evident most clearly in the appearance of what Luther calls "miracle men" or heroes.[19]

To Luther the three chief factors of history are the nation, the power that rules it, and the unexpected great man or hero (*vir heroicus*). In creation God gave all men an innate sense of justice, but this can be exercised in various historical circumstances only by persons especially gifted for that purpose. These persons are the creative leaders of history. In a manner of speaking, they are the incarnation of natural law. Their special gift is the ability to sense the demands of the particular situation. These "miracle men" represent the active agents in Luther's conception of history. An individual called to be a leader may do what others may not, he may and does pave his own way. Otherwise he is not a "miracle man" and does not fulfill the task he received from God. He is taught by God; God has placed in his mind what he must accomplish. God sends such "miracle men" when the situation demands them. He needs these heroes in his conflict with Satan who is also displaying his might here on earth. This conflict is a fluid one. In new, unexpected situations there is need for men who do not act according to accepted patterns and do not take the past as their example but are capable of opening new paths. This too indicates that Christian faith is no mere ideology but fellowship between God and mankind. God controls the course of history in a miraculous way.[20]

Miracle men however can accomplish great things only if God wills it. God's activity at this point has the character of predestination. Luther says:

> It depends upon the individual. If God wants to use him, the thing must succeed, even though he were a complete fool. But if he is not [God's] person or man, it will not succeed, even though nine Solomons sit in his head and fifteen Samsons in his heart.[21]

Success does not necessarily follow effort. True, a person with a good conscience is more heroic than one with a bad conscience. Also, faithful work can result in success. Yet one individual achieves greater results than another with less effort. There is a gulf between effort and success, and a crucial point at which it is determined whether success will follow or not. That point is the blessing of God, which is something man cannot control no matter how he tries. A morally impeccable life will not guarantee success. Certainty in regard to God's blessing is not granted even by God's own orders of creation. He has indeed decreed that children be born in wedlock, but not all married couples have children. He has decreed that peace must be maintained within the framework of political order, but in spite of it peace has not always prevailed in organized society. God has ordered that faith must come by the preaching of the Word, yet the Holy Spirit does not work through every sermon.

Everywhere in history Luther meets the personal will of God. God is the final rule for everything. As we attempt to explicate the logic of history, we must write above many important events: "God so willed." There seems to be no real connection between guilt and reconciliation, effort and success, justice and victory. Nevertheless the seeming irregularity of history reflects the justice or righteousness of God.

Theodicy is man's attempt to vindicate God's justice. By means of reason man attempts to order and determine God's universal rule. Luther resists such temptations. Zahrnt has expressed it in a striking way when he says that Luther turned the question upside down: in the face of each historical event he is concerned about the justification of man before God, not the justification of God before man.[22] By the latter is meant that the works of God are made understandable by rational standards; by the former is meant that man must submit to the judgments of God in history whether he understands them or not.

Luther feels that students of jurisprudence have the tendency to absolutize their own concept of justice and to expect its realization. He sees this happening in his own day. In each case the attempt is made to execute one's own idea of justice with a strong hand, and in each case the results are bad. Man's evaluation of history is according to his own meager sense of justice, while God's universal rule is according to his universal justice. His rule is equal to his justice. At times he can execute his justice in violation of the rights of the individual. This however is not an injustice toward that individual; the individual is simply given an opportunity to participate in God's universal justice. Submitting to God's will man knows that God alone is righteous, and no one is righteous before God. He who acts otherwise and insists on his own concept of justice is trying to make himself judge in his own case and to get out from under God's jurisdiction. To attempt this is to deceive one's self.

One of the central thoughts of Luther's theology is that God must be God. This includes the idea that in his activity God does not need to observe a pattern of justice understood and approved by man.

Here too it must be said that Luther's intention was not to construct a logical system. His concern was to help men in their affliction and anguish of conscience. For him theology had a practical purpose. Yet there was a definite focus around which his thoughts revolved. In all things God must be God, and under all circumstances man must remember that he himself is a creature, a temporal mite of a being. Man must never attempt to command God, either by his works or by his thoughts (Isa. 55:9).

## Chapter 6

# The Person and Work of Christ

In the beginning of his book, *Die Anfänge von Luthers Christologie* (1929), Erich Vogelsang shows that Luther's doctrine of Christ departs completely from the traditional Catholic doctrine. The leading Catholic theologians, Peter Lombard and Thomas Aquinas, begin their doctrine from above, with the pre-existence of Christ, and the doctrines of the Trinity and the two natures. Luther shows no interest in the person of the Savior except as it is related to the doctrine of salvation. The work of Christ is central and only in conjunction with it does Luther treat also the person of Christ.

To Luther the traditional scholastic approach was much too philosophical or, more precisely, logico-metaphysical. His search was for the biblical line of thought. To his way of thinking the scholastics dealt too lightly with divine matters. Like cobblers with leather, they lacked reverence for the subject itself.

## CHRIST—THE HEART OF THE BIBLE

It was not that Luther failed to grasp the scholastic presentation and thought patterns. On the contrary, he was well versed in them. But the creeds of the first Christian centuries had lost their original vitality in the hands of the schoolmen, and it was the dry forms in which they were known that Luther rejected. He had found a new basis for theological knowledge, which made the Bible the message of the crucified Christ. While the schoolmen drew deliberately from both reason and revelation, Luther set the word of the cross as the sole source of Christian knowledge, in spite of the fact that it was foolishness and a stumbling block to natural thought.[1]

The most extensive work representing Luther's early theology is his first lectures on the Psalms. In the traditional manner Luther finds Christ in the prophecies of the Psalms. All the prayers are understood as prayers of Christ. In the instance of the Psalms that cry for vengeance this leads into impossible situations. Traditional interpretation explained each verse in four ways. First, literally, or, as we would say, historically; second, allegorically, with free use of imagination; third, tropologically, in terms of the meaning of the verse for the individual in the present moment (this is the form that became most important to Luther); and fourth, anagogically or eschatologically, giving the meaning from the standpoint of final fulfillment.

It might be said that Luther became estranged from Catholicism when the tropological form of interpretation, with its emphasis upon the present moment, became the only significant one for him. At the same time Christ became the Lord and content of the whole Bible. When John 10:9 calls Christ the door and the way, Luther understands it now to mean that Christ is the only door and way to knowledge of God. No man on his own can reach the Divine Majesty. The cross is the substance and the goal of God's revelation. Christ is the "sun and truth" of the Bible. Not a single word of the Bible can be rightly understood apart from the cross of Christ. Luther says repeatedly: "The cross of Christ meets us everywhere in the Bible."[2]

In the tropological interpretation of the Bible Christ is present as Savior here and now. God's revelation in Christ did not happen in the past, nor will it happen in the future, for it happens yesterday, today, and forever. Luther sees God speaking to man's conscience in such a way that the past and the future become parts of the present moment. It cannot be said that once upon a time God was merciful to us or that at some time in the future he will reveal his wrath. The will of God is a single entity, eternal and unchanging. Christ is the only revealer of God, and the only Savior.

Luther views the justification of the sinner from this same christological vantage point. From the moment of his conception, before he had done a single deed, Christ was sanctified by God and was righteous. Tropologically this is true of the Christian also. In

Christ God sanctifies the Christian and makes him righteous. Only after this and on the basis of it come God-pleasing works. Participation in Christ is justification and regeneration. These insights are found already in the first lectures on the Psalms from the years 1513 to 1515. It seems then that Luther's famous treatise on good works, written in 1520, simply repeats these same thoughts. Succinctly stated, the whole idea is that good works do not make a good man but a good man does good works.

Many of Luther's thoughts, however, are a restatement of certain insights of medieval mysticism. Mysticism, too, brings everything into the present. It speaks tenderly of the soul's union with Christ, its being clothed with Christ. But the difference in emphasis is apparent. Luther does not dwell on allegorical portrayal of the spiritual birth. Christ comes to man in faith, not in ecstatic or ascetic exercises. Luther does not emphasize the sacrament and meditation; for him the preaching of the gospel is most important. Faith comes by hearing. Christ and the Word or gospel are practically synonymous. Luther believes in the regenerative power of God's Word. He speaks of spiritual birth and emphasizes God's activity and man's passivity much in the manner of the mystics. But while mysticism taught a many-staged way of meditation as a prerequisite for spiritual birth, Luther describes justification as God's work which needs no human prerequisites. To the mystics spiritual birth was the result of a long and painful process; to Luther it is the initial work of God in man. In justification God creates a new will in man. Especially in his early theology Luther identified faith in Christ with Christ in us. Vogelsang sees this as the heart of Luther's Christology. Seen from the vantage point of Christology, our justification, redemption, sanctification, and perfection are all accomplished in Christ and, as a matter of fact, they all mean the same thing.[3]

## THE CROSS OF CHRIST

It might be supposed that in his childhood Luther had learned to think of God as stern and demanding, and of Christ as the tender

Savior. The fact is that early in his youth it was Christ who was pictured to Luther as a judge, seated on a cloud and coming to judge the world; and from that time on Christ was for Luther as stern as God himself. Staupitz often urged Luther to fix his gaze upon the man called Christ, but Luther's deep sense of sin kept the picture of the stern judge to the front. In the course of the first lectures on the Psalms the word *iustitia* (righteousness) of the Latin text of the Psalms took on new meaning. Scholars have not agreed on the date of the crucial change. Hirsch thinks it occurred at the point of Psalm 31:1, while Vogelsang places it at Psalm 71. In recent research Ernest Bizer and Regin Prenter have presented differing views on the time of the "tower experience." In any case, righteousness, worthiness, or holiness now ceases to be a requirement, and becomes instead a gift. According to the traditional interpretation it was Christ who in the words of the Psalms was praying to God. Accordingly, the requirement becomes a gift first in the case of Christ, but—using the tropological principle and substituting Christian for Christ—the Christian also receives righteousness as God's gift. Christ was willing to be rejected by God. On the cross he cried: "My God, my God, why hast thou forsaken me?" Here Luther found the meaning of the creedal statement: "He descended into hell." Vogelsang feels that no one has dared to apply to Christ as seriously as did Luther the idea of utter rejection by God. No one has grasped as he did the meaning of Christ's suffering the curse and rejection of God. Descent into hell signifies the deepest point of Christ's humiliation. He took upon himself the lot and portion of the condemned in hell. Here is the wonderful comfort of Luther's theology of the cross.[4]

If traces of the detailed Catholic doctrine of the conditions for grace do remain in the early theology of Luther, they are to be found in the thought that one must submit unconditionally to the judgment of God and acknowledge that God is right when he passes judgment upon man. The deeper the understanding of the despair of the Crucified One, the more serious the judgment. Christ and the believer are united by the cross. The Christian, too, is led into deepest despair; he, too, must descend into hell, that is, experience the truth that God judges sin. This is more than pious meditation; the affliction, torment, and despair that go with judgment under God's wrath are real.

What does Christ mean to me now? This question led Luther's interpretation into new channels. A new light illuminated Christ's cross. In that light Luther saw the wrath of God and the love of God at one and the same time. Ordinarily we think of wrath and love as opposites which weaken or even cancel each other. Luther saw now that the punitive wrath of the Father is in the service of his love. Wrath and goodness are intertwined. Salvation is found in the cross, blessing in the curse, joy in suffering, and life in death. The Crucified One himself reveals all this in his earthly life and person. He assumed the punishment for our sake, not for his own.

Already in his early evangelical theology, where those thoughts are found, Luther rejects the idea that Christ is primarily our example. Gradually the alternatives become clear to him: either *Christus exemplum* (Christ the example) or *Christus sacramentum* (Christ as the sacrifice for us). With Christ as our example, we end up in despair; as God's gift to us he is our life and salvation. Luther indeed speaks of Christ as example, but not one we have to imitate; for it is God himself who conforms us to Christ's likeness. Our oneness with Christ is God's work from beginning to end.

Standing before the Crucified One, the young Luther's conception of Christ was changed; he was no longer the stern judge but the Savior. The judge took the punishment upon himself, so to speak. The picture of Christ colored by the scholastic view of God was replaced by the picture of God portrayed by the Christ of the Gospels.[5]

## RECONCILIATION

Christ's cross determined the substance of Luther's doctrine of reconciliation. Many have supposed that in this doctrine Luther follows in the steps of Anselm of Canterbury, who taught that the once-and-for-all atonement of the God-man has appeased God's wrath. In place of man's punishment for sin stands now the *satis-factio vicaria Christi,* Christ's reconciling act in man's behalf, which receives its absolute adequacy from the God-man's infinite personal worth. The forgiveness of sins thus procured is conveyed to man by the sacraments of baptism and confession.

Luther's doctrine of reconciliation, however, is fundamentally different. The idea of satisfaction means a weakening of the seriousness of judgment. Christ indeed bears the punishment of our sins; Luther regards the notion that God in his mercy does not punish sin as a misconception. God hates sin, and God's pardon is realized through punishment and judgment. Luther speaks of the "strange work" of God and of his "proper work." The idea of God's strange work is from the Book of Isaiah (28:21). With ingenious insight Luther complements this with the idea of God's proper work. In the former he sees God's judgment, in the latter God's grace and goodness. God judges that he might show mercy, and not until he shows mercy does he do his proper work.

The difference between Anselm's and Luther's doctrine of reconciliation or atonement becomes clear when we ask concerning man's appropriation of Christ's work. Why does God reckon Christ's merit to some and not to others? Anselm—and also Melanchthon—made man responsible. By faith man appropriates Christ's merit. This is a form of the ancient, traditional, semi-Pelagian doctrine. Luther answers differently. The vicarious atonement points to God as the sole subject of the act of reconciliation. Christ's work is God's work. What God in Christ has done for us he continues to do through Christ in us. Anselm, Melanchthon, and many others look upon salvation as a transaction between man and God, but Luther sees it as a conflict involving God and Satan, with man as the battlefield.[6]

Here we are faced with the great alternatives of grace and atonement. Guilt and atonement are the basic themes of nearly all religions. The idea that guilt must be atoned appears in various forms: ceremonial washings, fastings, self-denials, even human sacrifices. This indicates how deeply rooted in human existence is the sense of guilt. Related to the idea of atonement are the principles of blood revenge, an eye for an eye and a tooth for a tooth.

The early Catholic church had the gospel of Jesus, but nevertheless constructed a complete system for man's appeasement of God: holy water replaced the cultic water of purification, innumerable ceremonies met the need for cleansing, the sacraments took on new meaning, the mass became a sacrifice, and priests were elevated to the status of mediators between God and man in the manner of the priests of sacrificial religions. Catholicism perverted the gospel into a religion with a multitude of rites and ceremonies, whose center was man's activity directed toward God with the intent of reconciling him. God's mind had to be made favorable toward man. Entrance into monasteries was a tremendous sacrifice, with man offering his whole life to gain God's favor. Luther would hardly have experienced such deep despair of soul in the monastery had not Catholic Christianity been such a hopeless admixture of the religion of grace and the religion of appeasement. Augustine and Anselm had shaken the foundations of this system but had nevertheless left the religion of appeasement in charge.[7]

It remained for Luther to bring about the collapse of the Catholic system. Working his way to the fountainhead of the New Testament with his understanding of Romans 3:28, "For we hold that a man is justified by faith apart from works of law," Luther saw Christ's vicarious suffering entirely as God's work. In Christ's work God himself is active. Neither by faith nor by anything else we do can we add to Christ's vicarious atonement. No one in the history of Christianity has been more concerned than Luther about honoring God's work as God's work and not adding man's work to it.

Clearly Anselm's theory of atonement *(Loskauftheorie)* was out of harmony with Luther's view of the atonement as involving God and Satan. Vogelsang makes the interesting observation that in the glosses of the first lectures on the Psalms, which include Luther's quotations from earlier interpreters, he expresses views akin to Anselm's theory, but in the scholia (more extensive remarks), which reveal his own view, he never interprets the atonement along the Anselmic line.

According to the traditional scholastic view the sacrifice of the atonement appeased God's wrath. Since Luther placed stronger emphasis on God's wrath than earlier teachers of the church, it would seem that he would give special consideration to the reconciliatory aspect of Christ's death. To our surprise we discover that he does quite the opposite. The extensive first lectures on the Psalms make no mention at all of the reconciliation of God. Luther does not look upon Christ's death as appeasement of God's wrath in the sense of reparation for damages, which would make it possible for God to act according to his goodness. God's wrath remains in all its severity. But as God's strange work it is pressed into the service of his proper work. Wrath continues to show itself in punishment, but it is "wrath of mercy" *(ira misericordiae)* or pardoning wrath. Wrath is love that is not afraid to hurt, for it does so in order to heal.[8]

Atonement takes on new meaning. Ordinarily we mean by atonement and sacrifice a meritorious act performed outside God by man to produce a new, changed attitude in God. To Luther this is the coarsest form of paganism and ungodliness *(Widergöttliches)*. Under no circumstances are we to think of Christ the God-man as being outside God. Christ's person and work presuppose God's merciful and salvatory punitive activity. God's attitude toward us is revealed in the fact that he gave Christ for us. The incarnation is the revelation of God's mind. The atonement is not needed to change God's attitude, since it is his love that informs the atonement.

Bornkamm points to two revealing truths with which Luther opposed the notion that man can expiate his own guilt before God: 1) We cannot make restitution for a single past deed, and 2) we do not own the future.[9] In other words, Luther says that we can effect no change in regard to the past or the future.

The first truth is the easier to understand: we cannot undo what we have done. Confession will not eradicate the wrong that has been committed. "If one has deceived a person, the pain caused by betrayed trust and confidence cannot be, and is not, healed by a confession, no matter how honest."[10] We can remove nothing from our own lives nor from the lives of others. Over against the past we are powerless.

But the second truth is more difficult. We resolve to bestow two-fold love on our wronged fellow man in order to make atonement for our wickedness, not realizing that this is nonsense, for our future already belongs entirely to our fellow man. The future has no love, power, or sacrifice over which we might exercise a free hand. Nothing is left for our dispensation. There are no special deeds we might perform for the settlement of past debts. We are not our own; we belong entirely to God and our fellow man.[11]

Man always wants to do something to change God's attitude; he wants to bring a sacrifice to God. To Luther's way of thinking, every effort on man's part to expiate his sins is pagan and impious.

Yet Luther, too, is acquainted with the idea of sacrifice. In the Psalms he finds repeatedly the notion of a sacrifice of thanksgiving and praise. From this he concludes that sacrifice is not something man does to activate God, but something which originates in God's work and activates man. God works and gives, and man thanks and praises God for it. All man can do before God is confess his impotence and inability, and thank God for his goodness. We have nothing of ourselves; all is of God. We owe him therefore not only our thanks but our very selves. God does not want what is ours; he wants us. According to Romans 12:1 the thank offering to God means submission to God's operation and acceptance of God's judgment upon sin, the crucifixion of the old man and the reception of the new man from God.

Luther did not discard the idea of sacrifice but incorporated it in the idea of that daily dying and rising which characterizes the Christian's life, of which he speaks in his *Small Catechism*. This interpretation of sacrifice takes in the cross of Christ. The cross stands in the center of all; but in the light of the tropological principle it is seen not as something between God and Christ but as something involving our justification and sanctification. As something between God and Christ it would be an item in the theology of glory, but Luther refuses to pursue theology on that level. And he does succeed, at this point too, in staying within the theology of the cross. While Catholic theology always saw the sacrifice or surrender of man to God within the framework of merit, Luther could view Christ's work for us in a way that eliminated completely the element of merit from the idea of sacrifice as a whole. The christological and tropological interpretations became interwoven. Sacrifice signified mortification of sin and surrender of self in obedience to God. Sacrifice represents then the same mystery as the cross, the mystery of life and death. The sacrifice of the cross is simply the strange work of God. But punishment is unto life: Christ has become sin in our stead—that is why God has put him to death. He was offered for us by God in order that he might in like manner offer us to God. This is the interpretation we must give to Luther's striking statement, "Christ was offered for us, offering us in himself."[12]

## CHRIST AND THE POWERS OF DEATH

The preceding analysis is based upon the early phase of Luther's Christology, when Luther considered himself a faithful member of the Roman Catholic church. Being a professor of theology, he had the task of offering his students a church-approved interpretation of the Bible. Unnoticed by him, however, faithfulness to the Bible gradually became more determinative than faithfulness to former teachers of the church. In many instances he began to feel constrained to criticize these earlier theologians and to enter new paths. Unwittingly he was being estranged inwardly from his church.

In later years the central theme of Luther's Christology became Christ's struggle with the powers of death. Luther now saw the earthly life of Christ as one long struggle, but he also saw this struggle continued in the hearts of believers after Christ's ascension into glory. The repeatedly recurring statements about the devil, sin, death, and hell in Luther's writings are neither mythology nor merely archaic forms of speech. They describe the reality of man's relationship to God, that is, the struggles of faith. In the Christian's heart a struggle goes on between law and gospel, despair and trust in God, defeat and victory.

In the explanation of the second article of the Creed in his *Large Catechism* Luther defines Christ's lordship as follows:

> What is it to "become a Lord"? It means that he has redeemed me from sin, from the devil, from death, and from all evil. Before this I had no Lord and King but was captive under the power of the devil. I was condemned to death and entangled in sin and blindness. . . . Those tyrants and jailers now have been routed, and their place has been taken by Jesus Christ, the Lord of life and righteousness and every good blessing. He has snatched us, poor lost creatures, from the jaws of hell, won us, made us free, and restored us to the Father's favor and grace.[13]

Of this struggle and victory of Christ Luther speaks throughout his works. Without Christ man is a captive of sin and the devil. The description of man's enslavement in Romans 7 is, Luther agrees, the true picture of every man, converted or not. The bondage of the unbeliever is real, even though he is unaware of it, and the believer experiences his bondage in the midst of his struggles.

In the conflict Christ is alone, while arrayed against him are the devil and all the powers of death. The struggle is for man and in man. In theological terms this means that the work of Christ has to do with our justification. Atonement, salvation, and justification are intertwined, one within the other. It is impossible for Luther to view Christ's death and resurrection simply as past events. They have to do with each present moment and with each Christian. This is not to deny Golgotha as a historical event but to underscore the fact that as a mere historical event it lacks what is most important, namely, present actuality. Luther often speaks of the inadequacy of historical faith: it profis me not at all to believe that Christ once lived, died, and rose again. The meaning of Christ for me is that this moment he is my Lord and my Savior, who delivers me from death and the terrors of hell.[14]

The climax of the cosmic drama is the death and resurrection of Christ. God defeats the devil. The conflict is bitter, for the spiritual powers of this world are strong. Early Christians and the Greek fathers saw the redemptive work of Christ as a victory over the "powers." Luther speaks a great deal about these tyrants which Christ has conquered. Sin, death, hell, the devil, the law, and often also God's wrath appear as personal powers that tempt man and seek to lead him away from faith in Christ. Christ's conflict with these powers is sketched in sharp lines in the *Commentary on Galatians* (1531). The powers of darkness concentrate all their might against Christ without being able to overcome him, for he has on his side the greatest righteousness, namely, God's own holiness, power, and life.

Luther writes:

> This particular argument of Paul is therefore the strongest against the righteousness of the flesh. For it includes this invincible and irrefragable antithesis: If the sins of the whole world are on one man, Jesus Christ, then they are not on the world. But if they are not on him, then they are still on the world. Further, if Christ is guilty of all the sins which we have committed, then we are absolved of them, though not because of ourselves, our own works or merits, but because of him. However, if he is innocent and bears not our sins, then we bear them and shall die and be damned by them. "But thanks be to God who hath given us the victory by our Lord Jesus Christ. Amen" (I Cor. 15:57).

> But now let us see how two such contrary things can concur in this one person. Not only my sins and yours but the sins of the whole world, past, present, and future, attack him, proceed to condemn him, and indeed do so. But because in this same person, who is the highest, greatest, and only sinner, there dwells also an everlasting and invincible righteousness, these two then encounter each other; the highest, greatest, and only sin, and the highest, greatest, and only righteousness. They fight with such force and power that one of them must be overcome and retreat. The sin of the whole world therefore comes upon righteousness with full might and main. What happens? Righteousness is everlasting, immortal, and invincible. Sin, too, is an extremely powerful and cruel tyrant, dominating and reigning over the whole world, capturing and enslaving all men. In a word, sin is a strong and mighty god who devours all alike, learned, holy, mighty, wise, unlearned, and so forth. He, I say, assails Christ and proceeds to devour him as he devours others. But he fails to see that he is a person of invincible and everlasting righteousness. In this combat then sin must be vanquished and killed, and righteousness must overcome and live.

So universal sin is vanquished, killed, and buried in Christ, and righteousness holds the field as conqueror and reigns forever.

Similarly, death, an omnipotent empress of the world, who kills kings, princes, and all men in general, charges violently upon life, bent on utterly overcoming and devouring it. And what it intended actually comes to pass. But because life was immortal it overcame in being overcome and achieved the victory, vanquishing and destroying death. . . . Through Christ death is therefore vanquished and abolished throughout the world, so that now it is but a painted death which has lost its sting and can no longer hurt those that believe in Christ, who is now the death of death; as Hosea the prophet says, "O death, I will be thy death" (Hos. 13:14).

Likewise the curse, which is God's wrath upon the whole world, is involved in similar conflict with the blessing, that is, with the eternal grace and mercy of God in Christ. The curse therefore fights against the blessing, intending to condemn and nullify it completely, but this it cannot do. The blessing is divine and everlasting, and so the curse must retreat. For if the blessing in Christ were overcome, God himself would be overcome. But this is impossible; so Christ, the power of God, righteousness, blessing, grace and life, overcomes and destroys these monsters, sin, death, and the curse, without war and weapons, in his own body and in himself, as Paul likes to say. "Spoiling," he says, "the principalities and powers, and triumphing over them in himself" (Col. 2:15), so that they can no longer hurt those that believe.

And this fact, this "in himself," makes that combat more miraculous and glorious. It shows that it was necessary for all these things to be accomplished in that one person (namely, that the curse, sin, and death should be destroyed, and the blessing, righteousness, and life should succeed them), and that thus the whole creation should be renewed through this person. Therefore, looking upon this person you will see sin, death, God's wrath, hell, the devil, and all evils vanquished and destroyed. Since Christ reigns by his grace in the hearts of the faithful, there is no sin, death, or curse. But where Christ is not truly known, there all these things remain. Thus all who do not believe lack this immeasurable benefit and victory. "For this," as St. John says, "is our victory that overcomes the world, even our faith" (I John 5:4).

This is the principal article of Christian doctrine, which the sophists have completely obscured and which the fanatics obscure again today.[15]

Christ's conflict involves the deepest and most difficult question of theology, the antithesis between law and gospel. All mankind is under the law, including the unbelievers. Only Christ brings the gospel, and with it freedom. But the Christian also continues to be under the law, as well as under the gospel. Faith means continual transfer from the law to the gospel, from despair to hope, from darkness to light, and from death to life. Christ has freed us from the curse of the law by becoming a curse in our stead.

In rising from the dead Christ crushed the head of the devil and saved us from sin, from God's wrath, and from death and hell, granting us righteousness, life, and salvation. This no mere man could do. This is God's own work, and so Christ is of one being with God. Christ has life, and of himself he gives life; this is a divine work. God creates what is new; he has the power and the possibility for this. Christ's death on the cross was not a defeat but a victory. The victor is the Lord of glory. He who was crucified is no mere man but God, even though this fact is hidden from the devil. Christ's resurrection declares him to be true God and proclaims the defeat of the devil.

Christ's work is not directed toward the appeasement of God but toward the overthrow of the devil. In the very moment when the devil appears to have achieved his goal, he suffers defeat. The secret of Christ's victory is that he is God and not man. These thoughts constitute the main line of Luther's Christology.

## CHRIST AS MAN

Alongside this main line of Luther's Christology there is another which stresses the similarity (conformitas) between Christ and the Christian. This line has its origin in the true humanity of Christ. In Christ's humanity God comes to man. God speaks and acts, judges and pardons us in Christ. In him we see what God wants and intends. We learn prayer and obedience, patience and faith. Christ's history is man's history as God intended it and would have it. What God does to Christ he wants to do to all men. As Christ went through tribulation so must we. He leads us on the way of suffering. But our unity with him is also in love and service. This understanding of conformity is informed by God's work, not ours. It is quite unlike the Catholic idea of imitation, which has man striving to imitate Christ and the saints in order to gain God's favor. From such imitation Luther dissociated himself completely after his freedom from Catholicism. The likeness to Christ which he taught stems wholly from the fact that it is God who works all in all. By means of the cross and conflict God molds us in the image of his Son. In such a view Christ's humanity becomes vivid and near to us, being incorporated in our faith and prayers and empowering our will and conscience. Vogelsang states that neither the Greek nor the Roman church had been able to understand Christ's humanity in such personal terms. Precisely as the one who is oppressed and given into death Christ makes his human presence most real. What happens to him, happens also to us. As the oppressed and dying one he goes before us, thereby breaking the deadliest point of suffering.[16]

There is another way of viewing Christ—from the standpoint of suffering. Here his humanity has become divinity. In the gospel narrative of the Canaanite woman Luther finds a portrayal of the relationship between God and the afflicted, tormented conscience. At first Christ is silent before the woman's pleadings. Then he even turns away from her prayers. Finally he says to her that she belongs with the lost and condemned. But the woman perseveres in her trust and refuses to leave even after being rebuffed. Finally she submits to Christ's judgment, binding the Master with his own words. This shows our heart in the moment of doubt and despair (*Anfechtung*) when God is first silent, then refuses to hear our prayer, and finally in his Word takes a stand against us, and we feel in our conscience that he condemns not only our sins but us. Then we taste hell itself and feel eternally lost. Caught between the judgment and pardon of God, we must not lean on our feelings but in faith grasp the Word of God and cling to the deep and hidden pardon concealed in his judgment. This the Canaanite woman did. We must likewise submit to the judgment God pronounces upon us. Thus we gain the victory and bind God with his own words. The obstacle in the way of our being received into grace is our unwillingness to suffer God's judgment and to submit to it. Were lost souls able to do this, they would be saved in a moment.

The affliction and torment depicted here is similar to that which Christ experienced as one of us. The submission to God's judgment, in the midst of which one must learn to hear God's deep and hidden pardon, is likewise similar. But in this submission Christ is not as one of us; he is not on our side but on God's side. He stands in God's place, and Luther notes that nowhere is he shown to be as stern as here. Christ is Lord! Bearing in mind that Christ here portrays the manner in which God deals with Christians, we see the severity of God. But concealed in God's wrath and judgment is his grace.

In his treatise *A Brief Instruction on What to Look for and Expect in the Gospels* Luther says: "When you open the book containing the Gospels and read or hear how Christ comes here or there, or how someone is brought to him, you should therein perceive the sermon or the gospel through which he is coming to you, or you are being brought to him."[17] We must not stop where we meet Christ, for he leads us to the Father.

How can these two views be harmonized? Christ is as one of us, and yet he is God's Son and representative. This is doubtless a strange doctrine of two natures! Vogelsang interprets this to mean that Christ is tempted and troubled like one of us, so that as one like God he might help us in our weakness and temptation. He who is humanly tried, tries us divinely. He comes to our aid with a love that is wrapped in wrath and judgment.[18]

All this is difficult for man to understand and accept. But what comfort it gives to those who suffer and are in anguish! In this world of sin God reveals his true nature, that is, his love, only in severity and judgment. Once Luther called suffering the royal banner of the Christian, a figure his sixteenth-century fellow Germans appreciated much more than we who live in a democracy.

Luther was not satisfied with a historical faith in Christ. The historical standpoint keeps Christ in the past. For Luther, to whom pastoral care and practical Christianity were always the main thing, this was not enough. It was most important that Christ be seen as one who is present. His words in the *Commentary on Galatians* are characteristic of his view: "Faith justifies because Christ is present" *(Iustificat fides, quia Christus adest)*.[19] In faith and for faith Christ is really present. According to the fanatics Christ was really in heaven; and only spiritually was he within them. According to Luther Christ and faith must be united: "In faith we must be already in heaven, and Christ must dwell in our hearts." This must take place in reality, not just theoretically.[20] Christ's presence is possible because he has risen from the dead and has ascended into heaven. The great message of Easter is not an attempt to clear the name of a Savior debased on the cross and to reassert his glory. Rather, it points to the saving act of God which breaks through the curse and the judgment of the cross. As interpreted by Luther, the statement of the Creed that he "ascended into heaven" does not mean that he had risen "in a golden chair" into the heavens, or that he is sitting "as a swallow in his nest," but that "he is risen from the dead and ascended into heaven to begin his spiritual kingdom and to rule in us. . . . It is here on earth that he is active, here he rules consciences and souls with the gospel. Where Christ is preached and where he is known, there he rules in us, sitting at the right hand of the Father and at the same time in our hearts."[21]

In Luther's view the real presence of Christ is not a magico-sacramental presence or an emotional state but a presence that is operative in the Word, renewing and ruling consciences. This presence is realized wherever the gospel is preached and heard.

## Chapter 7

# Justification and Sanctification

Justification by faith as the core doctrine of the Reformation continues to raise the question: Does not free grace produce questionable ethical results? What happens to man's activity if in the end everything is forgiven anyhow? What will become of sanctification and the new life if forgiveness is not limited in any way?

These questions become more urgent as the various Reformation traditions are drawn into closer contact with one another in the ecumenical movement. Repeatedly it must ask: "Have the followers of Luther in grasping the heart of the gospel perhaps failed to draw the necessary practical conclusions? How did Luther understand the relationship between justification and sanctification?"

For background we must go to Augustine. Augustine points out again and again that the justified man is indeed righteous, yet also a sinner. He is partly righteous and partly sinful, an admixture of good and evil, spiritual and carnal. Righteousness in this life is partial and fragmentary, always permeated by sin. We are partly justified *(ex parte iustificati)*. But this righteousness of the justified man increases daily, reaching its completion in the next life.[1]

Luther states the matter in practically the same words, and yet his meaning is quite different. He, too, says that man is at one and the same time both just and sinful, but Luther does not have in mind partial righteousness and partial sinfulness. Both sinfulness and righteousness have to do with the whole man; both are total.[2]

## THE JUDGMENT OF GOD AND KNOWLEDGE OF SIN

Justification has its beginning in man's knowledge of his sin. God's judgment and wrath are directed against all sin, but the unbeliever is not aware of this. Man's acknowledgment that God

61

is right in judging him is the beginning of faith and justification.[3] This acknowledgment is already faith, a faith which accepts the first commandment. Revealing to man his sins and judging him, God seeks to impart to man his truth and righteousness. When man submits to this judgment God begins to renew him by his Word.[4] Natural knowledge of sin, which does not originate in the judgment of God's Word, can lead to some conception of the substandard character of human morality, but only God's Word felt in the conscience can show man his total corruption.

In judging man and receiving him into his grace, God delivers him from the spell of egocentricity. Man's false notions lead him astray in two directions: on the one hand he imagines that he is acceptable to God just as he is, on the other hand he imagines God to be a God of wrath who rejoices in casting sinners into perdition.[5] When man submits to God's judgment this judgment is revoked. The gospel, that is, Christ, is for the sorrowful and brokenhearted.

### FAITH AND UNBELIEF, OUTWARD AND INWARD

Unbelief is blind in matters of sin and holiness. It sees what is outward but not what is inward. Luther distinguishes between unbelief and faith as follows:

> The ungodly start in the matter of righteousness with the outward and then proceed to the inward. First they simulate works, then words, and later also exercise their thoughts. And this is their real goal. Then they immediately offer themselves as teachers, anxious to announce as holy and divine everything they think, say, and do, when as a matter of fact no man can work his way into the secret will of God. The saints begin from within, from his holy will, then follows meditation, then the outward act, and only after this instruction of others.[6]

Faith leads to inward holiness. Against the Catholic concept of holiness Luther found it necessary repeatedly to level the charge that it was aiming at outward holiness; it reflected natural man's rational mode of thought. Luther never tires of emphasizing that man wants to follow by native inclination the way of the Pharisees and fanatics, offering God his own holiness.[7] The holiness of faith is not visible to the eye. Faith fulfills the first commandment by seeking God and his holiness and depending solely upon it.

The Christian lives his life in a basic tension which cannot be removed: grace does not renew him into a totally new and perfect man. His faults remain.[8] Man's total sinfulness is one of the central insights of Luther's theology. This is stated in a simple way in the *Small Catechism:* "We sin daily and deserve nothing but punishment."

While seeking security in God in the monastery, Luther had been introduced through his monastic order to an entirely different view. Augustine, the father of this order, taught that the realms of nature and grace were so related that the more earnestly a soul turned from visible things to seek the treasures of the invisible world, the more he was freed from the power of his lusts and desires. Luther's struggle to find a merciful God brought him in contact with another and more basic alternative. His real problem had to do not with "nature" and "grace" but with the question: Can man love God purely or is he rather in the final analysis actually seeking his own even in God? What Luther says about spiritual lust *(concupiscentia)* clearly indicates the possibility that even the spiritual life can be corrupted by selfishness. He realized that knowledge, righteousness, purity, and piety are desirable and good, for which reason love often stops with them and ignores God. In his own words:

> We perform these works not because they please God but because they bring joy and peace to our heart or because they gain for us the praise of men. Thus we do not perform these works for God's sake but for our own sake. But tribulation puts our works to a test. For if we are criticized, or if God takes away the pleasant feeling of comfort associated with works of love, or if the inner harmony is dissipated, then we abandon the good works, take revenge on our critics, and set up our defenses.[9]

The question of the inward and outward deepens into the question of what really dwells within man. Luther became convinced that sinful lust *(concupiscentia)* dwells in the innermost part of man, and that man can never in his life eradicate this inherited sin or root of sin, regardless of what he does. Man is innately inclined to evil and turned away from God. In this state he remains guilty before God. There is very little difference between original sin and actual sin as far as Luther is concerned. The forgiveness of God means removal of guilt even though the root of sin remains.[10] Luther says that it is possible to make two contradictory statements about the sins of the Christian: no Christian has sins, and every Christian has sins *(Nullus Christianus habet peccatum et omnis habet peccatum).* Sin has been forgiven, and it must be rooted out. As forgiven sin it no longer accuses, but it still sprouts (Rom. 7:23). It tries continuously to bring forth the fruit of that former state which prevailed before Christ made us his own.[11]

In speaking of the sin that continues to dwell in Christians, Luther means to sound a warning: We have no ground for security even though sins have been forgiven; our righteousness is always an alien righteousness, and God's grace comes to us from without.[12] What is inward and what is outward in this connection was not a minor matter to Luther. Here we have one of the cardinal thoughts of the Reformation.

Since the Christian's righteousness is Christ's righteousness—in which the Christian is clothed by faith—it is always entirely a foreign righteousness. Our old nature is never completely eradicated, even though it is continually mortified. Two corollaries follow from this fact: first, all human self-assurance and pride is put down; second, the Christian is saved from despair inasmuch as he is not driven toward a perfection he cannot attain. The latter means real comfort to a person living in a world of sin, who must continually wrestle with the power of sin. Its significance, however, can be easily misunderstood, for what would be more tempting than to conclude that since the Christian is and remains a sinner there is no point in trying to live as a new man. Implied here is the absurd charge that Luther's conception of faith allows the believer living by God's grace to remain a slave to sin.

## REPENTANCE—DAILY WARFARE

The phrase "righteous and sinful at the same time" *(simul iustus et peccator)* implies continuous warfare rather than peace and rest. This insight must have come to Luther early, for it appears already in his lectures on Romans. Repentance is not merely release from the burden of conscience, and the reception of peace. It signals enlistment in the service of God *(militia Dei),* war against the devil and against the sins which beset us. He who is unwilling to engage in this warfare cannot be numbered among the soldiers of Christ.[13] The carnal man differs from the man of the Spirit in being totally flesh. He knows no conflict, for God's Spirit does not dwell in him.[14]

In Luther's treatise *On the Councils and the Churches* (1539) there is a paragraph in which he stresses the unity of repentance, forgiveness of sins, and the new life. He describes the antinomians who preach "finely" and "with real seriousness" about the grace of Christ, forgiveness of sins, and other parts of the second article of the Creed, but who avoid like the devil the third article, which deals with sanctification and the new life in Christ, feeling that men must never be frightened or saddened but must always have comfortingly proclaimed to them the grace and forgiveness of sins in Christ. Luther sees in this the granting of the premise but the denying of the conclusion. The result is that Christ is taken away and his work destroyed at the same time that he is being loudly hailed. "There is no such thing as a Christ who has died for sinners who, upon receiving forgiveness of sins, do not forsake sin and begin to live a new life."[15] Christ's atoning work has as its purpose to make us new. The gift of the Holy Spirit means not only that we have forgiveness of sins but also that we forsake sin.

Luther's underscoring of the necessity of sanctification during the so-called antinomian controversy[16] can easily make it appear that he was willing to compromise his view that the works of the law are altogether useless before God. Perhaps the new life can be brought forth by legal compulsion after all.

But no such compromise was involved. Once he had reached

clarity in the matter, Luther never taught anything else except that the Holy Spirit alone makes Christ a gospel for us. Without the Holy Spirit's operation Christ is for us only a law and our life is mere imitation and not the new life of the Spirit.[17] Were the law enough, one might suppose that the intention of God's commandments is to induce the ungodly to perform God-pleasing works. But Luther emphasizes repeatedly that God's commandments aim to awaken faith. Only in faith, that is, in right relationship to God, can man do God's will.[18]

Theologians at various times have handled this matter in one of two ways. Some have seen the purpose of the law to be simply obedience. They express it with the simple equation: law—imitation. Over against this interpretation we say with Paul and Luther: law—knowledge of sin—despair—justification—new life. However, none of these is in man's power. Emphasis upon the law can easily lead to legalism. The Holy Spirit must apply the law to man in his conscience, and when that happens man becomes afflicted and distressed. Where this affliction *(Anfechtung)* leads him cannot be determined in advance. In it man faces the possibility of falling into utter despair without finding freedom of the Spirit and new life in Christ. Spiritual affliction places man before completely new possibilities.[19] God or Satan may be its cause. If Satan gains access into the conscience with the message of God's judgment, the outcome is despair. If the Holy Spirit is the one who reveals God's judgment and man submits to it, the outcome is grace and freedom. But it is not a simple matter for one to find the way from God's absolute demands to Christ. As in justification man is transferred from servitude under the law to life under grace, so in sanctification he experiences continuous renewal. Day by day and moment by moment the sanctified new man is born in affliction and in submission to judgment. Mortification of the old man in us and vivification of the new is simultaneously justification and sanctification. If the substance of sanctification is something we produce, then, says Luther, it is indeed and simply something which is *our own;* it is not the "new" which God gives, but the old which serves no good purpose. The "new" of the new life is born again and again in justification, and its "parents" are God's judgment and man's affliction. All other forms of the "new" are imitations, expressions of bondage to the law, which itself is never "new." To imitate is to work with copies, but God has created each individual as an original. In judgment and justification he makes us into the new originals he wants.

### THEOLOGY OF PILGRIMAGE

Luther feels that it is easier to visualize the Christian's way when two truths are taken into consideration: 1) The Christian must not remain in his sins; yet in spite of this 2) the Christian remains a sinner. These two statements seem to contradict each other. The peculiar nature of the Christian faith is found, according to Luther, in this apparently irresolvable contradiction. He who lives in faith in God and Christ strives with all his powers to be free from sin. Yet he knows that there is sin in him. In fact, the more vital one's faith the more clearly he sees the sin that still clings to him.

Already in the first lectures on the Psalms Luther notes that to the extent that man does not desire to become better he ceases to be good. He who is righteous, let him be righteous still (Rev. 22:11), and let him who stands beware lest he fall (I Cor. 10: 12). Luther places much emphasis on Ecclesiasticus 18:7, which states that "when a man has finished, he is then only at the beginning."[20]

In Paul's theology the man who in Christ has already reached the goal must continue with the race. The reason for this is that the Christian lives under the conditions of two ages (aeons). The old and new ages alike condition him. Likewise in Luther's theology the Christian is ever en route, inasmuch as he is simultaneously righteous and sinful. Only the saints in heaven can relax and enter fully into their possessions.[21] In Luther's early evangelical theology Augustine's influence was very strong, and so we find there statements which interpret sanctification as a progressive series of events.[22] His later theology however shows a distinct aversion to all detailed scrutinizing of holy living. It is difficult to speak of progress, for there is no such thing as growth of the old man in holiness and perfection. The old man in us must be put to death daily and the new man arise, as the *Small Catechism* puts it. Our natural life is the life of the old man. No form of cure will make the old man into the new.[23] It remains old to the very end. As Luther sees it, the Christian must judge himself once and for all. The new man lives in us only as the alien righteousness of Christ. This righteousness never changes into a part of my personality (ego). If in our quest for such change we turn our eyes upon ourselves, we become "self-righteous servants of the law."[24] The new in us is Christ himself.[25] But under the conditions of this present life Christ does not control us so completely as to make it unnecessary for the old man to go through daily mortification. The new man never becomes a creature whom we might touch and see.

From a certain viewpoint Luther's teaching placed all outward piety under suspicion. In any given moment piety can be, as Prenter notes, an expression of the Spirit or of the flesh, according to whether the man in that particular moment is either Spirit or flesh. One cannot therefore speak of unambiguous growth toward genuine righteousness. Prenter is undoubtedly right when he says:

> When Luther speaks about the progress of sanctification, he thinks of something entirely different. He thinks of the fact that man on the way between baptism and resurrection constantly and anew takes leave of himself to take refuge in Christ's alien righteousness. In this refuge of faith in Christ, man is *Spirit,* new man, and all his past life up to this moment is at once considered as flesh, as old man. In this manner the Spirit, who knows only Christ's alien righteousness, is constantly struggling against the flesh, which wants to hold on to its own past life as an appropriation, its own righteousness. In the resurrection man shall be completely Spirit. Then the Spirit shall no longer struggle against the flesh. But on the way between baptism and resurrection man is Spirit and flesh.[26]

In the evaluation of holiness all that is outward must be suspect. No visible piety or concrete act as such guarantees that the mind or attitude itself is holy. On the contrary, with progress there is regress. In becoming better the Christian becomes worse. To reach the goal is to start all over again. Luther was quite aware that all this made no sense to man's wisdom, to the "sophists." That the Christian is simultaneously a sinner and a saint is contrary to reason. The human ideal is that life be altogether without sin. As a demand this ideal drives men into despair.[27]

## THE REAL BATTLE LINE

What we have said thus far about the pilgrim's daily warfare has not answered the question of sinlessness, the primary issue in sanctification. We have simply noted that Luther insists on the one hand that the man who has received forgiveness of sins must forsake sin and live a new life,[28] while on the other hand he looks upon the requirement of sinlessness as an absurdity that leads to despair.

Such sharply conflicting statements must be understood in the light of the situations which gave them birth. When Luther wrote that forgiveness of sins implies rejection of sin and new life, he was in the midst of the antinomian controversy (1537-1539). The gospel had been watered down to the point where any imaginable form of sin was permissible. Neglect of the law had caused all warfare against sin to cease. Against this background Luther stressed the importance of striving after the new life. We can hardly imagine that he had in mind absolute sinlessness as an attainable goal. The statements from the years 1531 and 1539 are only apparently contradictory. In neither case could Luther have taught a divinely acceptable sinlessness. The viewpoint may change but the seriousness of the warfare against sin remains uncompromised. This warfare is always related fundamentally to the righteousness that stands before God. It was for this reason that the affliction of unworthiness (*tentatio indignitatis*) was Luther's chief source of anguish. God demands the absolute; man is capable only of the imperfect and relative. And so Luther cries out: "Lord God, it is not enough that sin is forgiven. I would that it were completely annihilated, dead and buried."[29] From Augustine Luther had learned that the guilt of an act can be removed even though the act as an accomplished fact remains (Transit reatu, manet actu).[30]

The circumstances determined by sin, the state (habitus) of sin remains even though one has received forgiveness of sins. Holiness cannot be realized as a permanent state. At all times our righteousness is the "alien righteousness" of Christ. The real battle line in sanctification is to be found in the tension between the state of sin and the righteousness of Christ. Forgiveness cannot eradicate the fact of sin, since it cannot undo the act of sin. It removes only the guilt. All the devil has to do to bring about despair is to point to the facts of life, the reality of our existence. Forgiveness alone can free the Christian from the clutches of the devil. The Christian's holiness rests upon this foundation: "Let the devil, death, and sin be against me. I am still holy, for I believe in Christ and have learned to know him. I have a true understanding and use of the Word and sacraments. All this I have not of myself but as the gift of the Holy Spirit."[31]

This is the heart of Luther's faith. Holiness does not rest upon outward behavior or form of life. It is not to be identified with ethics (ethos). Before God it is always a matter of faith. But this faith man himself cannot create. Again, it is not the same as man's inner life. In reality faith is the antithesis of all that man is able to achieve. Faith rests upon the Word and promise of God. As commandment (law) the Word is a word of judgment, but as promise (gospel) it contains Christ. Even the word of judgment, however, is grace, for in it God comes to man. The commandment, too, is the activity of God directed toward the creation of faith in him and fellowship with him.[32] Our holiness and righteousness are never ours, for they stem from the turning of our eyes away from ourselves and toward Christ, who is our holiness and righteousness.

The substance of the gospel can be stated in this simple way; yet participation in the gospel is never a mathematical certainty.

Justification—the appropriation of the gospel—is always through the conscience. God's judgment in the conscience and the resultant anguish and despair *(Anfechtung)* involve the whole person, the total being of man, not merely his individual acts, even as sin also involves the whole person. By the same token the grace which is ours in Christ has to do with the whole person.

Sanctification can never be the sum of individual acts of repentance, even as it cannot rest upon individual good works. Sanctification is justification, but not in the sense of the simple putting on of the righteousness of Christ. It is submission to God's judgment and the bearing of the resultant despair and torment. But sanctification is at the same time trust in God in Christ. It is an act of faith in the true sense of the word, not of that faith which we ourselves are able to produce but of the faith which God gives.

The ensuing warfare against the devil is carried out on two fronts: outwardly against temptations of sin and inwardly against accusations of the tempter, which threaten to drive to despair. To live a life of holiness is to cling to the unseen, to trust in God's act in Christ, in the Word and sacraments. Briefly stated, sanctification is flight from man's works to God's work.[33]

Such a view of holiness, resting as it does on the Word and sacraments, placing primary emphasis upon objective factors and leaving the subjective spiritual signs on the periphery, can of course be looked upon as saltless and secular. But Luther's sensitive and often anxious and tormented heart led him to view man's relationship to God always from God's side *(coram Deo)*, with the result that man always found himself in the position of the judged. In his afflictions *(Anfechtungen)* one must place his confidence in the objective foundation of salvation, the Word and sacraments. Faith then becomes striving faith. Unless the knowledge of God's judgment remains vital, this way of sanctification can easily lead into superficiality and worldliness. But in the final analysis the alternative is no better. Where the point of departure is man, his piety and the marks of faith, the state of condemnation before God becomes secondary. Man's primary existence is then before men *(coram hominibus)* and his spirituality serves to exalt him above others. This has always and in all things been man's goal. Success in the achievement of this goal is not to be confused with sanctification.

In Luther's conception of holiness the issue is always faith, not works. To the very end man is in himself a sinner and under God's judgment. The severe criticism to which Luther's struggling faith was subjected in his own time has continued in later times. He has been accused of stopping at a halfway point. The fanatics and the Anabaptists accepted the Reformation because the Catholic church had not done full justice to faith; but they wanted to reform the Reformation because it had not permitted works to come to their own. In Pietism this new reformation broke out. But it was forgotten that Luther saw a more effective realization of holiness in the continuing work of the Holy Spirit than in all the emphasis upon works.[34]

The difference between Luther and Pietism is greater than is usually thought. Luther's "new" man is not the same as Pietism's converted man. The latter is a psychologically new individual, awakened into life by conversion, whose goal is to reach full maturity in holiness. The "new" for Pietism is a psychological reality in man. The struggle for holiness takes place between two levels of life, the lower life of nature and the higher life of the spirit. In Luther's view the situation is quite different. The "new" in the believer is for Luther not a higher nature or a new individual capable of sensible expression. The "new" in the believer is Christ's alien righteousness. The total old self, our old state of being— conversion and holiness included—is solely our own and therefore flesh. Insofar as our works are concerned, it cannot be anything else. The struggle for holiness is carried on in faith and involves Christ, who is really present, and our total self. Included in this self are the higher as well as the lower capacities of the soul and impulses of the will. No level of our personality is so high that it would not in the final analysis be dominated by self. In sanctification it is precisely this self that is striving against God *(homo incurvatus in se)* and must be beaten down. Luther always viewed man from the total point of view; to him man is an indivisible entity. In the view of Pietism man is a divided being and the struggle between the old man and the new is a struggle between two psychological levels within man.[35]

Because Luther does not see holiness primarily as a matter of works he has been charged, both in his own day and later, with passivity. Such a charge, however, is both shallow and unfounded. It is shallow because it is informed by a desire to make holiness perceptible to the senses, and a lack of confidence in God's hidden work in the believer's heart. It is unfounded because Luther's purpose was to direct men into the struggle for holiness, the struggle of faith against the devil, sin, and the flesh. This warfare can be called daily repentance. Though the primary focus may be not on works but on the conscience awakened by God, more is involved than merely Christ and conscience. Daily repentance comes to expression—and inevitably so—as works, though not as works of law but as works of the new man, as obedience of faith, as love.

## HOLINESS AND LAW

The new life can be realized only as conflict. This conflict has its ethical and its religious fronts. On the one hand the attack is against temptations, against the flesh and the world, and on the other hand the attack is against the works by which man seeks merely to enhance himself. Since the conflict is one of faith the attack is directed against that knowledge of self which bypasses Christ and leads to despair. How is the law involved in all this?

As a young theologian Luther had a rather optimistic view of man's ability to keep the law. Before long, however, such optimism gave way to a view according to which the law was given not to remove sin but to increase it (Rom. 5:20). The law leads to despair and is therefore in the service of death (Rom. 7:10). It is included among the powers of destruction.[36] The law as such is holy and good (Rom. 7:12); however, it never finds man as a neutral in the struggle between good and evil; he is always on

the side of evil, an enemy of God. Man cannot remain an innocent bystander, consequently he is judged whenever the law finds
him.[37]

The law not only reveals the situation of sin; it actually makes
the situation worse. When comprehended "after the flesh," it
leads to an evermore imperfect and carnal state. Being spiritual,
the law can be fulfilled only in faith. Where there is no faith,
there one becomes evermore involved in error and vanity.[38]

This whole series of thoughts is definitely Pauline (Rom. 7:9
f.). In regard to the civil and pedagogical significance of the law,
some have attempted to interpret Luther's concept of law altogether differently. They have remarked that in the *Small Catechism* Luther presupposes that the commandments can be kept;
nowhere does he say that the law is difficult to keep, much less
impossible. It is supposedly inconsistent therefore that Luther
should consider the law as a destructive power.

Because of its spirit and content Luther's larger *Commentary
on Galatians* must be considered a true exposition of his fundamental views. The main theme of this book is that the law has no
business in the conscience. By this Luther means that the law must
not determine man's faith-relationship to God. One of the arguments that Luther states repeatedly is that where the law prevails
there reason *(ratio)* dominates, and reason is the worst enemy of
faith.[39]

A number of insights led Luther to reject the law as an agent of
sanctification. Among them are the following:

1) The law does not make possible the fulfillment of its demands, for this requires free and joyful hearts and an inner desire
to do God's will, which the law cannot provide. The end result
then is a false state.

2) The law brings about a relationship to God in which reason
has the decisive role, resulting in a situation inimical to faith. Re-
ligiously speaking, reason means sinful man's enmity against God,
Christ, the gospel, grace, and faith.

3) Authorized by God, the law demands perfection and—be-

cause man is incapable of perfection—leads to despair. Thus the law becomes a destructive power and an ally of Satan. It is indeed God's law, and as such holy and perfect, but it becomes a destructive power because of sinful man who is unable to fulfill its demands.

4) The law was given to reveal to man his sin and to lead him to a true knowledge of self. But always it encounters a man who is fleeing from God and going against God's will. Man is not free to choose between good and evil, so the law cannot lead to holiness, that is, to ethical perfection.

5) The law receives positive significance in the quest for holiness when it leads, by way of ever greater knowledge of sin, to Christ. Therefore the law must not be ignored nor its importance minimized.[40]

### OBEDIENCE OF FAITH

In this world faith can remain alive only if it continues to strive. Its sights are on rest and security before God. Even before men, however, it cannot remain idle but finds it necessary to express itself as love of fellow man. Assistance to fellow man is not limited to meeting his physical needs and succoring him in his physical suffering; it includes helping him to faith. Here the great example is Christ himself, who came from God and drew us to himself and throughout his earthly life never sought his own welfare but only ours. In like manner we are to serve one another and to save as many as possible.[41] Luther writes:

> Faith receives, love gives. Faith leads man to God, love leads man to men. In faith man lets God do good to him; in love man does good himself to other men. For he who believes has all things from God, and he is blessed and rich. Therefore he needs nothing more, but devotes his life and work to the good and welfare of his fellow man. In love he does for his fellow man what God has done for him in faith—as though by faith he draws upon the good from above and by love he distributes good here below.[42]

Lutheranism has at times been called lazy, but a lazy Christianity finds no support in Luther. A true believer cannot be uncon-

cerned about his fellow man. The relationship to fellow man is
an essential part of faith.

To Luther the interrelatedness of faith and love was of first
importance. His separation from Catholicism signified a parting
of the ways also in this respect. He had adequate experience of
the fact that outward works were no guarantee of inner attitude.
The new insight taught him that even as our righteousness is
Christ's righteousness, so also our works of love are Christ's works
in us. They ripen of themselves as fruit on a tree. From this spon-
taneity it follows that works must come after faith,[43] and that if
there are no works then faith cannot be true but is "acquired"
(acquisita), in other words, self-made in some fashion. But the
matter of works must not be put into the form of a demand. The
demand as such would imply that faith is not real and needs something to complete it. True faith knows no demands, for the works
of faith come of themselves. Faith rejoices in being able to clothe
itself in works. Demands cannot improve the character of faith in
any way. Faith is true if the relationship to God is true. Demands,
however, are unable to improve the God-relationship. True faith
and premeditated works for merit are contradictory, for true faith
rests on what God does while works of merit reflect man's own
activity. Works that do not originate in faith are apt to lead a
person into false notions about the true works of faith; they lead
one to imagine works of faith where none exist. The distinction
between true and false works, however, is as difficult as the distinction between true and false faith. No theory is adequate. One
must believe, pray, and strive.

The works of faith issue forth from the spring of God's abun-
dant goodness. No human activity is comparable, for God and man
are not comparable and all that a man does is really done by
God.[44] For this reason even the thought of merit before God is
absurd. The grace of baptism already is so great that no human
works can compare. Thereby "daring fools gain heaven and are
blessed," that is, those who properly trust in this gift of God with-

out offering their own works as merit to God.[45] The works of faith come spontaneously.[46]

While Catholicism looked upon sanctification as a continuous activity on man's part, as cultivation of self, as "school," Luther saw it theocentrically: God does everything. Man's struggle is a struggle for faith, not for works. Faith involves the total man, totally. Faith cannot result in inactivity, for it lives by God's judgment and grace, which in turn give rise to the activity of faith. If something is lacking, it at once becomes a matter of faith. The activity of faith is the service of fellow man; the fellow man is therefore an inseparable part of faith. The aim of faith can never be merely one's own salvation.

## SUMMARY

According to Luther sanctification always involves faith, its birth and growth. Faith has its beginning in man's knowledge that God is right in revealing sin and judging the sinner. Such faith leads to the salvation of the sinner who acknowledges his sin. God justifies the man who submits to his judgment. But in judging and justifying a man God also begins the work of bringing him into harmony with his will. This work occurs basically in an invisible manner, even as faith itself is invisible. Dissatisfied with such invisible holiness, reason and unbelief seek constantly to produce holiness of works visible to the world.

Christian existence is characterized by a double aspect: the believer is a sinner, and the believer is righteous; in himself he is a sinner, but in Christ he is righteous. This insight of Luther reflects significantly Paul's concept of the two aeons (Gal. 1:4). Luther may not have been familiar with the modern form of Paul's doctrine of the two aeons, yet his often-repeated concept of "simultaneously sinful and righteous" is in substance close to this idea of Paul. In Christ the Christian is a "new" man and sinless; outside Christ he is an "old" man and under the power of sin. The continuing sinfulness of the Christian is not to be interpreted as helpless subjection to the dominion of sin. Rather it expresses the thought of Romans 7 that in man "dwells nothing good," but that because he is a new creature in Christ he is involved in a continual conflict between the old and the new. For this reason the new life is constant warfare. In this warfare the weapons of the Christian are the Word and sacraments. Through them he has unity with Christ, and in Christ he has forgiveness of sins. This peace with Christ deprives the tempter of his strongest ally, namely, the guilty conscience.

Reason would convert the struggle for holiness into an empirical victory, with the power of sin finally and completely destroyed. But perfect holiness is not attainable in this world and this age. Here the conflict must go on. Trust in the Word and sacraments does not signify retreat from the imperfections of life into an invisible realm of faith; it does signify the rejection of deceptive human possibilities, and construction on God's sure foundation.

Interpreted in this manner holiness may appear as something purely passive. Yet in Luther's understanding faith is vital and active. Luther could agree completely with James that faith without works is dead (Jas. 2:26), without implying that works must be elicited by law or some outward requirements. Works are genuine only if they are the fruit of faith and gratitude. Only spontaneous works witness to true faith. Thus the problem of holiness or sanctification is from beginning to end a problem of true faith, not in the sense of "orthodoxy" but in the original biblical sense.[47]

**Chapter 8**

# The Work of The Holy Spirit

The topic of the Holy Spirit and his work has a constant timeliness in the Christian church. There have always been those to whom faith is primarily certain significant experiences and the witness to which they give rise. We must note however that religious experience is a general human phenomenon and is not peculiar to Christianity. All world religions speak of religious feelings, unique experiences, and, in many instances, ecstatic moments. Thus ecstasy is not a peculiarly Christian phenomenon. Furthermore, all such experiences do not lead to a knowledge of God and Christ. The New Testament certainly does not lend unqualified support to psychic experiences in general. Paul for one speaks with reservations about the psychic realm, clearly subordinating it to the realm of the spirit for which it is merely a prerequisite. The psychic and the spiritual must not be confused.

To Luther theology was a matter of the heart and not of the intellect. From the beginning of his theological endeavor he valued experience very highly. He who has not experienced temptation and affliction, what does he know?[1] Here we have one of the difficult problems of Luther's theology: he insists on an experiential basis of faith, yet takes a stand against natural human feelings. Faith's experience of reality does not stem from natural human feelings but contradicts them. The saving reality of Christ and faith in him are in contradiction to everything that natural man can experience on his own. They have to do with the reality of God, which is beyond human reason.[2] Appropriation of grace is not the reception of an "infused quality." It cannot be attested by psychic experience; it must be believed unseen. As such it is a most arduous thing *(arduissima res)*.[3] Confidence in God's act and

79

gift turned Luther against Karlstadt and the spiritualists. Luther's theology and ecclesiastical reform passed between the Scylla of the objectivism and institutionalism of the Catholics and the Charybdis of the subjectivism and spiritualism of the fanatics.

## LUTHER AND THE FANATICS

In discussing this problem in his well-known book *Spiritus Creator* Prenter makes no attempt to give the history of Luther's conflict with the fanatics. He is content with delineating the contrasting points of view.

In his treatise *Concerning Heavenly Prophets* Luther argues that the fundamental error of the fanatics is that they reverse God's order. God works in two ways, outwardly and inwardly. Included in the outward operation are the Word and sacraments; included in the inward operation are the Holy Spirit and his gifts. God's order has the outward preceding the inward. The fanatics reverse this order, insisting that the inward gifts must come before the outward means. In fact, what in God's order is outward they consider inward, and vice versa.

The fundamental difference between Luther's understanding of faith and that of the fanatics involved more than simply the relationship of the outward and inward elements. In the background is a divergence in the conception of the "order of salvation" *(ordo salutis)*, to use an expression of seventeenth-century theology. As the first item in this order Luther sees the law, which reveals sin, crushes man, and awakens in him a longing for the life-giving Word which is the gospel. He who hears the gospel receives the gift of the Holy Spirit. However, this reception is nothing mechanical or automatic. The Spirit creates justifying faith where he wills; he does not always as a matter of necessity come with the hearing of the Word. The Spirit rules the Word but is not ruled by it. In his conflict with the fanatics Luther could stress the significance of the external Word and make the Spirit subject to the Word. Nevertheless he underscored unceasingly the sovereignty of the Spirit and the insufficiency of the external Word alone.

Yet he insisted that the Spirit operates only through the external Word. The Spirit alone can create justifying faith in us. He alone is responsible for the fact that in the whirlpool of afflictions we do not run away from God but rather cry, "Abba, Father." Not until he is under the Spirit does man become active in his relationship to God, and then he shares God's activity toward the world. Our primary task is to preach the Word, by means of which we ourselves are saved. Participation in the work of Christ's kingdom lays a cross upon us, for the gospel invariably arouses the hatred of the world. This cross purifies our faith and gives proper direction to our hope. In addition to the world, the "old" man in us also resists the efforts of the Spirit. Our immediate task is to mortify the old man. Both preaching of the gospel and mortification of the old man are the Spirit's work, in which we participate. Further, the Spirit's operation includes also the good works done for our fellow men.[4]

The order of salvation suggested here must not be understood in chronological terms. The issue is not man's spiritual development, that would presuppose an anthropocentric viewpoint, and in Luther's view we are dealing here exclusively with the uninterrupted activity of God. The direction is from heaven downward. God sends the Word and sacraments. Man is at the receiving end.

The fanatics' order of salvation is something else. It begins with the mortification of the old man, and this is understood as a prerequisite for justification and the gift of the Spirit. The Spirit is not received by the hearing of the Word, hearing as such being outward and unspiritual. In order to receive the Spirit man must destroy by repentance the sin that dwells in him. Luther interpreted this to mean that man is his own savior. Thus the fanatics do not teach how the Spirit comes to us but how we go to the Spirit. The viewpoint is decidedly anthropocentric. The direction of the order of salvation is from earth upward. Law is made into a way that leads to God; Christ becomes an example, and faith, nothing but imitation.

From the viewpoint of the fanatics the outward Word and the

sacraments are assigned an inferior role. Given as means through which the Spirit operates from heaven downward, they can indeed be ignored if man is capable of making his way upward to the Spirit on his own.

Nomistic imitation-piety has a spiritualistic conception of the Lord's Supper. Reception of Christ as a gift is made into a spiritual exercise. Christ's presence must be experienced emotionally. To Luther the "remembrance" of Christ in the Supper was the Spirit's work.

Luther attacked this anthropocentric nomistic imitation-piety of the fanatics. They did not understand the Spirit as the giver of the gospel and the comforter of the poor in spirit, but made him the reward of the perfect. In his conflict with the fanatics Luther saw that the stakes were high; nothing less than the gospel itself was involved: do we receive Christ as a gift or must we work our way to him?[5]

### THE SPIRIT AND THE OUTWARD SIGNS

The fanatics understood the Spirit as the opposite of the visible and the physical. Since the Word and the sacraments belong to this visible world, they could not possibly serve as instruments of the Spirit. At best visible objects could be useful only as symbols. Luther, however, clung tenaciously to the idea that the Spirit's operation is associated with visible and outward things (eusserlich ding).

Prenter stresses strongly that in the conflict with the fanatics Luther did not defend some kind of metaphysical unity of the Spirit and the outward means. No divine power is associated with the outward signs, the water of baptism and the elements of the Lord's Supper, which the partaker in the sacrament might automatically share. The Spirit is no impersonal power but God himself in his sovereign majesty. He is not metaphysically in the means of grace so as to be transferred then into us.

Luther stressed both the necessity of the outward Word and the sovereignty of the Holy Spirit, without seeing anything contradictory in this. He never looked upon the Word and sacraments as means possessing grace in themselves. They were effective where and when it pleased God (*ubi et quando visum est Deo*).

From his natural standpoint man tends to see an essential union between the Spirit and the outward signs. He sees the Spirit as a power given to man in the means of grace for man's use as he works his way to God. This view is as anthropocentric as the seemingly opposite view of the fanatics, for both see man working his way from his own level to God's level. The difference is only in the manner in which this is accomplished. For Luther it was impossible to think that the means of grace as such contained the Spirit and grace. Such an idea leads inevitably to the concept of *ex opere operato,* according to which the "act as acted"—for example, distribution of the Lord's Supper—is automatically effective. In Luther's consistently theocentric view the operation of the Spirit, though mediated by the Word and sacraments, is the activity of the living God.[6]

With this in mind we are compelled to ask how it was possible for Luther to emphasize as he did the necessity of the Word and the sign. An answer is found in Luther's use of the word "sign" *(signum).* The Word and sacraments are signs of revelation. They "contain" God's presence. The Spirit works through them, using them as instruments. The incarnation of Christ was a sign of revelation. Now the sign continues as the means of grace, so that in them the risen Christ continues his real presence in human form. Throughout this age God is among us under the veil of a humble sign, Christ's humanity. The sign is to us a visible seal or guarantee of God's (Christ's) real presence. At the same time it affects our life, for it is an instrument of the Spirit. It binds our whole existence to the divine event. We are recreated in Christ's image and our life is set within the frame of the eschatological event, which points to a future fulfillment.

The efforts of the fanatics to reach God without any outward signs, whether by the way of speculation or of moralism, are doomed to fail. Such ways lead to the naked God *(Deus nudus),* the God of the law, the infinite Divine Majesty; and to encounter him means death. God can be truly found in the outward signs. In them he is our God (God in Christ, God for us).

God's sign overthrows the mastery of the law in our God-relationship. Our aspiration from earth to heaven is nullified as God descends to us. Prenter writes:

> When we are under the law each one finds himself on his own step on the ladder toward God. . . . One enters the monastery, another makes a trip to Compostella. They all seek a corner where they are able to develop their own private piety. This is the way the sects get started. But the signs of revelation, which are God's way to us, are public. They seek us all where there is no distinction between us as to our distress and our perdition. Therefore the gospel is not preached in closed circles but *in media civitate.* . . . When God comes to us he does not hide himself in a corner where only the especially initiated or those especially fortunate may find him. No, he appears publicly before all.[7]

But not all outward things are signs of God's revelation. The Word distinguishes the signs of revelation from other visible signs. Christ is present everywhere, but not as a sign. The Word and sacraments are signs because God has willed the presence of Christ in the bread and wine as the Supper is received and in the Word as it is preached. The outward signs are God's veil. Only through them is God able to come to us and still remain God. Under the protective cover of the sign God is among us as the God of revelation, the Savior, and not as the Judge. When he is hidden in the outward sign his gracious presence cannot be demonstrated. It can only be received in faith. To the unbeliever the sign is merely an outward thing. In these signs God both reveals and hides himself. We can meet the living God in them only in the faith created by the Holy Spirit.[8]

## THE OUTWARD SIGN AND CHRIST

According to Luther the Holy Spirit's work is not concentrated on man. Luther does not speak of visible effects of the Spirit in man, nor of visions and revelations, nor yet of hidden union with God and new truths revealed by the Spirit. In speaking of the

Spirit, as always, he speaks of Christ and the revelation of God in Christ. Luther's doctrine of the Holy Spirit's work is an aspect of his Christology. Christ as man is a sign, even as water, bread and wine are signs. Faith alone sees God in Christ, even as faith alone knows the real presence of Christ in the sacraments.

The substance of Luther's Christology is found in two central New Testament passages: "In him the whole fullness of deity dwells bodily" (Col. 2:9) and "He who has seen me has seen the Father" (John 14:9). Christ is the incarnate God and as such the sign of signs. His humanity is the sign of God's revelation, a shell containing the Divine Majesty.

The Word and sacraments are signs of Christ's incarnation in the period between his resurrection and return. Were it not possible for Christ to be present in Christendom in the form of these signs, he would belong to ancient history and our faith in him would be merely historical. According to Luther historical faith is never saving faith. The real presence of Christ as mediated by the Word and sacraments is an absolute prerequisite of salvation.

The fundamental features of Luther's Christology belong of necessity together: Christ is everywhere present (ubiquitous), wherever the Lord's Supper is celebrated. The deity dwells in his historical person, and the Word and sacraments are signs of his revelation. By despising the outward signs, the spiritualism of the fanatics, says Luther, denies the very incarnation of Christ. The signs have been given from above, and to ignore them is to build the God-relationship from earth upward. Two ways are then open, the way of speculation and the way of meritorious works. Rejection of the signs given from above, the Word and sacraments, results in denial of the gospel and straying into idealistic metaphysics.[9]

Christ's incarnation shatters the basic antithesis of idealism for, as Luther puts it, man is at the same time spirit and flesh. The whole man is flesh and as such opposes the operation of God's Spirit. But the whole man again is both spirit and flesh under the lordship of God's Spirit.

In this light we are to understand Luther's thoughts about the bodily benefit of the Lord's Supper. These thoughts have usually been looked upon as erroneous. The background of Luther's concept of Spirit is on the one hand the doctrine of the Trinity and on the other the doctrine of theocentricity. The Spirit is always the Spirit of God. He must be viewed from the standpoint of creation, redemption, and sanctification. There is a consistency in the work of God's Spirit. The spiritual and the physical are not antithetical. Spiritual participation in the Lord's Supper brings with it always also a bodily benefit. Prenter says pointedly that in Luther's view the sacrament cannot be received even spiritually without assurance and hope of bodily blessing. This follows naturally from the fact that to Luther salvation always involves the whole man. The new creation which is ours through Christ is not merely spiritual but spiritual-corporeal, even as Christ himself. In salvation we receive the whole Christ, not a part of him. Here is the basic reason for Luther's antispiritualistic stand.[10]

The elements of the Lord's Supper, the bread and wine, possess no supernatural power. The operation of God's Spirit is not magical but historico-eschatological, a saving act whose subject is God's Spirit and whose object is man. The goal is the eschatological fulfillment of the Christian hope, the resurrection of the body. The Holy Spirit's work is "hidden in faith and hope until the last day." This total view includes justification and sanctification as an indivisible unity. The Spirit's work cannot be divided into parts and the parts viewed chronologically, as was done in the order of salvation (ordo salutis) of seventeenth-century theology. The "spiritual food" of the Supper is so powerful that by the last day it changes our bodily being into a spiritual being, with the resurrection from the dead as the ultimate fruit. Faith in the forgiveness of sins and in the resurrection of the body are inseparably associated with the bodily benefit of the Supper. The spiritual and bodily fruit of salvation become one. If the gospel is taken to convey but one gift, the forgiveness of sins, which is understood to be something spiritual while the bodily benefit of the Supper and the

resurrection of the body are regarded purely as naturalistic speculation, then we have a spiritualistic idealism altogether foreign to
Luther.

The bodily benefit of the Supper includes in Luther's view also
love toward fellow man. In both instances a spiritual thing is
joined with an event of the physical world, and in both a gift from
above is translated into a physical benefit. To receive God's gift
without loving one's fellow man is to Luther a denial of faith.
Faith and works belong together without need of a rational statement about the necessity of works. Here a return has been made
to the fountain of early Christian thought, away from the unfruit-
ful efforts of medieval Catholicism to distinguish between faith and
works.[11]

Luther's understanding of corporeal is informed by two ideas:
the corporeal is a necessary instrument of God in the service of
our fellow men, and the corporeal is associated with the fulfillment
of the Christian hope, the resurrection of the body. This fulfillment demonstrates the greatness of God's saving love, which seeks
us in the depths of our misery, in the jaws of death, and raises us,
spirit and body, into a new life of glory. Here is revealed the full
richness of the forgiveness of sins.

At this point we see most clearly the contrast between Luther
and the fanatics. The fanatics' antithesis between body and spirit
reflects the basic antithesis in Plato and Neoplatonism between
matter and spirit, with matter always signifying a lower form of
being which has no value alongside spirit and is in fact identical
with sin.

In the spiritualism of the fanatics man seeks to elevate himself
to heaven by his own works or experiences. Diametrically opposed
to this way of salvation is that revealed in the gospel, whereby
the Spirit of God descends into the life of helpless man, creates
faith, and brings about complete redemption in the resurrection
of the body on the last day. Certain outward signs are involved:
baptism, the spoken word, bodily participation in the Lord's Supper, vocational activity for the good of fellow man, and resurrec-

tion of the body. The way of salvation of the law gives little significance to these external factors, for in the foreground are mortification of the body, spiritual experiences, inner perfection, imitation of Christ, and immortality of the soul.[12]

As Luther saw it, the spiritualistic development leads away from Christ and into the hands of the God of wrath (*Deus nudus*). This is why he was so determined in his opposition to the fanatics, in a surprising way labeling spiritual experiences as marks of the proud and selfish, and as belonging to the way of salvation by the law.

## Chapter 9

# The Problem of Affliction

Recent studies in Luther's theology have shown that the matter of anxiety or affliction *(Anfechtung)* was more than simply an expression of Luther's mental and emotional make-up. It was a decisive factor in his theology and is associated with a whole host of theological problems.

Luther was a sensitive religious man; he was "sick because of God."* Already in 1505 when he entered the cloister his main concern was to find a gracious God. He was no stranger to moments of distress and torment. His strict upbringing had much to do with this sensitivity. He is undoubtedly referring to himself when in a sermon he describes the fear that is created in a child's life. "Where such fear enters a person in his childhood, it is difficult ever to dispel it, for when every word of father and mother causes the child to tremble, during the rest of his days he fears even a rustling leaf."[1] Purely physical factors played a part in this distress. Much has been written about Luther's illnesses, even mental illness. Statements along this line have been seized upon with great eagerness. The uninformed have taken the discovery of the basic Reformation insight to be the matter of a personal crisis, after which the appearance of anxious moments is not to be taken seriously. The facts, however, say something quite different. Luther's most serious experiences of anxiety and affliction actually occurred after the publication of the Ninety-Five Theses, and not during the early years in the cloister. Repeatedly these experiences led him into indescribable depths.[2] Yet at times he could boast of

---

*"*Jumalasta sairas*" suggests that even as a person can be sick because of measles Luther was sick "because of God," not in the sense that he was physically or mentally debilitated but in the sense that he had, so to speak, a bad case of God.—W.J.K.

them, saying that they placed him among the great religious heroes.[3]

Luther looked upon his experiences of affliction and distress as experiences of God's wrath. Vogelsang makes the striking observation that the term *Anfechtung* is not a doctrinal concept but a word that points to life in that borderland where doctrinal formulations are of little use. Every effort to conceptualize it is bound to fail, for it is something that cannot be expressed in general terms. Real affliction is experienced only where everything doctrinal and conceptual has been played out.[4] Affliction belongs to the most mysterious area of a person's spiritual existence. It appears and reappears in new forms, constantly taking the person by surprise.

Luther translates the Latin term *tentatio* as *Anfechtung*, even though it should properly be translated *Versuchung*, the German term for "temptation." *Versuchung* connotes subjection to a test, while *Anfechtung* has the connotation of an attack or assault. In a catechetical sermon Luther uses the term *Anfechtung* in connection with the sixth petition. Following medieval usage he understands it to mean temptation to carnal sin. The flesh, the world, and Satan tempt man with "wild and rough life."[5] The urging to such sins comes as an attack by the powers of darkness. Since in its main root the term *Anfechtung* reminds one of fencing [*fechten*], it is an appropriate term to describe this aggressive action by the enemies. *Versuchung* refers more to what occurs within man's soul.

On the basis of studies by Wolf and Vogelsang we know that Luther classified *Anfechtungen* in three groups: 1) the carnal, 2) the spiritual, and 3) those pertaining to election. His specific terms varied somewhat, so that those of the second group he can call afflictions of faith and hope (*tentatio fidei et spei*), of sin (*tentatio peccati*), or of unworthiness (*tentatio de indignitate*); those pertaining to election he calls, following Gerson, temptations to blaspheme God (*tentatio de blasphemia*).[6]

In Luther's own words traditional Catholic theology, with the exception of Gerson and Tauler, knew only the *Anfechtungen* of the first group. These carnal temptations Luther calls sarcastically "fox tails," so soft and mild did they appear in comparison with those of the other two groups.[7] A spiritual *Anfechtung* is something entirely different. He describes it as a supreme affliction, an *Anfechtung* of death. Vogelsang describes its inner character as an infinite threat by the eternity, holiness, and omnipotence of God. Man's total existence, his life and activity, his moral will and judgment, his faith and hope, in a word everything in him is threatened. "God's ever present judgment is the continuous judgment of man." This supreme affliction is at the same time the affliction of an evil conscience, or of sin, or of unworthiness. It results from God's entrance into the conscience.[8]

The *Anfechtung* of election is clearly distinct from spiritual *Anfechtung*. In spiritual affliction man asks about his worthiness or unworthiness before God. He who is concerned about his election, on the other hand, does not doubt the truth or reality of the gospel but rather suspects that from his very birth he himself has been outside the pale of the gospel.

We omit from further discussion the *Anfechtung* of the flesh, since Luther himself considered the other two kinds much more important and difficult.

### THE AFFLICTION OF UNWORTHINESS

Perhaps the most shocking *Anfechtung* of unworthiness described by Luther is one from the year 1518. He says that God and with him all creation are terribly angry. Man has no hiding place, no comfort without or within; everywhere there is nothing but accusations. He feels the weight of pending eternal punishment. He still yearns for help but has no strength left even to cry out for it.[9]

Total helplessness is the characteristic feature of *Anfechtung*. God alone can help, but man is unable even to turn to him. The only God man sees is the God without Christ. Luther writes:

But outside Christ man is the subject of many raving tyrants, who are not his kings but his murderers, and under whose dominion he suffers great misery and distress. These are the devil, the flesh, the world, sin, and in addition also the law and death and hell, all of whom oppress the poor conscience. On account of them it is in a difficult prison and lives a miserable life. For where there is sin, there is not a good conscience, and where there is not a good conscience, there is only uncertainty and constant fear of death and hell. Therefore the soul has no true joy or pleasure but fulfills what is said in Leviticus 19 [26:36]: "The sound of a driven leaf shall put them to flight."[10]

With God's wrath weighing upon him the afflicted soul, unable to cry for help, tries to run away from the affliction. But to his horror he discovers that "the world has become too small and cramped for him."[11] He can find no hiding place, for all creation threatens him with wrath and judgment.[12] The anguish of this deep affliction is so great that it threatens to drive him into total despair and blasphemy of God: he desires another god and even wishes that he himself would cease to exist, thereby mocking the highest Majesty. If he could, he would put an end to God,[13] but seeing that this is impossible, he realizes that God's wrath threatens to make an end of him. The affliction of despair is an *Anfechtung* of death.[14]

The wrath of God which man experiences in his anxiety has other features also. God makes himself as the devil, and the devil appears as God.[15] *Anfechtung* is compounded by the uncertainty as to whether it is meant to test faith, or is judgment pure and simple. One thing is sure: to the afflicted one God appears as his enemy *(in forma hostili)*.[16] And human nature cannot stand the weight of God's eternal wrath.[17] Seeking to know whether the wrath he experiences is of God or of Satan, the tortured soul is fully aware of the fact that God is the enemy of sin and that he himself is a sinner. Now, if from this fact he concludes that God is his enemy, he has fallen into "Satan's greatest temptation" *(maxima tentatio Sathanae)*[18] and believed the greatest lie. To top it all, Satan takes on the appearance of the Divine Majesty.[19] If the distressed and afflicted soul can see through all this, he has averted the greatest danger.

Seeing that *Anfechtung* has such treacherous chasms, what could Luther say about overcoming it? In the midst of affliction he was quite helpless, but in moments of peace and security he was able to look upon affliction as God's game, by which God wants to draw his child to himself. This is why the tortured soul must without further questions be assured of God's love and goodness.[20] The first thing one must do in affliction is run to God. Whether the messenger be the devil or man, trials must be seen as sent by God.[21] One must flee to the angry God, no matter how difficult or painful this may be. One must hope, even if there is no hope. One must attempt the impossible.[22] The distressed and afflicted soul does not feel that his voice is heard, so everything seems impossible.[23] One must flee to God by trusting him.[24] God is not angry with us and does not want our guilt to remain unforgiven. He is simply testing us to ascertain whether we will trust his grace rather than our own merit.[25]

It can hardly be stated more clearly that the same God who sends trials and judgments is also the God who offers grace. The soul in anguish must not yield to the common blasphemy of the ungodly which says that God has hidden his face. "For it is actually blasphemy to say that God forgets the wretched, turns his face from him and does not care about him, when in the first commandment he has commanded us to believe and hope, in the second to call upon his name in time of need, and in the third to wait for his action."[26]

In the deepest whirlpool of affliction Luther sets the God of law against the God of law. The distress is due to the judgment of God's law, which man knows in his conscience. But God also commands us to take him as God and therefore to believe and trust in him. The despair caused by *Anfechtung* is directly contrary to God's will; it is disobedience against God's first commandment. God is good!

The fact that the first commandment provides an escape from despair shows that our help is in God's Word. Here is revealed the magnitude and depth of affliction. The comfort that comes in the gospel does not help. The afflicted soul refuses to accept it, saying that he is unworthy. The help that comes in the commandment reaches deeper, for the refusal of help is shown to be disobedience toward God. *Anfechtung* is of such a nature that God alone can help. The afflicted soul must therefore take refuge in the God who meets him in the Word of the Bible. He who rebels against the first commandment utters the most terrible blasphemy possible when he cries, "You are not God!" The tortured soul may consider himself guilty of such blasphemy, but in reality he is suffering from the devil's whisperings in his heart.[27]

Unnumbered times Luther emphasizes the fact that God's Word is our help in *Anfechtung*. The devil tries to tell the man who receives the Lord's Supper that he is not worthy of it with the result that he becomes distressed and anxious about his unworthiness and looks for reassuring signs. To such a man Luther says, "Here you must set the cross before you and not permit your worthiness or unworthiness to bother you. Take care that you believe the true Word of God as a sure sign, and you will be and remain worthy. Faith makes one worthy; unbelief makes unworthy."[28] But then, worthy or unworthy, it makes no difference. "God does not give you anything according to your worthiness. He does not establish his Word and sacraments upon your worthiness, but out of pure grace he establishes you upon his Word and sign."[29] Such establishment upon God's Word and promise becomes more prominent in Luther's later works.[30]

With his emphasis on God's Word as the help of the afflicted Luther actually means that Christ, the heart of the sacred Word, is the helper. Christ himself was the most tormented and afflicted of all. The fact that he overcame assures us that we, too, will overcome.[31] Even on the cross he was able to pray and to thank God (Ps. 18:6). Such prayer is not natural; it is of the Spirit, and can be realized in all who are in Christ.[32] Luther says that Christ the man is like one of us for to him, too, the "holy mount of comfort" was in a sense unknown and incomprehensible.[33] In the words of Psalm 22:2, "My God, my God, why hast thou forsaken me?", Luther sees the Christ who was afflicted and tormented for our sake. When God's wrath revealed in the law, that is, death and hell, terrify and oppress man, this Bible verse reminds him of Christ and supports him like a sturdy staff. When Christ was thus stricken and distressed he learned compassion for the afflicted. Mercifully he entered into suffering and bore it not because of his own need but because of ours.[34]

In setting Christ before us as an example *(exemplum)* Luther stands in the best tradition of the medieval mystics, to whom the imitation of Christ's sufferings was common. Throughout his life Luther continued to speak of Christ as example, even though in his later years he placed the main emphasis upon what Christ has done for us *(sacramentum)*, because Christ as example alone leads invariably into despair.[35] And perfect imitation of Christ is impossible for us. In fact the desire to be exactly like God is the root of all sin. Our transformation into Christ's likeness is nevertheless the ultimate goal of all God's activity directed toward us. Vogelsang points out that this two-edgedness is the deepest question involved in the imitation of Christ. "It is the dialectic of law and gospel, and according to Luther everything depends upon understanding it."[36] By 1522 Luther had rejected the idea of imitation of Christ as a way of salvation.[37]

Christ as the one who overcomes our afflictions and distresses takes on new meaning in Luther's theology after 1528. Earlier Luther had seen in the suffering Christ the tempted and afflicted Lord who suffered under God's eternal wrath, tasting the *Anfechtung* unto death and hell. After 1521 Luther describes the Gethsemane experience primarily as conflict with the devil.[38] The description of Christ's redemptive work as conflict with the devil is found, for example, in the larger *Commentary on Galatians*.[39]

During the years 1522-1524 Luther placed more stress on the immediate feeling of Christ's presence as that which overcomes doubt and despair than he did ten years later, when he spoke more doctrinally and objectively about the same matter. (To the earlier period belongs the conflict with the fanatics.) Thus in the passage of the *Commentary on Galatians* to which we have just referred Christ is described in objective terms as our Redeemer from sin. Repeatedly Luther states that to the extent that we look into ourselves we are lost in the face of sin, despair, and death.[40] But though I feel nothing but sin and death, "I nevertheless believe in Jesus Christ and so am justified in the Spirit, and in those evil things I await the appearance of righteousness. Its beginning I already bear in myself."[41]

## THE AFFLICTION CONCERNING ELECTION

Nominalistic theology made God's unpredictable and inscrutable will the sole basis of man's reception into grace or rejection from it. Luther's *Anfechtung* in regard to election stemmed from this teaching, with which he had been acquainted from the very beginning of his theological studies. Taking into consideration the theological climate of his monastery, it appears strange rather than natural that his doubts and anxieties regarding election apparently did not arise until around the year 1515.[42]

Luther's lectures on the Letter to the Romans illumine his position on the issue of election. In explaining Romans 8:28 he states that the elect are not saved by accident but of necessity. Since God saves them in spite of their numerous enemies (Rom. 8:33-35), salvation cannot depend upon their merit but must depend solely on God's election and eternal will. He writes:

> How then, you see, would it be possible for man to overcome all this which would cause him to despair a thousand times, unless God's eternal and sure love led him through it all and unless the Spirit helped him in his weakness and prayed for him with unutterable sighs? You see, in the midst of such things man could not know what to do or how to pray. He would likely pray to be spared from such things, and that would be a foolish prayer, for it would be contrary to his salvation. Therefore "we do not know how to pray," especially in weakness, that is, in such sufferings.[43]

The affliction concerning election and the concomitant despair and helplessness were no strangers to Luther.

The devil wants to cast man into doubt and despair and to accomplish this he resorts to various techniques. The primary one involves the fact that man does not know who are the elect. The devil urges man to investigate the matter. Luther says:

> Thereby he leads man, as is his intention, beyond God to seek signs of the divine will and, becoming impatient when he cannot know if he is among the elect, to doubt the existence of God and to long for another god. Briefly, the devil plans to extinguish God's love by a windstorm and to kindle God's wrath. The more man follows the devil and permits the devil's thoughts to prevail, the more dangerous his state. Finally he succumbs, and begins to hate and blaspheme God. For when I desire to know if I am among the elect, what is that but to desire to know what God knows and thus to be like God. God then is not supposed to know more than I, and so he is not supposed to be God. Then the devil brings to mind how many heathen, Jews, and children of Christians are lost, and he tempts with such dangerous and imaginary thoughts to the extent that man, who otherwise would gladly die, now becomes unwilling. To be assailed with doubt concerning one's election is to experience the distress and affliction of hell, about which there are many complaints in the Psalms. He who here is victorious has overcome hell, sin, and death all at once.[44]

Here the affliction concerning election is seen as the devil's temptation to pride. Man wants to look into God's secret plan of salvation. Seen against the background of the sin of the first man, this is a violation of the first commandment.

Despair is the most important mark of the affliction concerning election. Terrified carnal wisdom drives to blasphemy when it sees that salvation is not dependent upon one's own doing and activity but rests entirely on an outside factor, the election of God.[45] The encounter is no longer between God's knowledge and man's knowledge but between God's will and man's will. This *Anfechtung,* too, is the devil's work. God permits the devil, the world, and the flesh to tempt his own, in order to compel them to put their entire trust in his mercy.[46] The affliction concerning election is in many respects similar to the affliction of unworthiness. In the latter the despair stems from unworthiness as such, while in the former it stems from impotence in the face of tempta-

tion by the devil and the flesh. Impotence then is seen as a sign
that one does not belong to the elect.

The substance of the affliction concerning election Luther describes very clearly in his statements about the *Anfechtung* of
death in his so-called second commentary on the Psalms. Whereas
in other afflictions hope and faith contend with each other, here
in the afflictions concerning election the conflict is with the devil
and even with God himself and all creation. Satan fights against
man with his last and best-equipped forces. He does not drive us
to despair, knowing that such an attack would raise our resistance,
but he attacks our very ability to resist, trying to nullify our efforts at recovering hope. He makes our hope appear ridiculous,
as though it had been lost long ago. Thus faith and hope, which
ought to carry on the battle, are themselves subjected to attack:
That which prevents us from carrying on the conflict must be
overcome at greater cost than that which forces us into conflict.[47]

This is perhaps the profoundest and most striking description
possible of the peculiar nature of the affliction concerning election. Despair results ultimately from the threat to the power of
faith and hope to stand firm. The issue has to do with the continuation of the conflict itself. This being the case, it is no wonder
that Luther later viewed unbelief and despair as the ultimate and
most difficult forms of *Anfechtung*. He who has overcome them
has entered fully into the knowledge of God's will and can say
with Jacob, "I have seen God face to face."[48] Luther says that affliction concerning election drove him more than once into the
deepest chasm of despair, tempting him to the point where he
wished that he had never been born.[49] The thought that one does
not belong to the elect is not merely a foretaste of hell but an
actual experience of its terrors. The soul is virtually in hell already.[50] While other *Anfechtungen* can result in the strengthening of faith, the affliction concerning election destroys the very
pillars of faith. Man stands face to face with the "naked God"—
to use Luther's language—and the "naked God" is a terror to man,

for man can deal only with the God who has revealed himself in Christ.

Luther's lectures on the Letter to the Romans (1515-1516) do contain statements about the affliction concerning election, but the form and tenor of the presentation is objective. The purpose of this affliction is to make man humble. In its grip one is to learn to put his trust in God's mercy alone. Proud confidence in one's own ability and will disappears. This affliction, too, then stems from God's fatherly love. God leads his own safely through such affliction into the assurance of faith.[51] The positive meaning and effect of *Anfechtung* is implied even more clearly in the thought that one must be grateful for it. Luther points to Psalm 51:17: "The sacrifice acceptable to God is a broken spirit; a broken and a contrite heart, O God, thou wilt not despise." One must trust in the reality of the God of promises, and turn away from the fearful God of foreknowledge. Then one is blessed and among the elect.[52]

Such pastoral admonitions indicate that Luther was by no means helpless in the face of the affliction concerning election. We find the same clear instruction in his later writings. He states that we must not view hell and eternal perdition as such—not even in those who are judged—nor be concerned about the multitudes that may not be among the elect; for such reflection may crush us, unless we are on our guard. For this reason Luther suggests that we practice a little violence at this point and simply close our eyes. After all, what benefit is there in reflecting upon all this for a thousand years and bringing ourselves to ruin. In the end God must be permitted to be God; he knows more about us than we ourselves. So Luther urges:

> Therefore fix your eyes upon the heavenly picture of Christ, the Christ who for your sake went to hell and was rejected by God as one damned to eternal perdition, as he cried on the cross, "Eli, Eli, lama sabachthani. My God, my God, why hast thou forsaken me?" Behold, in that picture your hell is overcome and your election assured, so that if you but take care and believe that it happened for you, you will certainly be saved in that faith. Do not therefore permit this to disappear

from sight. Cling to Christ and not to your own resources, and you
will be in him forever.[53]

Recognition of the enemy is already partial victory over *Anfechtung*.[54] When the enemy is seen to be the devil, the way to victory is clear. One must know that God does not originate the affliction concerning election, for such affliction is completely re-
pulsive to him. When God initiates something, its purpose is to
help man keep his commandments and do his will. But concern
about one's election is not among the things that God has orig-
inated; far from commanding it, he actually forbids it.[55] The afflicted needs to discover that his anxious thoughts about his own
election are not from God at all. They are from the devil, who
seeks to lead man into one of two sins. The first sin is to press for
certainty concerning God's counsel and decision as they pertain
to him. Such a person actually hates God and would not have God
be God, for he refuses to permit God to know more than he himself.[56] The second and greater sin is to want to know God's counsel and hence be like God. Such a person does not want God to
be his God. This is the greatest sin.[57] Luther suggests that as a
way out of the affliction concerning election we should not even
enter into conversation with the devil about these matters. We
must turn a deaf ear to him, as did the men in Daniel 3:15-18.
In any case man must not try to force his way into the secret counsels of God, lest the glory of the Divine Majesty cast him into the
dust. That of course is what the devil has in mind when he en-
courages man to scoop dry the ocean of divine wisdom.[58]

The bottomless chasms and the numerous occasions for defeat
to the contrary, *Anfechtung* has in the final analysis, says Luther,
a positive and good purpose. It serves to push man closer to God,
teaching him to know God's love and goodness. It gives man an
experiential knowledge of God's wrath and judgment, but thereby leads him into a new and deeper experience of God's love.[59]

# Chapter 10

# The Spirit and the Word

Through the Reformation the Word was reinstated as the cardinal principle of faith. The Pope was replaced in spiritual matters by the Word, and in earthly matters by civil authority, the only recognized authority in the secular realm. Here we are concerned with Luther's understanding of the substance and power of the Word.

## THE DYNAMIC WORD

It was under rather dramatic circumstances that Luther was compelled to clarify the nature of the revolutionary power of the Word. While he was in seclusion in the Wartburg, one of his fellow workers, Karlstadt, initiated radical reforms in Wittenberg. Paintings were removed from churches, altars were smashed, and general disorder created. Had this been permitted to continue, the whole evangelical cause might have been lost. Luther therefore decided to come out of seclusion. He arrived in Wittenberg on March 6, 1522, and on the following Sunday preached his first sermon for restoration of order.

Many of Karlstadt's reforms Luther considered proper, but he could not agree with the manner in which they were carried out. Christian love demands that we avoid extremes and violence in all matters of reform. As Luther puts it:

> No one should be dragged away from it [the mass] by the hair; for it should be left to God, and his Word should be allowed to work alone, without our work or interference. Why? Because it is not in my power or hand to fashion the hearts of men as the potter molds the clay, and fashion them at my pleasure.[1]

Luther points out that man's word can reach people's ears only, not their hearts.

> And since I cannot pour faith into their hearts, I cannot, nor should I, force any one to have faith. That is God's work alone, who causes faith to live in the heart. Therefore we should give free course to the Word and not add our works to it.[2]

Thus it is not possible, Luther feels, to command the papal church to surrender its false mass. This can only happen by voluntary action. The Word must be preached, which today touches one heart and tomorrow another, and so they are won gradually. The principle must be that God wins the heart with his Word, and when the heart is won the whole man is won. In this connection Luther points to Paul, who in Athens discovered altars to idols. "He did not kick down a single one of them with his foot. Rather he stood up in the middle of the market place and said they were nothing but idolatrous things and begged the people to forsake them; yet he did not destroy one of them by force. When the Word took hold of their hearts, they forsook them of their own accord, and in consequence the thing fell of itself."[3] Since the Word brought forth heaven and earth, it must be trusted to renew churchly customs. As far as his own efforts were concerned, Luther says:

> I simply taught, preached, and wrote God's Word, otherwise I did nothing. And while I slept, or drank Wittenberg beer with my friends Philip and Amsdorf, the Word so greatly weakened the papacy that no prince or emperor ever inflicted such losses upon it. I did nothing, the Word did everything.[4]

### AN INSTRUMENT OF THE SPIRIT

Clearly the Word itself does not possess this great power. It has its power as an instrument of the Spirit. The question arises whether Word and Spirit are so related that the Spirit always works in the Word or whether each also operates separately.

Luther acknowledged no operation of the Spirit without or outside the Word. Against all unmediated revelations of the Spirit he placed the written word of the Bible. Yet the Word without the Spirit, Luther insists, is ineffective. Unless God himself speaks to the heart when the ears receive the Word, the Word is nothing more than an external thing, a human word. The Word does not receive its power from man. Without the Holy Spirit's operation no one can rightly understand God's Word. The outward Word, the written word, is weak and fragmentary in itself. It becomes God's Word under the operation of the "inner Word."

The value of the outward Word as such then is rather small. In comparison to the inner Word it is but a symbol. However, this is not the entire story. Unless the starting point is the outward Word, the Spirit and the inner Word are all but completely dissipated. Again and again Luther returns to the fact that the outward Word is an instrument of the Spirit. In fact, it is an incarnation of the Spirit. As the rays of the sun have heat as well as light, so the outward Word includes the Spirit. The Word is followed by the Spirit. This order must not be changed. First the Word, then the Spirit.

Here we have what appears to be a contradiction. On the one hand Luther emphasizes the sovereignty of the Spirit, so much so that the outward Word is on the verge of becoming a mere consequence of the Spirit. But on the other hand he stresses the outward Word to the point where the operation of the Spirit is in danger of being made into a mere attribute of the outward Word. How can this apparent contradiction be resolved? Is it simply that the stronger emphasis upon the Spirit's operation occurs in the earlier writings of Luther, those which reflect the stronger influence of Augustine, while the greater stress on the outward Word in the later writings stem from his experience with the fanatics?

After detailed study of the problem, Prenter observes that the Augustinian emphasis upon the Spirit continues unweakened throughout Luther's writings. In the later period it is more strongly combined with the outward Word. But Luther had effected this combination even before the conflict with the fanatics. Luther's own development then offers no basis for a solution of this problem. Orthodoxy resolved the problem by confining the Spirit to the outward Word. Verbal inspiration fixed the Spirit in the Word, whether it was in use or not. Another well-known solution is equally foreign to Luther. According to the so-called historical understanding of the Bible those portions of the Bible which have "religious value" are God's Word.

Exclusive emphasis upon the sovereignty of the Spirit leads in principle to predestination, inasmuch as the Spirit operates in whomever he wills. If the Spirit, on the other hand, is bound to the outward Word, the decision is transferred to the individual who hears the Word. Neither alternative represents Luther's view. He combines the two lines of thought even at the risk of tension. The tension that is created, however, testifies in its own way to the fact that paradoxes are part and parcel of living faith and cannot be eliminated by any thought process. Were this not true the very presuppositions of faith would be destroyed.[5] The tension is eliminated only in Christ.[6]

## CHRIST—THE HEART OF THE WORD

Luther's concept of the Bible centers in Christ. The whole Bible testifies of him. He who does not notice this sole purpose of the Bible has heard only external voices, the "flesh" and "shell" of the Bible, not its "spirit" and "heart." The Bible contains much that is "expanded" and "imperfect," figures and shadows, material that is not directly to the point. But in the middle of all the shadowy and unreal stands Christ, the real message of the Bible. In him we have "epitomized" and in "perfect" form the message of the whole Bible. The expanded and imperfect Word is "law," the abridged and perfect Word is "gospel." The same truth could be stated in terms of the antithesis between flesh and spirit. The imperfect Word does not give what it is supposed to give. The perfect Word, the gospel, gives grace. The law intends Christ, but the gospel alone conveys him.

In Luther's theology law and gospel do not refer to specific parts of the Bible. Rather they represent two viewpoints or stances. The Bible always places its reader before the face of God. The message of this sacred book is as serious as life and death. For this reason only faith can understand the true content of the Bible, the gospel. Without faith the sacred Word is the mere shell of the Bible, not the kernel, not the Spirit's Word but empty and Spiritless knowledge. This is the result of man's proud and false stance.

The antithesis between law and gospel is reflected in man's two opposite stances of pride and humility. With sin continuing to grip us in all possible ways and forms, we must repent again and again, moving away from ourselves and our own wisdom, perfection, and goodness. Without this struggle of faith engendered by the Holy Spirit, we cannot comprehend the message of the Bible as Word of the Spirit, as gospel.

Christology casts significant light upon all this. Through the Holy Spirit's influence Christ is in the external Word, even as he was in Jesus in the days of his flesh. Luther looks upon the Bible as the spiritual body of Christ. In it the risen Lord is in our midst. Transfigured by the Spirit, the Word proclaims to us the central truth of Christology, the resurrection of Christ. In speaking of this transfiguration Luther can say that the resurrection and glorification proper take place here on earth in the Word of the gospel, not in heaven. The Holy Spirit transfers the resurrection from God's hidden world into the world of the gospel. In this Word the risen Lord lives the resurrection life in our midst. Thus the resurrection of Christ is not a distant metaphysical event but a saving event to us and in us.

Christ then is the heart and the secret of the Word. In the incarnation he came into the world—or, to use another figure of speech, in the incarnation this Word was spoken into the world. We encounter his humanity in the outward Word; in this Word the Risen One himself is among us as God's gift. From this it follows: 1) that without the living Christ the outward Word is merely dead letters, and 2) that the Spirit can work only through the outward Word. Without the outward Word Christ cannot be proclaimed. The gospel has a sacramental nature, that is, it has also a visible part, the written Word. Without it Christ is but an idea which we can treat as we would any other idea.

No man can receive Christ on his own, whether by investigation, hearing, inquiry, or search. For the knowledge of Christ all books are too small, all teachers too weak, all reason too dull. Only the Father can reveal and impart him to us. By his own reason and with his own capabilities man cannot rise to heaven and please God. The outward Word is set over against man's thoughts and works as something foreign to man, but in this Word God comes to man that man might receive him in faith.

What has been said about the Word can equally well be said of the Sacrament of the Altar. Without the Word the real presence of Christ would not benefit us, for without the outward Word we would have no sacrament. Of equally little benefit would be the incarnation of Christ, were it not communicated to us by the outward Word which faith can receive. The outward Word is the point of contact for faith. In it the Spirit approaches us and enters into us in a concrete manner. If the outward Word is the promise, the inner Word signifies fulfillment. Thus at the crucial point of faith the question is not of our works and accomplishments but of a gift offered for our reception.[7]

### THE SPOKEN AND WRITTEN WORD

We are now in a position to appreciate Luther's strong emphasis upon the spoken Word. Luther points to the fact that Christ spoke a great deal and wrote not a word. Likewise the apostles spoke more than they wrote. The message of the New Testament was not written on inanimate tablets of stone but was given as an oral Word. In a remarkable way Luther anticipated the chief argument of Form Criticism in our own century that the gospel pericopes were originally individual sermon texts, oral tradition, and were later collected into the present Gospels. In his *Church Postil* Luther remarks bluntly that the writing of books is quite "unlike the New Testament." The proper order would have been to have everywhere good, learned, spiritual, and industrious teachers, who orally interpreted the ancient writings and communicated their Spirit.[8] The law is dead words written in books, but the gospel is a living sound.

On the one hand we have then the law and writings; on the other hand, the gospel and the oral Word. The Word as it is spoken must broadcast the gospel which is hidden in the writings, that is, in the law. Prenter concludes that in Luther's view the written Word is law. It offers us some history and at best calls us to imitation. As mere writing it leaves us to ourselves, to our own possibilities. The oral Word, on the other hand, is gospel. It proclaims Christ and conveys him to us as a gift. The living Word promises the descent of the Holy Spirit upon us and his operation in us. The difference between law and gospel has to do, however, only with the form, for the substance of both is Christ. The law contains Christ as a demand; the gospel contains Christ as a gift. Prenter summarizes Luther's thoughts as follows:

> The outward form of the law is the written Word, its inward form the wisdom of the flesh. The outward form of the gospel is the preached Word, its inward form the Spirit of God. . . .
>
> The outward form of the letter corresponds to knowledge—that which the wisdom of the flesh can make into its mastered object. In this sense all of Scripture, as the written Word, can be made into inward knowledge. But to the same extent that the Scripture is made an object of knowledge it also becomes law. It places us on our own resources to realize this knowledge. Outward preaching is something entirely different from this inward knowledge which is an expression f man's own ability. In the outward preaching the Word meets us as something over which we never become master; it meets us as an alien power, which gives us what we never could take of ourselves: the living Christ as a gift. This applies not only to the hearer but also to the preacher. It is the impossible he does when he preaches the gospel; it is not the display of his own knowledge and power.[9]

Hardly any one in the whole history of Christendom has seen more deeply than Luther into the problem of the Word and the Spirit. He says that the study of books often conceals the proud will to master the Word without the aid of the Spirit. Therefore the best Christians are not those who have read the most, for without the help of the Spirit the written law leaves man untouched, still self-dependent.

Only when preached is the Word the gospel that offers the

whole Christ. When heretics refuse to hear the gospel preached by the church, they refuse to receive the whole Christ. They prefer to follow their own taste and sense, and for this reason their faith takes in only the historical fact of Jesus. They know that he was born and that he died, but they do not know that he lives as Lord. Ernst Wolf has explained that this affirmation of Luther is directed against medieval imitation-piety.[10] Imitation is consistently legalistic and has an incomplete Christ. The written Word leads to a piety undersigned by the law and by man's own works, taste, and critical acumen, in other words, by man's own ability. The oral word *(verbum vocale)* on the other hand leads to piety in which the crucial place is occupied by Christ as a gift, Christ as a sacrament; and the signature is that of the Spirit. The oral Word, however, is not just any word that the preacher may utter, but the Word of the gospel by which faith lives. Should someone presume to possess such complete faith that he no longer needed to hear the proclamation of the Word, he would be incapable of hearing God's Word for he would resist it as false.

The man who is not always ready to receive a new message or gospel from God is deceived by his false preparedness and led astray by his own false ideas. But this vitally necessary Word, this message or gospel, is hidden under a lowly and strange garb. In revealing himself God always veils himself with his opposite. Thus Christ, the revelation of God, came in distress, death, and the sufferings of hell.

True faith is always in the making. A "finished" faith receives only the historical Christ, the Christ of imitation-piety, and not the living Lord, the whole Christ. The believer whose faith is a finished product loses the whole Christ. By the true or whole Christ is meant the message of redemption about the Christ who lives now for those who are now under the judgment of the law. This message is so hidden from the world that it must be proclaimed by word of mouth. Prenter says that if the reality of Christ were not hidden and different from all other reality, we would end up in unevangelical Christ-mysticism. In this world of sin and suffering God reveals himself only in translation, that is, concealed in his opposite. This accounts for the antithesis between faith and sense perception. Man tries to establish contact with Christ by means of his own thoughts and critical faculties, but since Christ's presence is hidden such contact is possible only in faith.[11]

A twofold conclusion may be drawn. First, the living Word speaks in the present and person to person, thus proving that Christ is the risen Christ who lives and speaks and imparts himself in his Church. Second, Christ is a real presence only as the Christ of faith, the hidden Lord, who is the opposite of everything that is grasped and felt, sensed and experienced, and who is apprehended only by faith. The living, spoken Word brushes aside all attempts at final possession of Christ, whether in the form of scholastic theology, imitation-piety, a movement of spiritual awakening, the dated conversions of Methodism, or Pentecostalism's baptism of the Spirit.

The written Word and the oral Word are both needed. Both are means of revelation and of the Spirit. As Christ became flesh, so the Word takes on written form; and as Christ lives and is active in this moment, so the oral Word serves as an instrument of the Spirit. The written Word points to the redemptive acts of God, the history of Israel, the coming of the Messiah, his death, resurrection, and ascension. All this is history, and it is proper and right that it be verified in the same way as all other historical events, by written historical sources. But since the incarnate Word is not merely history but also revelation, it must also appear as oral proclamation, otherwise it remains a thing of the past. In proclamation it becomes actual.

These views may seem surprising since much of Protestantism is dominated largely by the doctrine of the verbal inspiration of the Bible and an exclusive reliance upon the written Word. To Luther the real presence of Christ is the decisive factor, and the Spirit alone makes him real. The Spirit, however, is not in our power. The real presence of Christ is a miracle of the Spirit, but in the performance of this miracle the Spirit uses the Word, whose center is the history and resurrection of Jesus. Using the letter, the written Word, as his instrument, the Spirit in proclaiming history, does what the Spirit alone can do—he creates faith. In Luther's theology the Word and the Spirit belong together.

# Chapter 11

# The Church

Thank God, a seven-year-old child knows what the church is, namely, holy believers and sheep who hear the voice of their Shepherd. So children pray, "I believe in one holy Christian church." Its holiness does not consist of surplices, tonsures, albs, or other ceremonies of theirs which they have invented over and above the Holy Scriptures, but it consists of the Word of God and true faith.

These are Luther's words in the Smalcald Articles (Part III, Art. xii). Bornkamm observes that theologians have no doubt often thought with envy and suspicion about that "seven-year-old child" who had such a thorough grasp of the concept of the church. History at any rate shows that this concept has undergone many changes in Protestantism. In the days of the patriarchal state the church represented the spiritual care which the father of the country exercised over his subjects. During the period of absolute monarchy the church was a part of the absolute order. The state dictated to its subjects both the content of their faith and the conduct of their life. In the Enlightenment the church was primarily a society of believers for the maintenance of public worship. Romanticism saw the church as an expression of interest in and fostering of the emotional life. Church leaders and members were related to each other as artists and adherents. As a result the church became a religious communion of like-minded people, which demanded complete freedom in a nonconfessional state. This is perhaps the situation in which Protestantism finds itself today in most countries.

As part of its Old Testament heritage, the New Testament uses the designation "God's people" as a name for the church. To begin with, only Israel was God's people. Adopted by the Christians, the designation quickly broke through all national lines. In the early years of the Christian era, however, the idea of the church, like other Christian ideas, was molded by its environment. The Greco-Oriental mystery religions influenced it in a significant way; religion was a mystery with occult powers in which one participated by means of certain cultic rites. The concept of the church of this early era was also strongly influenced by the Old Testament. Both Judaism and Roman Catholicism are founded on a well-defined juridical system. Canonical law supplies the basis for the Roman ecclesiastical institution.[1]

The Catholic church considers herself the true church because she has the true cult. The Roman mass is both a mystery and a continuation of the Jewish temple service. The Old Testament sacrifice has become a bloodless sacrifice of the mass. The Catholic priest is a leader of the mysteries, and bears the office of the Jewish temple priest; this is why he is set so far apart from the laity of the church. In the ordination the priest is supposed to receive an indelible character *(character indelebilis)*. As the guardian of the sacrament he remains unmarried, so as not to profane it. As early as the second century it was thought that the church became concrete in the bishop. Eventually there developed the more definite idea of the bishop representing the church in all matters of doctrine and polity.[2]

The German theologian Friedrich Heiler, a convert from Catholicism to Protestantism, has analyzed the Roman Catholic idea of the church in his famous book *Der Katholizismus*. He finds in it the following seven elements: 1) primitive religion, 2) religion of the law, 3) juridic-political church institution, 4) rational theology, 5) mystery liturgy, 6) ascetic-mystical ideal of perfection, 7) evangelical Christian faith.[3] Synthesis is characteristic of Catholic thought and practice. In spreading among a new tribe or people it receives from them a sufficient number of terms and beliefs to make possible internal penetration into the life and religion of these people. Since the program has been one of repeated synthesis without counteracting reformation and since tradition is given an important place as a matter of principle, a constantly growing baggage of pagan beliefs is handed down from century to century. As a result of this synthesis the Catholic church has always been able to give to all groups whatever they ask. Those on the primitive level have received religious nourishment appropriate to them; aesthetic people have enjoyed the most important products of Western culture in various fields; philosophers and other intellectuals have been offered as spiritual fare the best fruits of human knowledge. Thus the church has been deeply involved in the development of Western culture. The gulf between the church and cultural life has not become as pronounced as in the Protestant world. The Renaissance opened up a gulf between freedom-seeking humanism and the Christian church, a gulf which the Catholic church has been attempting for two hundred years to remove, and with some degree of success.

True, the Roman Catholicism of today is not what it was in Luther's day, but its main features have changed very little. Knowledge of them gives us the background for understanding Luther's contribution in connection with these issues.

## THE COMMUNITY OF SAINTS

In his extensive literary output Luther repeatedly presents his thoughts on the nature of the church, though never in a completely systematic way. Already his initial major work, the first lectures on the Psalms, contains numerous statements concerning the church. Catholic and Protestant scholars have come to opposite conclusions in regard to them. From the Catholic side Grisar has argued that Luther's concept of the church during the early period (1513-1515) was more Catholic than Protestant, while Holl is of the opinion that the first lectures on the Psalms have a concept of the church which Luther never surrendered. Fagerberg is willing to straddle the issue by saying that during these early years Luther was more dependent upon the Catholic tradition than Holl is ready to admit, but that at the same time his concept of the church has more permanent features than the Catholics admit.[4]

Luther's intention was never an outward church organization. In opposing the many errors of the Catholic church he had no desire to create a new church organization, but only to renew the original apostolic church. The important thing was the church of the Spirit, the inward church. The institutional church was only a form and servant of the church of the Spirit. To Luther the church was above all the community of saints. This thought Protestantism has not always maintained in its vitality, but today the ecumenical movement is again raising it to a position of honor.

The community of saints, *communio sanctorum,* is confessed in the Apostles' Creed. The key to the understanding of this concept is the word "saints." The Catholic church taught that the saints were in heaven; Luther brought them down to earth again, as Holl has strikingly put it. According to the apostolic understanding every believer is a saint in Christ. Therefore no distinction is to be made between saints and ordinary Christians. There are two kinds of saints all right, but they are the living saints and the dead ones.[5]

In the Smalcald Articles (Part III, Art. iii) Luther describes the saints in the course of his discussion about true repentance. He rejects the traditional Catholic acts of penance by which one seeks to free himself from actual sins, "such as wicked thoughts to which they consented . . . wicked words, and wicked works which man with his free will might well have avoided."[6] No thought is here given to Christ or faith, since one hopes by his own works to overcome sin before God. The idea that everyone should be able to enumerate all his sins was to Luther impossible. Beyond that it was terrible torture. Referring to Romans 3 and Acts 17 Luther observes that the Bible teaches us to know sin in the sense that "we are all utterly lost, that from head to foot there is no good in us, that we must become altogether new and different men."[7] In the light of this biblical kind of total repentance everything in us appears as sin; nothing is uncertain, for there is no need to sift out the items for which we need no repentance. With Christians repentance continues until death and is carried out not in our own strength but in the power of the Holy Spirit. The gift of the Holy Spirit "daily cleanses and expels the sins that remain and enables man to become truly pure and holy."[8]

Saints do not live in monasteries and chapters, for such institutions are human inventions without any foundation in God's Word. It is completely erroneous to label them as forms of life "superior to the ordinary Christian life and to the offices and callings established by God."[9] It is equally erroneous to think that saints know no temptations.[10] "The true saints were no logs or stones, as the sophists and monks imagine, but people who were tempted and who knew the desires of the flesh, for their flesh lusted against the Spirit, as Paul says."[11] Those who fall in weakness, no matter how often, are forgiven. But those who choose to remain in sin are of a deceitful spirit.[12] Saints are sinners engaged in continual repentance. Holiness is hidden in weakness, which means that God's saints are hidden.[13] They are ordinary people. They are not to be worshipped in the Catholic fashion but served. Luther says, "The saints are the hungry, the thirsty, the naked and poor, who have wife and children and who suffer shame. Help them, work for them, use your tongue to protect them, cover them with your coat, and help them to honor."[14]

In the explanation to the third article of the Creed in the *Large Catechism* Luther deals with the meaning of *communio sanctorum*. He thinks that these words are a later addition to the Creed intended to explain the preceding word *ecclesia* (church). He does not like the word *ecclesia,* he says, because its German equivalent *Kirche* (church) had come to mean a consecrated building. He says he prefers to call the church by the name *heilige Christenheit* (holy Christendom), since these words best express the unity of all who are baptized and believe.[15]

The church is above all the community of saints. Luther says, "I believe that there is on earth a little holy flock or community of pure saints under one head, Christ. It is called together by the Holy Spirit in one faith, mind, and understanding."[16] To him the chief thing is always the inner nature of the church as the community of holy, believing people. In his important treatise *On the Councils and the Churches* (1539)[17] Luther does not touch with a single word on the church as an outward institution, but discusses only the inner nature of the church, which is the unity of holy people in Christ. This shows the contrast between the Roman church and Luther. In the Roman view the Christian church is primarily a large outward institution with the Pope as its head as the vicar of Christ on earth. Over against this idea of the outward institutional church Luther throughout his life emphasized the community of saints as a unity of hearts in one faith.

Protestant scholars have noted the danger which accompanies a false emphasis on the church as a community of persons. If the church is considered to be the sum total of its members, we are in spiritualistic subjectivism. This danger is inherent in the so-called church association concept. The Christian church did not have its birth after the manner of a temperance society, with people uniting around a common interest. The foundation of the Christian church is Christ himself. He is the tree to whom we are grafted in baptism. He was before a single member of his church existed. According to Luther however—even at the risk of subjectivism—faith is a prerequisite. But faith does not imply merit before God, for it is God's work in us.[18]

Luther faced enemies on two fronts, the Catholics on the right and the fanatics on the left. While the Catholic church emphasized the juridical order as the foundation of the church, Luther stressed the Word as the only thing essential for the being of the church. Against the Anabaptists, who relied on an inner Word and immediate revelations, Luther underscored the unique significance of the outward Word. In each case the Word meant something slightly different for Luther. To the Romanists Luther insisted that the Word is sufficient and that alongside it canon law is secondary. To the fanatics his emphasis upon the Word was meant to say that revelations are not enough and do not provide an adequate foundation. The Word alone is sure. Aulén puts it well when he says that Luther always carried within him a picture of the gospel making its way in the world, creating the community of saints by awakening faith. The gospel or Word is an instrument that God uses in creating that which is "new" in the individual; by the same instrument he creates the church. Luther stated the matter also in another way, saying that the Holy Spirit has in this world the church as a mother which gives birth to and bears every Christian through the Word of God. The church of Christ on earth is the product of the preaching of the gospel; it is a creation of the gospel (*creatura evangelii*).[19]

In Luther's view a sinner can come to Christ only with the help of the gospel that is proclaimed in the church, the community of saints. Luther adopts the basic Catholic idea that outside the church there is no salvation (*extra ecclesiam nulla salus*) but gives it a new content. Luther does not mean that membership in the church organization is a condition of salvation. He means that the gospel or the saving Word is to be found only in the church of Christ. His words are:

> Any one who is to find Christ must first find the church. . . . Now the church is not wood and stone, but the company of people who believe in Christ. . . . Christ is certainly in their midst. Outside the Christian church there is no truth, no Christ, and no salvation.[20]

The church was to Luther a religious reality. To the individual the church must be first of all a divine institution of salvation, which exists prior to individual Christians. The church both gives birth to and receives the Christian. There can indeed be no salvation outside the church.

In Roman Catholicism the church organization dominates. The Word is a tool of the church, rather than the church being a tool of the Word, that is, of the Holy Spirit in his saving work. To Luther the significance of the Word or gospel is so total that he can say that the whole life and substance of the church is in God's Word (*tota vita et substantia Ecclesiae est in verbo Dei*).[21] The regular function of the gospel is to be "the oral Word, by means of which he [the Holy Spirit] proclaims forgiveness of sins in the whole world." The gospel comes to us also in the sacraments, but even in them the promise or the Word is more important than the sign. The Word or gospel is also their real substance.[22]

Luther's concept of the church is bound inseparably with his view of revelation or God's Word. Christ himself is the reality present in the Word; the Word is primarily Christ himself. The Word, Christ, and the church form a unity. The full authority of the church consists in the fact that in the church it is Christ himself who through the Holy Spirit continues to reveal God in the present moment, proclaiming the gospel and thus gathering the Christian people on earth.[23]

In the light of Luther's bitter attack against the Roman church it might appear that he could see no connection whatsoever between the papacy and the church of Christ. This is not so. He had no desire to leave the Catholic church. In fact, he acknowledged it as his spiritual mother. In its bosom he had been nurtured. He had no desire to sever relations with the church. It was simply that he could not accept the false conception of the nature of the church entertained by the papal and priestly party. Even though he later rejoiced that he did not have to remain in the "den of robbers" of the Roman church, he was glad nevertheless that he had not left the church voluntarily but had been excommunicated. As "the Lutheran church" came into being, he refused to accept the idea that he and his supporters were the only true church. The name "Lutheran" never pleased him. In the midst of internal and external conflict it became ever clearer to him that the church of Christ cannot be bound to any individual, time, or place. The church could not be an outward organization. The church as the community of saints was something altogether different, a living reality that continues from age to age. Throughout the darkness of the papal era God had preserved for himself a little flock, among whom the gospel continued to live. "The

Creed teaches us that a people of God must be on earth and remain until the end of the world. This is an article of faith, which cannot cease until that comes which it believes, as Christ promises, 'I am with you even unto the end of the world.' "[24]

Luther called the Roman church holy, even though he had to fight against its many errors. Here he followed Paul, who called the church in Philippi holy, even though it lived "in the midst of a crooked and perverse generation" (Phil. 2:15). The church of Rome was a church, even though it was "in the hands of wolves and robbers, that is, spiritual tyrants." For in its midst had been preserved "baptism, the Lord's Supper, the word and text of the gospel, the Holy Bible, the holy offices, and the names of Christ and of God."[25] The boundaries of the community of saints in the Christian church do not coincide with the boundaries of some outward ecclesiastical organization. The lines are drawn according to the reception or rejection of the Word. Like the individual Christian, the church too is "simultaneously righteous and sinful." "The church is indeed holy, but at the same time it is sinful. Therefore it also believes in the forgiveness of sins and prays, 'Forgive us our trespasses.' "[26] Christian holiness is shared by all churches and all Christians. The church is holy, but only in faith in Christ. It has no holiness of its own; it is neither visibly nor perfectly holy, for its members stumble and fall in many ways.[27]

## COMMUNIO AS PARTICIPATION

As we have noted, the church of Christ is to Luther a *communio sanctorum*. The word *communio* can be translated by various terms and with various meanings. Luther gave it among others the meaning of participation or sharing. Thus the term points to the fact that in the church of Christ all things are held in common. Membership in the church means participation in common treasures, but it also includes sharing in distress and anguish. This connotation of *communio* revealed to Luther the richness of what the early Christians knew as community in the body of Christ.

Christians are one body in Christ. Thus they are also united with each other. This unity is the most intimate possible, for there is but "one baptism, one Christ, one sacrament, one food, one gospel, one faith, one Spirit, one spiritual body, and each person is a member of the other. No other brotherhood is so close and strong."[28] The uniting factor is faith, which makes the believer and Christ one person.

Community eliminates all distinctions in the church. The gulf existing in Catholicism between the clergy and the laity disappears, for Christ does not have two kinds of bodies, an earthly and a spiritual. The special distinction attached to life in the cloisters disappears. Referring to Galatians 3:28, Luther says, "All must boast only of Christ, in whom there is no man and wife, no maiden and spouse, no widow and single, for all are one in Christ." The church as the body of Christ is a community of faith, love, service, suffering, and sacrifice. The life of the Christian is as a matter of fact the life of Christ in this world.[29]

In Luther's view of the church as the community of saints, the church as an organization or a hierarchy all but disappears. The community of believers in Christ becomes dominant. Christ's holiness is the believers' holiness; his perfection is their perfection. They have no nature of their own which would exalt them above others. They are new people, but only in Christ, that is, only in faith. Without Christ and apart from faith they are only sinners.

Orders of worship have value only as they serve in creating and sustaining faith. Their sole meaning is in their helping men into unity with Christ and strengthening them in this unity. As something we do for God they are worthless, for God does not need them. Any attempt to influence God by means of them is magic; it is the proffering of human works to God in the matter of salvation. Righteousness of works is idolatry, no matter what form it assumes. God's thoughts of us are thoughts of love. This we see in the incarnation of Christ, his life, death, and resurrection. By our acts of worship we cannot in the least add to God's love. Any effort to do so brings God's wrath upon us, for it means that we are refusing to receive in faith the Christ whom he has made our Savior, and instead are offering to him something of our own. He who seeks to justify himself by his works despises God's greatest gift, since he wants to replace Christ with something of his own. This Reformation view represents a radical reform of worship, but it is in accord with the attitude of the first Christians toward Jewish temple worship (Heb. 10:11-25).

Equally radical is Luther's rejection of a line of thought that stems from the Oriental mystery religions. The priest is not a guardian of occult knowledge nor does he represent a holiness greater than that of ordinary people. His holiness—like that of any member of the church—is the "alien righteousness" of Christ. "There is no distinction," as Paul insists (Rom. 3:22).

The Anglo-Catholics of England, who belong to the extreme right of Protestantism, make the sacraments and the offices of the church decisive. Over against them, on the extreme left, are those who conceive of the church in an individualistic way as an association in which the prerequisites for membership are personal decision, experiences, works, and religious and moral qualities. Between these two extremes we find innumerable variations. Luther's concept of the church is often supposed to be somewhere among them. As a moderate view it supposedly wants to avoid both the extreme "objectivity" of the right and the exaggerated "subjectivity" of the left.

But what is this "objectivity"? The term has reference to the institution of the church, the sacraments, the offices and ceremonies which sanctify the secular life. By means of them man is supposed to be made acceptable to God—which is precisely the view Luther wanted to destroy. And to what does the "subjectivity" refer? To man's experiences and efforts, the decisions of his free will. As determinants of a man's relationship to God Luther rejects these with equal firmness, for they too involve work righteousness. The two alternatives represent, in Luther's view, the same righteousness of works in different forms. Again we must say, "There is no distinction."

We have arrived at the seemingly strange conclusion that both alternatives—that of "high churchliness" and that of "low churchliness"—represent, in Luther's view, two forms of the same thing. The fault is with the man-centered starting point. Having become entangled in man-centeredness we find it difficult to understand Luther's God-centered views. He proclaims to us the gospel, God's act and God's love. In his concept of the church, as in all aspects of his thought, his great main theme is: It is God who does it.

Luther is not operating here on the basis of some truths he himself invented. The whole New Testament bears consistent witness to God's activity for our salvation. "All is from God, who through Christ reconciled us to himself" (II Cor. 5:18). More consistently than perhaps anyone else in the history of Christendom Luther built his concept of the church on this foundation alone.

## Chapter 12

# The Spiritual Office

In the chapter on Luther's concept of the church the Oriental mystery religions were considered as a factor in the development of ancient Catholic theology.[1] It was due to this influence that the Catholic priest became the officiant of certain occult rites. His knowledge of the mysteries raised him above other people. In ordination he received, as Catholic theology saw it, an indelible character; and living in celibacy he was crowned, as the common people saw it, with saintly glory. The Roman Catholic priest is primarily an officiant of the sacrifice of the mass; the sacraments are his real task. This includes the hearing of confession and pronouncement of absolution. In general, the essential feature of the Roman view is that the churchly office guarantees purity of doctrine and proclamation.

## THE AUTHORITY OF THE OFFICE

Among the essential features of the Protestant Reformation is the insight that the spiritual office receives its authority and power from the Word and sacraments, not from the church. God's Word is central, not the institutional church. God himself, using his Word as an instrument, is active in his church.[2] Thus the church is not an institution or organization but an organism. The Word and sacraments, however, need as their instruments the men who hold office. Herein lies the justification of the spiritual office.

Luther dealt with these questions in his *Address to the Christian Nobility* (1520). Here he attacks the ecclesiastical organization by pointing first of all to the three walls which the Romanists had erected around themselves. They had argued, first of all, that they were not subject to the judgment of secular authorities, because the spiritual office is above the secular. Secondly, they said that the Pope alone had the right to interpret the Bible. Thirdly, they had invented the pretext that no one except the Pope had the right to call a general church council. By appealing to the general ministry of all Christians Luther breaks down all three of these walls.

In attacking the first Luther writes:

> It is pure invention that pope, bishops, priests, and monks are to be called the "spiritual estate"; princes, lords, artisans, and farmers the "temporal estate." That is indeed a fine bit of lying and hypocrisy. Yet no one should be frightened by it; and for this reason—viz., that all Christians are truly of the "spiritual estate," and there is among them no difference at all but that of office, as Paul says in I Corinthians 12, We are all one body, yet every member has its own work, whereby it serves every other, all because we have one baptism, one gospel, one faith, and are all alike Christians; for baptism, gospel and faith alone make us "spiritual" and a Christian people.[3]

Every Christian is "spiritual" by virtue of his baptism. Ordination by bishop or priest cannot place him in the spiritual estate, since he already belongs to it. From the standpoint of the doctrine and practice of the church of Luther's day this was indeed a radical and revolutionary argument. Yet Luther drew this interpretation from the New Testament, thereby eliminating the distinction between priest and layman.

Ordination in the Catholic system has fundamental importance since it imparts to the priest the power to consecrate the elements of the Sacrament and the ability to perform the accompanying sacrifice. Luther understood episcopal ordination to mean that the bishop as a representative of the church and in the name of the church takes one of its members and appoints him to exercise in behalf of others a right which all members of the church possess.[4] The primary emphasis is on the call and not on ordination. He who has received a call has the office even apart from ordination.

Circumstances can vary the call. In his interpretation of the apostolic office in his *Commentary on Galatians* (1519) Luther, following Jerome, distinguishes four types of the apostolic spiritual office. The first type is represented by those who have received their call directly from God without human mediation. The second includes those whose call from God came through men, as in the case of the apostles' disciples and followers. The third type are those who have been called by men but not by God. Finally, there are those who have been called neither by God nor men but by themselves, the false prophets and false apostles.[5]

Luther refused to permit his doctrine of the general ministry of all Christians to be made into a principle of disorder. He writes:

> Just because we are all in like manner priests, no one must put himself forward and undertake, without our consent and election, to do what is in the power of all of us. For what is common to all, no one dare take upon himself without the will and the command of the community.[6]

The general spiritual ministry incorporates the idea that Christians, though alike before God, differ because of their spiritual functions. The stations they have received are not alike, even though there is no difference in their personal status.[7] Luther knew well that the office of the minister or priest was divinely willed and ordained, while that of the Pope and bishops—like the brotherhoods and orders—were self-assumed burdens. The offices of the Pope and bishops were of human origin, as surely as was the practice of celibacy which regularly accompanied them.[8]

The divinely-willed functions of the priestly office are preaching and administration of the sacraments. The minister is installed primarily in the office of the Word. In this office he is the shepherd who feeds and protects his flock, the protection being needed against false doctrine. To Luther this makes the office of preaching the highest office. Alongside preaching, a minister's baptizing, conduct of public worship, and other ministerial acts are secondary. Naturally, for preaching has to do with the Word that creates faith.[9]

The Roman Catholic and Reformation concepts of the spiritual office differ therefore in this respect that the former views the church and the spiritual office as founded upon the Pope and the hierarchy, while the latter sees the church and the spiritual office as resting on the Word and the congregation. The former sees the church anchored "above," the latter sees it anchored "below." While the former grants the Pope the authority in all questions of principle, the latter makes God's Word decisive, underscoring the importance of true preaching of the Word in the church.

## THE OFFICE AND THE COMMUNITY

There has been very little disagreement as to the substance of Luther's clear statements about the spiritual office. But there continue to be differences of opinion in regard to how, in Luther, the ministerial office and the general ministry of Christians are related to one another and how they differ from one another. When we follow the studies made during the past century, we discover that the earlier Luther was thought to support a strictly official ministry. The spiritual office, with all its diverse functions, was ordained by God. Thus God ordained that preaching, baptism, absolution, and excommunication should by his decree be the permanent function of specific persons. Among those who held this view of Luther's doctrine of the ministry was Julius Stahl. He regarded the divine authorization as alone decisive, leaving any congregational commissioning entirely out of the picture.[10]

Among the representatives of an opposite view was J. W. Fr. Höfling; to him the sacramental office of the church, according to Luther, was not an aspect of divine order but resulted by inner necessity from the general ministry. A. W. Dieckhoff saw a change in Luther's view taking place around 1523, making it necessary to speak of Luther's earlier and later views. In the earlier period (1520-1523) Luther supposedly emphasized the general ministry over against the Roman Catholic concept. Later he continued to speak of the general ministry of Christians but rejected its false application to the spiritual office.[11]

For the first thirty years of our century most scholars accepted

Höfling's interpretation of Luther's view and made the general ministry of all Christians the basis of the special ministry, which existed solely for reasons of outward order. In the 1930's three German scholars, W. Elert, M. Doerne, and E. Wolf, each one independently, pointed out that Luther believed in the divine origin of the spiritual office, yet did not minimize the importance of the general ministry of all believers. Whereas the earlier view had presented the divine origin of the office and the general ministry as alternatives, this new view placed them together.[12]

Among more recent scholars G. Hök has reached practically the same conclusion. To him Luther's view has two spiritual offices, one within the other. In the narrower sense the spiritual office, *ministerium ecclesiae,* is represented by regularly ordained office-holders, while in the broader sense all Christians are messengers of the gospel. In the spiritual office the preaching of the gospel and the public administration of the sacraments take place in the name of the church. Installation into this office is by ordination.[13]

In defining the spiritual office Luther again had to face enemies on two fronts. Taking his stand against the Roman Catholics, he wanted to reject the idea that the office of the minister is that of an officiant at the sacrifice of the mass. To this end he emphasized the general task of all Christians as preachers of the gospel. In opposing the fanatics he underscored the thought that is best expressed with the words "office of the church." The ministerial office is a specific function of orderly congregational life. It may appear that Luther changed his mind with the situation, but this is not how we must interpret him. Rather we must say that to Luther the word "office" had a twofold meaning: the office of the church and the office of the gospel. According to the former the office is a function of the church, according to the latter it is an aspect of the general ministry of all Christians.[14]

As we try to understand Luther's conception of the relationship between the general ministry of Christians and the office of the ministry, we must bear in mind that he can use the same concept in the same writing and even in the same series of arguments with

several meanings. His statements are not unclear but they must
be studied in their own immediate context if their meaning is to
be discovered.

Thus in studying Luther's treatment of this problem in his
treatise *The Babylonian Captivity of the Church* we discover that
he does not look upon ordination as a sacrament. No priest has
the right to withhold the Word and sacrament from any one who
requests them. All Christians have a right to them.[15] Similarly,
comfort and forgiveness can be received through any Christian, for
if we confidentially unburden our conscience to a brother and reveal to him the wickedness of our heart we can receive from that
brother's lips as from God himself the word of comfort.[16] Here
the general ministry of all Christians does not mean an emergency
measure, for absolution is included among the ordinary functions
of the Christian. Thus the general ministry of Christians is given
a place of honor alongside the official ministry. One might gather
that in this treatise Luther attributes very little value to the official
ministry. This is not so. While he stresses the freedom of Christians in contrast to the absolute power of priests, bishops, and the
Pope, he nevertheless places the *ministerium ecclesiasticum*
(churchly ministry) above the general ministry of Christians. He
writes:

> Let everyone, therefore, who knows himself to be a Christian, be
> assured of this, that we are all equally priests, that is to say, we have
> the same power in respect to the Word and the sacraments. However,
> no one may make use of this power except by the consent of the com-
> munity or by the call of a superior. (For what is the common prop-
> erty of all, no individual may arrogate to himself, unless he is called.)
> And therefore this "sacrament" of ordination, if it is anything at all,
> is nothing else than a certain rite whereby one is called to the min-
> istry of the church. Furthermore, the priesthood is properly nothing
> but the ministry of the Word—the Word, I say; not the law, but the
> gospel.[17]

Luther then does not deny the special office of the church but
rather presupposes it. It is necessary and is not to be identified
with the general ministry of Christians.[18]

According to Brunotte the officeholders and nonofficeholders are distinguished in two ways in this treatise on *The Babylonian Captivity of the Church*. First, the fact of vocation separates them, for a divine task, a task of the church, is given to the officeholder. The nonofficeholder does not have such a task. Second, the officeholder is called upon to use the power of God's Word, that is, a power which belongs to the church as a whole. Contrariwise, the right of each Christian to the power of the Word consists in the right to administer the Word which applies to each one only personally or individually. This general right of Christians cannot be surrendered to someone else, for it is the personal right of each one. The spiritual office, the office of the minister, consists then of another kind of assignment.[19]

We reach essentially the same conclusion in studying Luther's treatise on *The Right and Power of the Christian Congregation or Community to Judge All Teaching and to Call, Appoint, and Dismiss Teachers* (1523). The main thought of this treatise is that the Christian congregation cannot be without preachers and teachers. For this reason the congregation has the right to call a preacher of the Word of God. From this it follows that a minister cannot authorize himself for this work but must be called to it by others. It also follows that the authorization to preach is received from the congregation and not from an individual or individuals. This implies that the right of office is not based upon the general ministry of Christians, and that the bishop does not possess the right to call a minister. Only the congregation as a whole possesses this right. After the call has been extended by the congregation, the bishop simply installs into office and verifies the call. In emergencies a minister may be called without episcopal verification, and again a bishop may find it necessary to call a preacher without congregational participation, so that souls will not perish for lack of God's Word.[20]

Scholars have shown that Luther maintained these views to the end of his life. In various writings he may have adjusted his statements to changed circumstances but no change is evident in the main points. Among these is the recognition that the credentials of the officeholder are not to be identified with the general right of Christians to spiritual functions. The spiritual office continues as something in its own right, even though the polemic against the Roman Catholic concept of the priest continues throughout Luther's life. The spiritual office was established by Christ and must be included among the things specifically willed by God. Luther believed in the general ministry of Christians to the end of his life, but without narrowing or weakening the special function of the spiritual office.[21]

## THE POWER OF THE KEYS

In Luther's view the power of the keys constitutes an essential aspect of the function of the spiritual office. It deserves special consideration.

The officeholders exercise the power of the keys in behalf of the congregation and not because they have received some special authority to rule over men. Christ's keys or the true keys signify to Luther the office and the authority to convey to repentant sinners what Christ has procured with his blood. These keys contain Christ's blood, death, and resurrection. They signify grace, and when they are used it is Christ himself who is doing the retaining and remitting of sins. When Christ's disciples have bound and loosed, it is Christ himself who has bound and loosed. Christ has no other keys besides the ones he has given to his disciples. Luther writes: "Why are you staring heavenward in search of my keys? . . . Peter's mouth is my mouth, and his tongue is my key case. His office is my office, his binding and loosing are my binding and loosing. His keys are my keys, and I have no others, nor do I know of any others, says Christ."[22] Again and again Luther says that God forgives sins through the oral word.

When Luther speaks of the keys, he has in mind particularly the key that looses. Yet the binding and loosing keys must not be separated. Both intend the salvation of men. The binding key works in the area of the law, while the loosing key works in the area of the gospel.

Over against Christ's keys or the true keys Luther sets the false keys of the Pope, which are like painted images compared to the real thing. Whereas Christ's keys are for sinners, the Pope's keys are for the governance of those who consider themselves righteous and sinless. The Pope has established laws and demands works of men. His power is legislative; by his keys he extracts works. Christ, however, uses his true keys not to demand works but to grant grace. Thus the Pope's keys and Christ's keys reflect the antithesis between works and faith.

In Luther's interpretation the papal power of the keys leads to interesting conclusions. Luther observes:

> If we grant that to bind means the same as to make a law, then to loose, on the other hand, must signify to annul and abolish law. . . . Now, if the Pope and his church has the power to make laws, he must also have the authority to annul them. For if the law is applicable to the process of binding, it is equally applicable to the process of loosing. Well then, under such conditions the Pope might annul the Ten Commandments of God as well as the Gospels and all of Scripture and release and free the whole world from them.[23]

But Christ says that not one iota will pass from the law. Only one possibility therefore remains, namely, that the Pope is able to annul his own laws. "That is true," Luther admits, "but it is not enough, for the key which looses, that is, the power to forgive sins, would not be equal to the key which binds, the power to retain sins."[24]

A particularly evil situation prevailed among the Catholics in Luther's opinion, for they doubted the trustworthiness of the loosing key. In the Catholic view the binding key is always trustworthy but the loosing key never is. The Pope therefore cannot err in placing a man under the ban; but in declaring absolution he can never do so unconditionally, for such absolution presupposes true contrition and no one can ever be sure in regard to his contrition.

Power to rule and power over knowledge were included in the power of the keys among the Catholics. Accordingly it was understood that the Pope had the power to command and forbid whatever he wished in heaven and on earth, to crown and dethrone emperors, kings, and princes. He also had the power to empty purgatory if he desired. Such power, however, Christ has not given to Peter or to his successors, Luther felt. Christ's power is not of this world (John 18:36). Christ says, "The kings of the Gentiles exercise lordship over them; and those in authority over them are called benefactors. But not so with you. . . ." (Luke 22:25 f.) The Pope's exercise of temporal power confused the earthly and the spiritual governments.

The earthly monarchy of the Old Testament was not intended to be permanent but to serve as a type and shadow of the spiritual monarchy of the New Testament. It reflects not some outward power but the power of Christ over sin, death, and the devil. For this reason the papacy is from beginning to end an error. Included in this error is the notion that the power of the keys involves power over knowledge. The Pharisees had the key of knowledge; all that meant, however, was that they themselves did not enter the kingdom of God but prevented others from doing so.

The Pope maintains that he possesses the true keys, that he has the power to bind in sin and loose from sin. Christ indeed gave such power to Peter, but not to Peter and his successors personally. The power was given to Christ's church, and so the congregation has power to bind and loose; it has the right to apply the law and the gospel to the individual. This occurs when the minister of the congregation rightly fulfills the preaching office. The true keys thus cannot be separated from preaching.

Since the Pope based his power on the fact that Jesus gave Peter the power of the keys, Luther naturally included in his polemic against the papacy his interpretation of Matthew 16:18 f. He stresses that the keys were not given to Peter personally but to the church as a whole. In Luther's opinion this is evident already from the fact that Peter's faith was not dependable. Soon after he had received the power of the keys from Christ he had fallen from faith and had to be reprimanded by Christ. The faith of the other disciples was equally undependable. The faith of the church, however, will never disappear from the earth; this is what Christ meant when he said that the gates of hell will not prevail against it (Matt. 16:18). Luther sees the decisive role of the congregation indicated in Christ's admonition (Matt. 18:17) that in difficult situations the appeal be made to the congregation. The reason is that the power of the keys had been given to the whole congregation, which included all the baptized and not only the bishops. To begin with, the Pope was merely the bishop of the church in Rome. The main point of Luther's polemic is directed against episcopacy in general.[25]

Luther's thoughts on the spiritual office and the power of the keys are a vital part of his whole theology. They reflect in characteristic manner his struggle to replace the Roman doctrines and practices which had developed over the centuries with those of the early Christian era.

## Chapter 13

# The Sacraments

Since the Roman Catholic church is a sacramental church, the main nerve of its theology is found in its doctrine of the sacraments. The development which led to this sacramentalism reached its climax in the theology of Thomas Aquinas. Augustine did not foster this development, but rather appears to have taken a critical stand against it. He teaches, for example, that baptism works forgiveness of sins but not in an automatic sense, for it presupposes that God brings the man to conversion and a right mind. An evil heart nullifies the effect of baptism. Baptism is indeed the sacrament of regeneration, says Augustine, but this regeneration is of water and not of spirit. The sacramental act and its spiritual effect are two distinct things. The effect is essentially dependent upon the subjective state of the one who is baptized.[1]

In Thomas Aquinas' theology the Catholic doctrine of sacraments received its classical form. The seven sacraments of the church are in actuality *mysteria verbi incarnati* (mysteries of the Incarnate Word). They are sacred symbols (signs) which effect salvation. As form is united with matter (Aristotle), so the Word of God is united with certain perceptible elements and a sacrament is born. In a natural cognitive way the sacraments put man in touch with the Spirit in order that he might receive God's grace. This makes the sacraments means of God's grace *(causa instrumentalis gratiae),* in which the spiritual and physical components are fused into one event. While Aquinas presents his doctrine of grace without speaking of the sacraments, he still means that the grace mediated by the sacraments is in no way additional or special grace. Being a quality or participation in God's nature, grace can be conveyed to man only by a spiritual-physical sacrament.[2]

In the 1510's Luther seems to have paid little attention to the sacraments. Evidently their significance for him was enhanced as his responsibility for the future of the Reformation movement increased. On the one hand, the distress created by this responsibility called for God's objective and dependable act to overcome it. On the other hand, in the polemical period, which was also a period of reconstruction, the ancient heritage of the church proved necessary and useful. Clearly the sacrament of the Lord's Supper in its current form did not fit into the theology of the Reformation. The sacrament was replaced by the Word, and the sacrifice of the mass was replaced by faith. In the light of the emerging Reformation theology the sacrifice of the mass was seen as man's offering to God for the propitiation of sins.[3] So completely did the general Catholic concept of the sacrament dominate Western theology that it was impossible for Luther to be negatively influenced from the outside in regard to the value of the sacraments.[4] The only explanation for what happened is Luther's own personality and his struggle in the monastery to find a gracious God. During the years 1513-1518 all theological problems became to him increasingly serious, a matter of life and death. They involved his very existence, for he sensed that in all things he stood in the presence of the holy God.[5]

In his first lectures on the Psalms (1513-1515) Luther shows no particular interest in the sacraments. "Sacrament" was primarily a "mystery" in the New Testament sense. It may be a mystery of revelation; however, the pulse of the church is not felt there but in the preaching of the Word. Preaching brings forth children for the church. Luther's doctrine of the sacraments places the Word above the sacraments. As he saw it, the Old Testament had many ceremonies, of which the church of his day recognized the seven sacraments, but in the future there would be only the Word. The life of the church is in the cultivation of the Word and sacraments, but the preaching of the Word is absolutely the more important of the two.[6] This emphasis upon the Word continued in the years following these first lectures on the Psalms.[7]

## BAPTISM

In a treatise of 1519 Luther has already in outline the doctrine of baptism he presented ten years later in his *Small Catechism.* In baptism man is born spiritually. He becomes a child of God and a righteous person. Sin never disappears in this life, so spiritual baptism, which signifies the drowning of sin, must continue throughout life and is not finished until in death. Luther says that "this whole life is nothing else than a spiritual baptism which does not cease till death."[8] He describes the eschatological character of baptism thus: "Spiritual birth and the increase of grace and righteousness, even though it begins in baptism, lasts until death, indeed, until the Last Day. Only then will that be finished which the lifting up out of baptism signifies."[9] Many fail to understand this and become remiss and negligent in the killing of their sinful nature.[10] For this reason Luther feels it necessary to stress the necessity of carrying on the conflict, and he does so repeatedly. He describes baptism as the covenant which God made with man for the purpose of putting sin and the flesh to death:

> You pledge yourself to continue in this desire, and to slay your sin more and more as long as you live, even until your dying day. This, too, God accepts. He trains and tests you all your life long, with many good works and with all kinds of sufferings. Thereby he accomplishes what you in baptism have desired, namely, that you may become free from sin, die, and rise again at the Last Day, and so fulfill your baptism.[11]

Luther points to the fact that baptism also contains comfort:

> Now if this covenant did not exist, and God were not so merciful as to wink at our sins, there could be no sin so small but it would condemn us. For the judgment of God can endure no sin. Therefore there is no greater comfort on earth than baptism. For it is through baptism that we come under the judgment of grace and mercy, which does not condemn our sins but drives them out by many trials.[12]

The word of promise, or the testament, to which the sign—water or bread and wine—is joined, is the very basis of the sacrament.[13]

The word "testament" entered the picture at this point in an interesting way. Luther found it in the words of institution of the

Lord's Supper ("new covenant in my blood"). The Greek word *diatheke* is *testamentum* in the Latin translation. This Latin word inspired Luther to interpret "covenant" as a "will" which Christ has drawn up for his own. A linguistic and factual error produced nevertheless a right result, inasmuch as the sacraments do certify God's gift of forgiveness of sins. The idea of testament expressed the real meaning of sacrament in Luther's earlier theology.

While the sacrifice of the mass had introduced the idea of merit into the Roman Catholic doctrine of the Lord's Supper, the gift contained in baptism had remained untouched. God in the richness of his mercy, says Luther, "has preserved in his church this sacrament at least, untouched and untainted by the ordinances of men, and has made it free to all nations and classes of mankind."[14] The chief thing is expressed in Mark 16:16: "He that believes and is baptized shall be saved." Baptism works upon the desperate, conscience-stricken man. We cannot explain the substance of baptism by asking what it is but by examining what it conveys to him who is baptized. Baptism takes in all of man's life and means that sins cannot condemn him, except the sin of unbelief.[15]

Baptism is from beginning to end God's work. Luther underscores this fact as follows:

> For man baptizes, and yet does not baptize. He baptizes in that he performs the work of immersing the person to be baptized; he does not baptize, because in so doing he acts not on his own authority but in God's stead. Hence we ought to receive baptism at human hands just as if Christ himself, indeed, God himself, were baptizing us with his own hands. For it is not man's baptism, but Christ's and God's baptism, which we receive by the hand of a man. . . .[16]

In the Roman Catholic system the sacraments were signs of grace which conveyed grace to men unless obstacles were placed in the way. Luther considered belief in signs as ungodly and unchristian. He felt the need to distinguish between signs and figures. There are a number of signs in the Old Testament, such as Abel's sacrifice, Noah's rainbow, Isaac's circumcision, and others. These have a sacramental character, since promises are affixed to them, and therefore they presuppose faith. Vestments, vessels, foods, houses, and the like, things that belong to the order of worship, are legal symbols. These require not faith but obedience to the law. God's promises are to be found scattered throughout the Bible, beginning with the Old Testament. But at no time does a sign as such save, neither in the Old nor in the New Testament. Only faith that clings to the promise saves.[17]

Emphasized in this way, faith can of course be understood as man's work and the whole of salvation as centered in man. But the fundamental message of the Reformation is to be found in the fact that no human accomplishment must be made the basis of salvation. All deeds of merit are invalid. Not even humiliation and brokenheartedness make one deserving of grace before God. He who thinks he can produce saving faith by himself is declared to be self-deceived.[18]

Luther's emphasis upon faith is an attack against the Catholic emphasis upon the sacramental sign. The sign loses practically all meaning in Luther's treatment of the promise and faith:

> Therefore let us open our eyes and learn to pay heed more to the Word than to the sign, more to faith than to the work or use of the sign. We know that wherever there is a divine promise, there faith is required, and that these two are so necessary to each other that neither can be effective apart from the other. For it is not possible to believe unless there is a promise, and the promise is not established unless it is believed. But where these two meet, they give a real and most certain efficacy to the sacraments. Hence, to seek the efficacy of the sacrament apart from the promise and apart from the faith is to labor in vain and to find condemnation.[19]

Luther interprets the meaning of baptism as death and resurrection. His reference is Romans 6:4: "We were buried therefore with him by baptism into death, so that as Christ was raised from the dead by the glory of the Father, we too might walk in newness of life." He calls this death and resurrection the "perfect and complete justification," implied in such terms as new creation, regeneration, and spiritual birth. Luther says:

> This should not be understood only allegorically as the death of sin and the life of grace, as many understand it, but as actual death and resurrection. For baptism is not a false sign. Neither does sin com-

pletely die, nor grace completely rise, until the sinful body that we carry about in this life is destroyed . . . so that faith is truly a death and a resurrection.[20]

Baptism is an eschatological event, looking forward to the Last Day when God's work in us will be finished. This work begins now but reaches fulfillment then. The practical significance of baptism into the death and resurrection of Christ is twofold: as a gift, baptism proffers forgiveness of sins; and as a task, baptism prompts daily the death of the old man and the rising of the new.

Baptism reflects the whole goodness of God, which follows a person from the cradle to the grave. In the baptismal rite it is God himself who acts, even though he puts on a costume of human activity. With his word of grace he awaits man even before man is born. Grace is by its very nature prevenient grace. Especially in the distress of affliction and anxiety *(Anfechtung)* and in the face of death baptism is of great comfort. Luther feels that God actually commands us to praise our baptism.[21]

## LORD'S SUPPER

In a treatise on the Lord's Supper published in 1520 Luther speaks of the mass as the only order of worship appointed by Christ. "Where the mass is used, there is true worship; even though there be no other form, with singing, organ playing, bell ringing, vestments, ornaments, and gestures. For everything of this sort is an addition invented by men."[22] The substance of the Supper Luther interprets in this treatise as a testament. Testaments are certified by the seal and mark of a notary; Christ has affixed to this testament the most powerful and precious seal and sign, his own true flesh and blood under the bread and wine.[23] The bequeathed blessing is indicated by the words of institution: remission of sins and eternal life.[24] Since mere words could not sufficiently assure us of this, "we poor men, living as we do in our five senses, must have along with the words at least one outward sign."[25]

Luther discusses the importance of the sign also in his book

on *The Babylonian Captivity of the Church.* The sacrament has
no other purpose than to confirm with an outward sign the forgiveness of sins proclaimed in the Word. This earlier phase of
Luther's doctrine of the Lord's Supper extended to the year 1524,
and was informed by his attack against Roman Catholic sacramentalism.

By the sacrifice of the mass the Roman Catholic church implied
that in each celebration of the Lord's Supper the priest offered
Christ in a bloodless sacrifice once more to God as the sacrificial
Lamb, with the bread being changed into the body of Christ and
the wine into his blood. Luther felt that this whole idea de-
tracted from God's work and inverted the very substance of the
Supper, making the whole thing from beginning to end a horribly
ungodly practice. Man pretended to do what God alone can do.

After 1524 the attack was directed primarily against the fanatics
and their spiritualism. Now the central thought became the real
presence of Christ in the Supper. One might suppose that Luther's
rejection of the Roman Catholic doctrine of transubstantiation
would lead to surrender of the idea of the real presence of Christ
in the sacrament. But this did not happen. The doctrine of the
real presence, which he had held prior to 1524, he taught with
even greater emphasis in the conflicts that arose after that year.

Only from the theocentric viewpoint can we rightly understand
Luther's doctrine of the Lord's Supper. God, not man, is the host
at the Supper. God has offered his Son as the sacrificial Lamb,
and as a sign of this we celebrate the Supper. The Roman Catholic
mass, in which the priest presents Christ as a bloodless sacrifice to
God, has upset the whole matter. To Luther this sacrifice of the
mass is the "worst abuse" of the sacrament.[26] His main argument
is that in the sacrament man does not sacrifice to God.[27] To the
extent that the sacrament is made into a means whereby man seeks
God's favor, man has declared himself an equal of God, a creature
with a free will. Such action makes unbelief out of faith, and
idolatry out of divine worship. This is what had happened, Luther felt, in the Catholic sacrifice of the mass; the sacrament had

been put into man's hands for the purpose of appeasing an angry God.

Luther's theocentric viewpoint and his emphasis upon the real presence are intimately related. This is evident from the discussion between Luther and Zwingli in which Zwingli defended a symbolical interpretation of the sacrament while Luther underscored God's action and the real presence. To Luther the words of institution were God's own words and therefore creative words inasmuch as, when God speaks, word and the act cannot be separated from one another.

God's word always presupposes faith on the part of man. This is true also in the Lord's Supper. The presence of the body and blood of Christ in the Supper is not visible but hidden, as the Word and faith give us to understand. Luther knew that no local demonstration of the real presence of Christ was possible. Yet he clung to that presence with all his strength, for unless Christ is really present in the Supper it is no "meal" of grace and does not convey God's gift. As truly as God's Word contains the real gospel, so the Supper is intended as a visible sign of the gospel. The real presence of Christ is the substance of the gift of the Supper given by God from above.

The Roman Catholic doctrine of transubstantiation has the same goal, emphasis upon the real presence of Christ, but it seeks it along the line of *opus operatum*.[28] In Roman Catholic thought the sacraments are "effective signs," because the presence of Christ is realized in the performance of certain acts. The emphasis is placed on man's activity. Man takes God's place, and faith is unnecessary, since the doctrine of transubstantiation makes the body and blood of Christ into a visible presence of Christ.[29]

Luther's doctrine of the Lord's Supper is not to be placed in an artificial way somewhere between the Roman Catholic doctrine of transubstantiation and the symbolical view of the Swiss. It grows from the same ground as the rest of Luther's theology, the ground of theocentricity, the Word and faith.

# Chapter 14

# The Foundation of Social Ethics

The ethical problems in Luther's theology are difficult for three reasons. First, the ethical subject is not easily identified, since the new man in us is not static but in a state of being born. Second, every act intended as ethical is under suspicion, inasmuch as its ultimate value depends upon the purity of motives. Third, true ethical deeds are spontaneous, for they are deeds of the new life, they therefore cannot be planned or predicted or thought out in advance.

On this basis it seems as if nothing specific could be said about Luther's ethics. And yet it can be argued that the Reformation accomplished more in the area of ethics than in the area of dogmatics, and was in respect of the former truly a comprehensive "cleansing of the temple." A completely new evaluation of all values is implied in the famous fundamental statement of Luther's theology of ethics: "Good works do not make a good man, but a good man does good works." Here we have the basis of Luther's ethical viewpoint as a whole. The man who does good works is the man who has been justified through faith. Ethics rests on faith and gratitude.

One can always resort to the argument that all ethical responsibility is destroyed if any criminal can be justified through faith at any time. Why should any one behave morally rather than immorally, if the free gift of righteousness has no moral conditions? The question itself of course is wrong, because it makes of man's relationship to God a business proposition in which the greatest possible profit is sought with the smallest possible investment. In Luther's theology faith is never a coin with which one might operate an automatic saving machine. Faith is the gift of the

Holy Spirit; no man can acquire faith for himself, it can only be given to him. With faith man receives also a new attitude, the most characteristic mark of which is gratitude for grace received.

Rightly understood, Luther's ethics is an ethics of gratitude. The righteousness which is received again and again as a gift becomes again and again the reason for gratitude, and from this is born the desire to help and serve one's fellow man again and again. Perfection cannot be demanded of the works of the new life, for they are not planned in advance but are born on the spur of the moment to meet the demands of the situation. Imitation of the works of saints cannot be in harmony with God's will, for the saints lived in their own particular time and place and had their own particular response to their environment. With the life of saints and monks no longer the ethical ideal, the whole traditional Roman Catholic ethical system was changed. The celibate life and spiritual exercises of the priests and monks no longer represented the ideal life; marriage and secular vocations were no longer marks of a lower morality. The traditional ethical dualism was replaced by a new dualism, that of the earthly and spiritual governments.

### MOSAIC LAW AND THE SOCIAL ORDER

When he left the road marked out by the Roman church, Luther was forced to reconstruct his whole theology. What norm did he find for the solution of the problems of social ethics? Did he use the Mosaic law as a guide in these matters?

The clash between Luther and Karlstadt on the issue of the relevance of the Mosaic law in the contemporary social situation turned out to be difficult and deeply significant. To Karlstadt all the regulations of the Old Testament law were divine oracles. As far as he was concerned there were no distinctions, one could not accept some of the regulations while rejecting others. Karlstadt felt that by appealing to Moses to prove his doctrine, Christ had acknowledged the content and function of the ancient law. With the new power of the gospel man is enabled to keep the law.

Karlstadt could think of no other way of salvation. In his mind the heart of the gospel is to be found in Christ's words to the scribe: "Keep the commandments." Christian freedom was obedience to the law in the spirit of Christ.

From the very beginning Luther's view was altogether different. He was compelled to apply the doctrine of the law and Christian freedom critically to the Bible itself. He had to differentiate between the Word of God and the Word of God. In each instance it was necessary to ask whether or not a certain Bible passage applied to me, benefited me, obligated me. If all Bible passages referred to me, then I would have to build an ark, as Noah did, or I would have to rise in the morning and set in the evening, as God commanded the sun to do. God speaks to the fish of the sea and the trees of the forest, in fact, all creation is full of God's talk, but what he says does not touch me.

At this point Luther makes the simple deduction that the Word of God as such cannot be binding on me as the revealed Word of God. To be that it must be directed to my historical situation, for otherwise it cannot touch my conscience with the power of the Divine Majesty. The law of Moses is directed to things that do not pertain to us Gentile Christians, for Moses mediated God's Word to the Jewish people, not to us. The signs which God gave in Old Testament times were different from the ones given to us under the New Testament. The people of the Old Testament had circumcision, Abel's sacrifice, and Noah's rainbow; we have the death and resurrection of Christ. We must not imitate signs, for what God speaks to us is our freedom in Christ. Freedom of conscience means that we need not rely on any righteousness of works.

But how is the relevance of the law established, if it is not a special revelation of God? Karlstadt could well ask Luther, "Do you want to repeal the first commandment and the commandments that have to do with adultery, murder, and stealing?" Certainly one could not look upon these simply as commandments given to the Jews?

Luther could have answered Karlstadt by pointing to the traditional division of the law into ceremonial and juridical commandments. But he did not. To him the Mosaic law was a single unit. The ceremonial and juridical codes were part and parcel of the Decalogue. The whole Mosaic law aimed at the fact that God wanted to be God alone. To acknowledge a single point of the Mosaic law was to be subject to every point. The relevance of the Mosaic law stemmed from the fact that what it forbade, murder, adultery, stealing, and the like, was forbidden by the inner law in the heart of every person. According to Luther our Lord himself said as much when he said: "What you want people to do to you, you do to them." Christ combines the unwritten inner law and the Mosaic law. Paul does the same thing when he states that love is the fulfillment of the law. Even the heathen know by nature that wrong is not permissible. If man did not have this witness in his heart, we would have to preach to him a long sermon indeed before he would repent.

From this Luther made an important deduction: when Moses is preached we can apply it to ourselves only to the extent that the commandments are a naturally effective witness to our conscience. Otherwise we are to remain Gentile Christians and obey our own rulers and masters, letting Moses be the lawgiver of the Jewish nation. Thus the Mosaic law has material that corresponds to the inner law and binds all men, and also material that has to do with the national law of the Jews and does not bind us.

How did Karlstadt's line endanger Christian freedom? We can find the answer by continuing with the thought that to Luther the Mosaic law was of great value because it reflected admirably the unwritten law of nature. Luther's specific point was that the law of Moses must be highly regarded because of its usefulness. We need it to clarify the law within us. However, if we make it a matter of conscience by taking the Mosaic law as such as God's revelation, then our consciences become enslaved in works. Works are for the service of our fellow men; they are not for

God's pleasure or for the procurement of our own salvation. If the law and works are made into demands upon the conscience, then Christ died in vain. Works must be taken as a matter of fact (*secundum substantiam*) and not as a matter of conscience (*secundum conscientiam*), for by them we serve our fellow men.

The difference between Luther's interpretation of the relevance of divine law and that of Karlstadt stemmed from the fact that while the latter looked upon the whole law as direct divine revelation and therefore legally binding on all, the former dared to restrict God's revelation in matters of jurisprudence to the Jews only. Luther saw clearly that unless this position is taken God himself is made to bind our consciences with legal ordinances and the Old Testament way of salvation. But God cannot act against himself. The choice which Luther made was the only possible one.

Because of Luther's wonderfully elastic method of interpretation, he found significant help in the fourth commandment of the Decalogue. This commandment demands obedience not only toward parents but also toward all rulers, and hence also toward the ruler whose subjects we happen to be. The nation and citizenship are part of God's will and order. This means that God's will includes the present life situation. Therefore what the Old Testament law says to a specific situation in the past does not apply to a specific situation in the present. There is no such thing as divine civil law. Because of changing circumstances and new situations, we need something more specific than a rigid general law.

Luther's view is colored by broad tolerance. There is no difference in principle between Jews and Gentiles. What God revealed to the Jews the Gentiles have by nature in their hearts. They possess a great deal of knowledge about it in their oral and written tradition. Luther resorted to this simple insight in his polemic against the legalism of the fanatics. The law which the Jews received from heaven, however, was not merely an abstraction of what the Gentiles possess by nature, for it reached down to the

smallest details of everyday life. While the Gentiles were compelled to interpret on their own the law written in their hearts,
God himself undertook to order the details of life for the Jews.
The circumstances of the Jews and the Gentiles are then as far
apart as heaven and earth. Chance and fortune guide the history
of other nations; God's will is hidden from them, for they do
not have the Word. But God's people are ruled by the Word.

The fanatics objected that Luther was rejecting the gracious
gift of God's law at the expense of the laws of various peoples.
To this Luther answered in several ways. He stated, for example,
that the Mosaic law had been given for pedagogical purposes. God
wished to demonstrate how well matters of government could be
handled in a nation's life when he himself took care of them.
The Jews could boast of this and say, "Behold, what I do I
myself have not chosen but God wills it so." However, we
Christians are no longer in Moses' school. We are free to choose
between the law of Moses and other laws. Our place of refuge
and assurance is not the divine law but the divine word of grace.[1]

Luther's stand seems of course rather free, unbelievably free.
It makes the social order a matter of reason. The Mosaic law
is binding, because it is in harmony with the law of nature.
Already in creation God gave man the gift of reason, making
it possible for him to establish families and states.[2] However,
even though these orders of life are founded in God's will, the devil
constantly interferes with them. Luther knew that the devil blinds
man to the point where he can no longer see the law written
in his heart. This inward law, furthermore, is not to be equated
with the Old Testament.[3]

In any case it is clear to Luther that the Mosaic law is not
meant to bind all nations in all ages with all its ordinances. As
he interpreted it, the commandment of God never signified something which man could rationally incorporate into some system.
Nor is it something man is able to keep. On the contrary, the
law is the eternal speech of God, which has but one object,
namely, the birth of faith.[4] Man cannot fulfill God's command-

ment because its purpose is to crush that which man is in himself. It always encounters man as one who is running away from God. No forms of life or forms of worship can fulfill God's commandment. Faith alone can do it, never works as works.[5]

## THE TWO GOVERNMENTS

In beginning our discussion of Luther's social ethics, we mentioned that he replaced the Catholic dualism [double morality] with a dualism of his own, that of the earthly and spiritual governments. (The word here translated as "government" is the German word *Regiment,* which means "governing" or "rule," but which Luther used in a way which makes translation awkward if not difficult.) Luther made the switch not because of any desire for new labels but out of concern for fundamental principles of Reformation theology.

Luther distinguishes two kinds of righteousness. The righteousness of faith *(iustitia actualis)* has to do with man's relationship to God; the earthly righteousness *(iustitia civilis)* has to do with man's relationship to his fellow men. Rulers, statesmen, philosophers, and lawyers are concerned with the earthly righteousness. Included in this kind of righteousness-before-men are all those conventional customs and forms of behavior which priests, parents, and teachers seek to inculcate. In general, it includes all human ordinances which do not have to do with man's standing before God. Luther places in this area of civil righteousness both the demands of the Ten Commandments and the righteousness which comes from the law.[6]

The righteousness of faith, or Christian righteousness, is something quite different. Luther never tired of emphasizing that these two kinds of righteousness must be kept distinct. The righteousness of faith is not to be confused in any way with earthly righteousness, which today we would call good citizenship. The latter has to do with the laws of the emperor, the decrees of the Pope, and the commandments of God; the object in each case is a certain specific act. The righteousness of faith is not of this world, nor does it depend on certain ceremonies, or even on the law of God. For it has nothing to do with works; it is entirely a gift of God in Christ.

Corresponding to these two kinds of righteousness are two kinds of government or two realms, the "earthly" and the "spiritual," which Luther describes in his 1526 treatise *Whether Soldiers, too, Can Be Saved* as follows:

> God has established two kinds of government among men. The one is spiritual; it has no sword, but it has the Word, by means of which men are to become good and righteous, so that with this righteousness they may attain everlasting life. This righteousness he administers through the Word, which he has committed to the preachers. The other is worldly government, through the sword, which aims to keep peace among men, and this he rewards with temporal blessing.[7]

What led Luther to formulate his conception of temporal society and of the earthly mission of the gospel in terms of two realms or governments? In the background may be the medieval doctrine of the two swords, the spiritual and the secular. He was also acquainted with the traditional division of church, state, and family.[8] His monastic order preserved the tradition of Augustine, so he was familiar with the work of this influential church father, *The City of God,* and its central idea of two groups of people, the children of light and the children of darkness. But considering Luther's readiness to break away from traditional views whenever they were incompatible with his understanding of the Bible, it is doubtful that he would have given such a central place to the two governments in his description of society and the world had he not had other reasons besides tradition.

The idea of the two governments is directly related to problems involved in biblical interpretation. Luther received no peace from the difficult passages of the Sermon on the Mount which speak of oaths, turning the other cheek, and so forth. He was not satisfied with the traditional Catholic interpretation that these difficulties represented merely evangelical counsels *(consilia evangelica)* for those who wanted to reach greater perfection. It was impossible that Jesus' demands should be mere counsel. With such compromise of the difficult passages on the Catholic side, the fanatics and the Anabaptists on the other side made these passages into ordinances which were binding upon all men. As a result they refused to take oaths and to enter military service. Some of the fanatics, while refusing as a matter of principle to heed their ruler's call to military service, claimed the right to armed resistance against established political authority. Luther's rejection of such biblical interpretation was not prompted by a desire to please the rulers, as some have argued, but by what he found in the sacred Scriptures as a professor of biblical exegesis. Romans 13:1-7 and certain Old Testament passages which contain God's command to his people to take up arms became important to him, but he gave special attention to passages which related how Jesus and his apostles used strong words against their enemies. He paused before the statement of the Sermon on the Mount which asks us to turn the other cheek, but he also noted John 18:22-23, which shows that Jesus refused to submit to a beating when he was innocent.

On the one hand Luther confronted the Sermon on the Mount with its demand that a Christian must bear suffering at the hands of wrong. On the other hand he faced the harsh realities of the world. His search for a synthesis of the two extremes resulted in his doctrines of the two *Regimente*.[9]

The idea of the two governments reflects Luther's view of the world and his concept of history. It is not the fruit of any philosophical explanation of the world—cosmological and metaphysical problems play no decisive role in Luther's theology—but has to do rather with matters of this visible world.[10] Luther points out that men had turned things upside down. The bishops had neglected their proper task, that of caring for souls by the preaching of God's Word, and had instead become earthly princes exercising lordship over castles, cities, and countries. And earthly rulers had taken on spiritual responsibilities, trying to lord it over souls.[11] The realm of faith is one of freedom, and the realm of outward order is one of justice and force. The boundary between the two is a real boundary, as real as that between Leipzig and Wittenberg.[12] Princes must remain princes; and bishops must remain bishops, whose rule consists not in exalted power or violence but in service.[13] Both realms are a graphic reflection of God's lordship in this world: he has authority in temporal, external matters; and with his Word he attends to the inward care of souls.

In his early theology Luther does not use the term "governments" but speaks as an Augustinian of two "kingdoms." The kingdom of Christ *(regnum Christi)* is the kingdom of grace. Over against it stands the kingdom of this world *(regnum mundi),* that is, humanity estranged from God and ruled by Satan.[14] The dependence of Luther's doctrine of the two *Regimente* upon Augustine is evident. As has been noted, the leading idea of Augustine's chief work, *The City of God,* is the eternal antithesis between the children of light and the children of darkness. Abel and Cain were the forefathers of these contending factions of the human race. Both societies *(civitas Dei* and *civitas terrena)* have their superterrestrial relationships. The divine society includes those who live according to God's will, while the earthly society is constituted by those who are "of the flesh."[15] Medieval Roman Catholicism used this Augustinian doctrine to its own advantage. The divine society was being realized in the Catholic ecclesiastical institution. Since everything in it was of God, the earthly emperor also must submit to it obediently. The earthly society, the state, signified the rule of Satan. This explains at least in part the bitterness of the investiture controversy. The church was not just eager for unlimited authority; it was simply a case of the independent state and its highest representative, the emperor, symbolizing Satanic power.

Though as a Catholic Luther belonged to the Augustinian order where the Augustinian heritage was cherished, and though his earlier writings describe temporal society as largely satanic,[16] his theology presents the doctrine of the two realms in an essentially different form. The earthly realm, too, is God's realm. In the conflict with Satan, God controls both realms. Good and evil must not be distinguished, therefore, according to the boundaries of the two realms, for in God's great conflict with Satan the front line is fluid, so that good as well as evil is found in one as well as in the other.[17] If with Augustine we equate the two kingdoms with two groups of people, we must of course say that the earthly kingdom does not include those who will be saved. The quotation given above from *Whether Soldiers, too, Can Be Saved* clearly shows that in Luther's view the word "government" does not refer to groups of people but to forms of action, or orders. By one we gain the righteousness which leads to eternal life, while by the other we achieve the righteousness that is meant for this world. The latter, good citizenship, is the condition for social order and peace.

Both governments are instruments of God in his exercise of universal lordship. In acknowledging the temporal social order as "God's left hand,"[18] Luther punctured the traditional monastic ideal. Scholars are not agreed as to whether in Luther's view the earthly and spiritual governments are on exactly the same level.[19] Clearly the issue hinges on the meaning of *Regiment*. If it means primarily two kingdoms, the spiritual kingdom is of course incorruptible, glorious, and eternal, while the earthly kingdom is imperfect and full of evil. This view is basically Augustinian, as we have noted, and is found in its clearest form in Luther's early theology. On the other hand, if the word *Regiment* means an instrument in God's hand for the maintenance of order, it is not difficult to understand Luther's emphasis upon the necessity of the earthly government and its equality with the spiritual government.[20]

Modern man finds no difficulty in the idea that the power which maintains social order is to be called the earthly government. But it is difficult for modern man to see the need for calling the totality of spiritual things a spiritual government. For one thing, this makes the preaching office much too "official." Things of the spirit, we feel, belong to the inner life, for which the designation "government" is inappropriate.

As a divinely established order the spiritual government points to the honor in which God holds the preaching office. It means that our knowledge of Christ comes not by way of "inner illumination" but by the preaching of the Word. God's gifts are received in a God-determined manner. To find its way into the hearts of men the gospel takes on the form of a government. Only in this way does it gather and preserve the church of Christ. The spiritual office is then an inseparable aspect of the gospel itself.

But God's presence and sovereignty are realities also in the earthly government and not only in the spiritual. In the earthly government, too, the divine and the creaturely are intertwined; the earthly government, too, is ordained and willed by God. He uses it to govern the earth, so that the hand which maintains justice in the world and protects men from evil forces is God's hand and not man's. Though men abuse the offices of the state and function in them contrary to God's will, these offices still remain divine ordinances. Compared to each other the two governments are as far apart as heaven and earth, yet God hides himself unreservedly also in the earthly government, so that it, too, is an *eytel göttlich ding* (purely divine thing).

In substance these two governments correspond to the two kinds of righteousness. The earthly government has to do with the righteousness which prevails in this world and whose reward is temporal blessing *(zeitlich gut)*. This righteousness, good citizenship, is willed and ordained by God, even though it is not sufficient for eternal life.

The righteousness proffered by the gospel and received as a gift is something altogether different. The proclamation of the gospel is the purpose of the preaching office, which is the heart of the spiritual government. However, one must be extremely careful not to identify the spiritual government with the church, for the church has also its temporal aspect which does not belong to the spiritual government (church discipline and finances and organization). By describing the preaching activity of the church as a spiritual government Luther wants to place special emphasis on the freedom of the preaching of the gospel, for involved in the necessary distinction between the two governments is the insistence that the judge and the mayor must not determine how the gospel is to be preached. With the gospel God attends to the spiritual government, forgiving sins, justifying and sanctifying men. The fact that the earthly government is from beginning to end God's government does not justify its adopting spiritual patterns of action or its applying the gospel to matters of this world.

If that were done two evils would result. First, the gospel would disappear from the earth, for it would become a new law. Both the right and left wings of the church—the Catholics, and the spiritualists and Anabaptists, respectively—provided Luther with examples of this. Second, the world would go to ruin under the gospel. As Luther puts it:

> If one wanted to govern the world according to the gospel and eliminate entirely all secular justice and law enforcement . . ., tell me, what would he thereby do? He would free the wild, wicked beasts from their shackles and chains. The wicked would then abuse Christian freedom under the guise of the Christian name. . . . To attempt to rule a whole country or the world with the gospel would be the same as if a shepherd let loose together in the farmyard wolves, lions, eagles, and sheep and allowed them to move about freely, saying, "Graze here and be pious and peaceful among yourselves, the farmyard is open and there is adequate pasture. There are no watchdogs for you to fear." The sheep would indeed live in peace, but they would not live long.[21]

The error would be equally great, if Christians were placed under the law. They would then be put to work to earn a righteousness that would satisfy God.[22]

In stressing the need to keep the two governments apart Luther divorced himself in a twofold sense from the medieval view. First, he acknowledged the spiritual character of the spiritual realm of life. The church must give primary attention to the preaching of the gospel. Such issues in the history of Catholicism as the ecclesiastical state and the investiture controversy are beyond the pale of Luther's program. Second, he gave a certain kind of recognition to the autonomous character of the political realm.[23] To this we shall return later.[24]

Luther always spoke of two *Regimente*. It might be more accurate, however, to recognize three areas or realms of power. The first would be the kingdom of God as it was before the Fall and as it appears renewed by Jesus Christ; the second would be the world as the kingdom of men in a state of sin and under the rule of Satan; and the third would be that area of God's authority which we call the temporal sphere. This threefold division, suggested by Bring,[25] reveals the basic intention of Luther's social ethics better in many respects than the presupposition of only two realms. It must be noted that it is not a matter of indifference whether we speak of two "kingdoms" or of two "governments." The idea of two kingdoms implies two distinct groups of people, in the Augustinian sense; and membership in these groups is predicated on the inner character of man or his inner qualities *(habitus)*. When we speak of three spheres or realms of power the thought is that in addition to the two forms of God's rule, the earthly and spiritual governments, there is also Satan's sphere of power. The kingdom of God is a present reality in the gospel of Christ, even though it is only on its way toward final realization. Satan's sphere of power is also a reality, but everywhere it is limited by God's earthly government. This gives expression to the thought of the "fluid front" in the conflict between God and Satan, a thought which Luther stressed repeatedly.[26] Related to this mobile warfare in the context of social life is the demand for daily repentance and daily renewal of life on the part of the individual. This interpretation of the *Regimente* makes clear how and for what reason the spiritual and the earthly governments are antithetical. The spiritual government aims at forgiveness of sins and thereby at achieving the God-pleasing righteousness, while the earthly government maintains outward discipline and order with an iron hand.

Yet the two governments are intimately bound together, for both are expressions of God's love. By means of both God fights against the kingdom of Satan. On the one hand he wants to topple the satanic rule of terror over men's consciences *(iustitia christiana)*; on the other he wants to remove from the world the confusion Satan has created and replace it with an order of his own *(iustitia civilis).* In the divine perspective the unity of the two governments is evident. But it is apparent also from below, from man's perspective. God wants man to live as a subject of Christian righteousness, which involves more than merely the receiving of the forgiveness of sins. Neither pleasure-filled inactivity nor self-chosen activity is in harmony with God's will for man. God expects man to engage in faithful fulfillment of his vocation.

## Chapter 15

# Marriage

The Catholic teaching about marriage contained two radically different emphases. Marriage was, on the one hand, one of the seven sacraments of the church, a holy ordinance of God, so that opposition to marriage was opposition to God's own order. On the other hand, married people lived on a lower level of life, inasmuch as only the priests, monks, and nuns living in celibacy could attain the higher level. Destroying as it did the proper order of life, celibacy resulted in thousands of instances in outright hypocrisy.

In this area also Luther's task was to rip apart the net of ancient tradition and reinstate the original order of creation. This was not a simple task, so deeply rooted was the tradition. Through the years Catholic scholars have attacked Luther particularly at this point, and this is not surprising inasmuch as any changes in this area touch all of life in such a crucial way that repercussions are felt in all areas of social ethics.

## THE FUNDAMENTAL ISSUE

In attempting to clarify Luther's attitude toward marriage, it is best to start with the criticism Luther directed against the Roman Catholic doctrine of sacraments. In his book on *The Babylonian Captivity of the Church* (1520) Luther refuses to consider marriage a sacrament. Marriage lacks the words of promise and the divine institution necessary for a sacrament. By means of an external sign man partakes in the sacrament of Christ's death and resurrection, but this cannot be said of marriage. The Bible indeed speaks of marriage as a great mystery (Eph. 5:31 f.) But this passage refers to the relationship of Christ to his church. In the

157

Greek language the word for "mystery" is *mysterion*, which in the Latin Bible is translated *sacramentum*. On the basis of this similarity of words marriage was made into a sacrament, even though the passage in Ephesians has no such meaning. Already the church fathers spoke of the sacramental character of marriage. Marriage then became a covenantal sign to guard against sinful sexual lust, even though it was not established as a sacrament instituted by Christ until the Council of Trent (1545-1563).[1] When Luther took a stand against the traditional Catholic view, he was not motivated by a concern for proper interpretation of the Ephesians passage. He had a different reason. As a pastor he had learned that the canons concerning marriage placed heavy burdens upon the shoulders of the people, and so around 1520 he undertook a closer examination of the whole issue. He saw very soon that he could not support his church's traditional views on marriage and sex. He had to cast aside former teachings and to declare a new word of freedom.

Initially Luther took a stand against celibacy for purely practical reasons. Certain evangelical ministers had married, and the matter became the subject for public discussion. The Catholics naturally attacked such practice vehemently. The evangelicals had to defend themselves. It was impossible for Luther to stand on the sidelines as a spectator. In his theses on celibacy Karlstadt had made marriage a condition for ordination. At the same time he urged monks and nuns to marry, suggesting that in so doing they were committing a lesser sin than by remaining unmarried. Karlstadt thus wanted to make Christian freedom into a new law. By now it had become clear to Luther that the life and example of the saints must not be made binding on any one. He understood the ethical significance of the gospel to mean that imitation must be rejected and each must find his own way as God opens it to him.

Luther saw that celibacy was not an early Christian ideal but a relatively late phenomenon and in no way obligatory. A voluntary vow of celibacy was still possible and permissible as far as he was concerned. But even at this point he soon found need to reexamine his view and to reject all vows of celibacy, voluntary or not, for they conflicted with nature and the freedom of conscience.[2]

## THE GOSPEL AS LIBERATOR

As a monk Luther had discovered in sex an irrepressible power, a tyrant generally uncontrollable by prohibitions or force. He became convinced that nature, as God had implanted it in us, made it impossible for a person to remain chaste outside of marriage. He felt that there were very few young people who had not yielded to temptation. Since the sex drive is particularly strong in youth, early marriages are desirable. Except in instances of special divine election, efforts at continence led either into irregular satisfaction of the desire or into mental torture and inner agony, if not outright immorality. Thus man became a "martyr of the devil."

It is another question of course what Luther meant by sexual purity. In his youth, as we might expect, he looked upon marriage as sin and celibacy as the desirable ideal. Like Paul he saw celibacy as the liberator from numerous cares and troubles. It provided more opportunity for prayer and cultivation of the Word. But early in the 1520's the leaf turned. Luther sensed that the pure estate was marriage and not celibacy. Purity is a matter of heart, which shows itself in thoughts, words, and deeds. Thus understood, marital chastity is the only possible purity. As Luther says, "If you wish to preserve morality, husband and wife must first of all live together in love and concord, so that they love each other wholeheartedly and with complete honesty."[3]

One of the fundamental insights of Luther's sexual ethics was, therefore, that total continence and rejection of the demands of sex are normally impossible. In the rare instances where they do exist they are exceptions to the rule and require a direct gift from above. Without this gift the attempt at total continence may result in an outward chastity which is nothing but the cover for inward lust. In such a case there is no reason to boast of ethical perfection.

For Luther lifelong vows of celibacy were normally in sharp

contradiction to faith and to Christian freedom of conscience. Luther's counselor at this point was Paul, with his message of Christian freedom. Taking into consideration human weakness, one must not coerce or even urge any one to make promises in ethical matters. Not celibacy as such, but all forms of permanent vows of celibacy are in opposition to a wholesome view of life and to God's will. They are crimes against the grace of Christ and the Holy Spirit. If any one believed that by such vows he gained the special favor of God, he was deceiving himself, for these vows conflict with God's Word, ordinances, and order and are outright mockery and arrogance before God.[4]

Vows of celibacy therefore are not based on God's Word. On the contrary, they falsify man's relationship to God and subject man to compulsion and to groping after merit before God. Here we encounter the same criticism of the Catholic concept of holiness that appears regularly in other connections: man's quest for holiness is directed toward self-perfection, which draws the whole of holiness into the magic sphere of egocentricity and man's search for merit.

The fight against celibacy involved proclamation of the freedom of the gospel to men enslaved by false ideals. After the vow had been made celibacy became to many an unbearable ordeal. They realized that they had entered into an impossible state. In throwing open the doors of the monasteries Luther had no intention of promoting the cause of false freedom. He knew only too well that compliance to the demands of flesh and blood can easily lead a person astray. Satan was everywhere on the go, also outside the walls of monasteries. But Luther feared the enslavement of consciences with "ungodly monastic vows" as much as he feared the power of Satan in everyday life.[5]

## SANCTIFICATION OF SEX

In his reforms in matters pertaining to marriage Luther had against him the century-old views and customs of the church. Easy or superficial adjustments were not enough. It was a question not merely of the permissibility of sex life or of the value of marriage, but also of sin, of the Fall, and of salvation.

Through Augustine a dualism of spirit and matter had found its way from Neoplatonism into the doctrinal system of Catholicism. In the light of this dualism the Fall was interpreted as a metaphysical catastrophe that plunged man from the realm of the spirit into bondage of the body. Salvation signified liberation of the soul from the body. To realize this salvation man must fast, torture his body, and abstain from satisfying his sexual needs.

The Reformation threw this whole system into the crucible. The Fall was not a metaphysical misfortune. The antithesis between spirit and matter is not to be identified with the antithesis between holiness and sin. Man is created to live in faith but he is also created to live in the world of time and matter. His salvation is liberation not from matter and the body, but from the power of Satan and the slavery of sin.[6]

The implications of all this are clear. Efforts to realize the ideal of celibacy, together with the whole monastic institution, were consistent with the Catholic system but not with Luther's new view. Since God himself has placed us in it we must not deny this material world. While Catholicism thought of sin as something in the "flesh," Luther stated pointedly that the soul of man was more "fleshly" than his body, inasmuch as it is there that sin resides.[7] The soul is proud, self-sufficient, able to get along without God, and in rebellion against God. For this reason liberation from the body, were that generally possible, would not in the least free us from sin. And in a wider perspective, the philosophical division of matter and spirit, body and soul, is artificial and contrary to facts. When we speak of man we must always speak of the whole man. Sin is sin of the whole man, and salvation is salvation of the whole man. Luther realized this in a fundamental way when it dawned on him that sin and impurity are not associated merely with the outward physical life. The soul too is contaminated by sin. This is evident even in the matter of sexual continence, for it is clearly possible to avoid immorality in the body and yet involve the soul. The example of the saints was no guarantee that there was no sin in the monasteries. "Who can remain strong and pure there?" Luther cries. The power of sin in man is total; so is the corruption. "Flesh" denotes everything that is subject to God's wrath and judgment; it is the total enslavement of the whole man with his thoughts, actions, and all that is his. As a slave of sin man is estranged from God; he is without the Holy Spirit and lacking in all divine virtues (*virtutes*). There is no divine spark (*synteresis*) in him; he is altogether evil. "Spirit" on the other hand is man in subjection to the operation of the Spirit of God. Man has a conscience which is what makes it possible for the preaching of repentance to take effect.[8]

God acknowledges the world of matter. He does not limit his activities to the realm of the spirit but is active in time, matter, sacraments, the church, and real people. Matter or "flesh" is not intended as the permanent sector for Satan's activity; it is to be set aside for God once more. This includes sexual life also; it too is to be set aside for God, or sanctified, and not cast aside.

Luther sees human involvement in sin beginning with the first moments of life. This is his understanding of Psalm 51:5: "Behold, I was brought forth in iniquity, and in sin did my mother conceive me." Yet he does not interpret this passage to mean that conception and birth as such are sin. Copulation in the marital state is not sin, Luther insists, refusing to agree with those who charge that marriage is a legitimate form of adultery. A person cannot commit adultery with his own spouse. Marriage is a guard against adultery. The difference between marital relations and free or extramarital relations is precisely the fact that the former alone is based on God's own decree. Because of this divine decree marriage is holy, a divine estate and a great treasure.

Luther had inherited his statement of the problem of sexual intercourse from Augustine, in a form which made lustless intercourse the ideal. In his great work *The City of God* Augustine goes into a detailed description of the life Adam and Eve lived in Paradise before the Fall. Succinctly it was life without sin, that is, without lust. Luther gave up this view but not completely.[9] The Catholic view still colors his presentation of the problem in *The Babylonian Captivity of the Church* (1520). The biblical statement that man was conceived and born in sin Luther interprets to mean that the inception of a new human being may in certain instances be associated with such lust and evil desire that a sin no less terrible or no less a crime in God's sight than adultery is committed. The tempter has taken control of man's desires. The fact that the sex drive is strong gives Satan an effective point of contact. The sexual act can easily be given such license that harmony with God's creative purpose is destroyed.

One can readily understand why sexual sins were regarded as so great and so difficult to resist that the alternative became: celibacy or hopeless resignation to the power of sin. Luther's greatness manifests itself in his courage to see a different alternative: God-pleasing life in marriage *or* a self-chosen way that leads either into deplorable asceticism or sin. Since sin is always violation of God's will and order, and since the problem is not one of matter vs. spirit, the alternative of sexual activity *or* asceticism is not identical with the alternative of sin *or* holiness.[10]

It is interesting to note in what decisive manner God's Word illumines this whole problem. In principle the fundamental factor in the distinction between adultery and marriage is the Word. The person who is married has submitted to the order which God has ordained in his Word, while the adulterer satisfies his desire in a manner contrary to God's Word. Without God's Word marriage too would be impurity, corruption, lust, and sin.

Concerning those who despise marriage Luther said:

> Let them ridicule and continue in their evil will, those pure hearts and great saints! Let them be iron and rock, as they boast! But you, do not deny that you are a man with flesh and blood. Then let God judge between these angelic, strong heroes and you, a sick, despised sinner.[11]

Luther's statements about marriage point to an insight that we encounter repeatedly in his writings, namely, that the divine dwells in humble quarters, in the ordinary affairs of life, in weekdays, in what is despised and insignificant. Marriage and adultery have their physical aspects in common, but as founded in God's Word and ordinance marriage alone is the holy and pure form of life. Therein God sanctifies those who take the marital cross upon themselves. The old man is mortified, and the new man raised to life. All that God has created is holy, pure, and glorious, and sex is no exception. The work of the Creator must be given the honor it deserves and demands as the work of the Creator.[12]

### "LET EACH HAVE HIS OWN WIFE"

Luther recognizes the potency of the sex drive but makes no attempt to explain it; he simply accepts it as a natural necessity. This is perhaps the most fundamental thesis of his ethics of marriage, and with it he restored the ancient truth expressed in the words of Paul: "It is better to marry than to be aflame with passion" (I Cor. 7:9).

In a sermon on marriage from the year 1519 Luther speaks of three kinds of love: false, natural, and marital.[13] The first is selfish love which seeks its own honor and advantage. Natural love unites the family and the circle of relatives. Marital love is the erotic attraction of opposite sexes. The third form Luther sets above the other two. He describes marital love as admiration of beauty, a burning emotion, and a desire to possess the other wholly. This is true love between a man and his fiancée as well as between husband and wife. Such glowing feeling and sensual pleasure is the love which draws total strangers together, often in an incomprehensible way. Usually Luther looked upon the matter of getting married as a very practical thing, the counsel of the parents being decisive. In this particular sermon, however, he says that young people must be permitted to marry for reasons of mutual attraction and love.

Luther gives full recognition to the romantic and physical aspects of marriage, yet he sets the following three considerations above all others in his definition of marriage: marriage aims at guarding against adultery, at procreation, and at nurture of children. Special attention is given to the first: marriage is primarily a preventive against moral temptations and lapses, a protection and medicine against evil, against unpredictable lust. Included in this consideration is a certain guide for marital life: one must guard against the sin of selfishness. But here too Luther wants to maintain freedom of conscience. Marriage as "protection and medicine" simply underlines the thought that sex is a violent natural force.

Procreation and nurture of children must be accepted even by Luther's worst enemies as representing wholesome and sober objects of marriage. After all, it is a question of the Creator's own order. Where these are acknowledged as the purpose of marriage, there a solid foundation has been established. In the procreation and nurture of children we also encounter the marital cross on which the old man is crucified that the new man may arise.[14]

The idea is commonly held that the realm of nature or the area of the first article of the Creed is clearly distinct from the spiritual realm or the area of the second and third articles. Luther's broad sense of reality is manifested in his ability to see both realms as spheres of the one activity of God. In his natural life, fulfilling the purposes of his creator, man becomes a cross-bearer and finds that he needs Christ. God's "strange work" and his "proper work" form a unity, and both reveal God's love.

Catholic sexual ethics attempted to escape the physical realm of life in order to realize an often impossible ascetic ideal. Luther found the right way in the routine of everyday life. This was a tremendous discovery, for it glorified the creative purposes of God.

Does this recognition of the natural basis of marriage mean that marriage has its own naturalistic autonomy? The answer must be a negative one, for Luther sees marriage as founded entirely on God's Word, receiving from it its rights and rules. We must not even talk about naturalistic autonomy, for where God's Word has authority and power, there my fellow man is assigned the first place and "I myself" take second place. The form thus given to

marriage is so noble and refined that one need not look to biology
or psychology for higher guidance.

Some have suggested that Luther's reforms in marital and family life stemmed from his own moral or human weakness. Roman
Catholics have entertained the notion that Luther merely surrendered to the demands of the flesh when he permitted the marriage
of priests, monks, and nuns, all the while knowing that celibacy
was the holier form of life. But there is no reason to draw such
conclusions. From Luther's sermons and writings we gain a clear
and consistent picture. Occasional statements may have diverse
connotations, but this is true in regard to the statements of any
living person. Luther's basic view does not rest on human weakness or ascetic bankruptcy but on God's Word, on the acknowledgment of God's creative will, and on an awareness of God's order.
Here too the Reformation was empowered by the word of the gospel. This is what accounts for the overthrow of the century-old
traditions.

Reforms in this particular area of life touched a tender spot in
the ethical system of the Catholic church. We understand therefore the bitterness with which Luther was criticized. But we can
accept with confidence his solution of the problem of marriage.
God does not will the institution of monasticism. A minister may
be the head of a family as naturally as a farmer may be. As a
spouse, the minister is like any other Christian.

The Christian home is specially rooted in God's will, for it is
there that the people are born, raised, and trained whom God uses
as salt of the earth and light of the world. Luther did not deny
the celibate state as such. He knew that Paul was unmarried. But
he opposed the kind of celibacy in which by permanent vows a
person sought to gain merit in God's sight, for such celibacy denies
both Christ and faith. Then too he opposed celibacy as a state in
which self-centered contemplation is considered more God-pleasing than ordinary service to one's fellow man, for such a celibate
state contradicts love.

According to Luther's view marriage is normally the form which sexual life between man and woman assumes and as such it is an ordinance of God. Only in such exceptional cases as Paul, Anthony, Bernhard, and Francis of Assisi can one remain unmarried and not lose both faith and love.

## Chapter 16

# Vocation

As was noted in chapter fourteen, to understand what Luther says in the area of social ethics one must be acquainted with his concept of the two governments. This concept points to a division in society. At times men are placed exclusively under one government or the other, at least so it appears. Some people do not have the gospel, yet have their earthly task or sphere. The boundaries of the earthly government in such an instance may coincide with the boundaries of a nation, as in the case of the Turks. On the other hand, some look upon the Christian preacher as belonging entirely to the spiritual government because of his purely spiritual function. And yet he too is a member of society and belongs within the sphere of earthly government also. It becomes clear then that, in Luther's view, the two governments represent two viewpoints.[1]

God makes provision for this world through the law and the gospel. The law takes shape in outward organizations which compel men to works and outward righteousness *(iustitia civilis)*. The gospel assumes form in the church which grants men the forgiveness of sins *(iustitia christiana)*. To see the unity of the governments one must view them from above, with respect to God: he is active in both governments, and both express his love. God has so constituted all the tasks of life that through them man benefits his fellow man; in this way God's creative work goes on and his love reaches out in ever wider circles. Through the preacher he dispenses forgiveness. And so both governments serve as channels of his gifts and love. From man's viewpoint the unity of the two is evident in the fact that man receives God's good gifts through both the earthly and the spiritual governments, that is, from both the state and the church.[2]

Clearly then one's vocation is by no means an isolated or accidental phenomenon in God's universal government but an essential part of it. Since vocation is an aspect of God's exercise of his sovereignty through the law, all secular work is of a serious nature. "He who does not work, let him not eat" (II Thess. 3:10). But vocation has its inevitable cross, whether it be the vocation of a ruler, husband, father, or anyone else. And the cross has its peculiar purpose: to crucify the old man in us. Thus is realized the significance of baptism: the old man in us must die and the new man arise in its place. The raising of man into the newness of life God accomplishes through the gospel.

## THE CENTRALITY OF THE FELLOW MAN

Our vocational activity must be directed toward all men, in other words, toward the people of "this world." We serve them in the love of Christ, and are rewarded with the same ingratitude that he received. But this is the only form in which the love of Christ can be real, for as soon as we limit our service to those who are in some way saintlier than the rest we narrow the circle of love and shut out the effective operation of Christ's love. Thus in the cloister it is impossible to serve all men, for here the very purpose of works is changed; they are done in order to make oneself holy, and hence become acts of worship directed toward God rather than men. But, says Luther, faith alone is to be directed toward God; a fundamental error has occurred. Luther feels constrained to say that when God wants to save a monk he compels him to occupy himself with earthly things. Furthermore, in attaining to the duties of marriage and many other temporal tasks man becomes uncertain and helpless. Thus the way is paved for faith, for one is compelled to believe and trust in God.

In his vocation a person is active in behalf of his fellow men. Through such activity man distributes gifts of God's love to others for their welfare. Thus vocation compels man to look to God and to take hold of his promises, and trains him in both love and faith.[3]

The cross and the law collaborate to crucify man; the gospel gives him power to arise and live. Works are directed toward fellow men; faith is directed toward God. With faith thus directed from earth upward, why does love, which is part and parcel of faith, direct itself horizontally to fellow men? Some have attempted to show how love is born of faith. Wingren states that Luther purposely never gives such an explanation. After all, we cannot say why God became man; he was happy in heaven. Yet Christ was born into this world, loved man, and died on the cross. Just as all this is inexplicable, so is the fact that faith gives birth to love. God became man; that is the nature of God's love. And faith becomes love; that is the nature of faith. Man receives the Holy Spirit when he believes the gospel of Christ, and in the power of the Spirit he loves his fellow men without duplicity and guile, and willingly shares their burdens. Love keeps no record of its works for it thinks only about the fellow man, and when it does good its deed appears as a gift and not a work. Love looks upon service to others as a privilege, not a duty. A person possessed by such love does not direct his attention to the love itself but to his fellow man. To be preserved, such love must constantly be given new life by faith. Without Christ and the Spirit man is under the law, and under the law vocation is enforced labor completely lacking in joy. The old man in us tries to be perfect and righteous in all that he does. The new man knows only one righteousness, the forgiveness of sins. The old man is under the law, the new man is in faith.[4]

When the fellow man is again made central in ethics, the gospel of Jesus is revitalized. We recall what Jesus said about the separation on the Last Day. The righteous will ask, "Lord, when did we see you hungry, thirsty . . .?" They had paid no attention to their works. They could not even remember having met a fellow man in distress. They had rejoiced in others and had helped them without being aware of having done so.

The traditional Catholic teaching fixed man's attention on works and their value in God's sight. This formulation of the question derives from ancient philosophy, and is remarkably well suited for the purposes of the old man in us. By nature we want to achieve the greatest possible results with the least possible effort. Such utilitarianism ruins morality. In contrast, Luther's ethical teachings resurrect the New Testament ethos. In faith the Christian breathes God's free air and lives in the immediacy of God's presence. He does not push selfishly toward goals, yet works of love are actually produced. Were we to ask Luther what we should do, he would answer, "You must do the task at hand."[5] He would point out that to be in harmony with God's will our activity need not seek high places, or be remarkable or great; often it need not even be spiritual. God's will and purpose have to do with inconspicuous earthly activity, activity which we often overlook.[6] A person fulfills his vocation in the insignificant which, coming from God's hand, is most significant. The new man in us does his work, whatever that may be, with heartfelt joy *(ex animo et cum gaudio)*. Where the gospel and faith prevail, there our fellow man ceases to be an irritant and we serve him with joy.

The law makes every effort to dominate and dictate to love. It tries to make love, the queen, into a servant girl. The law tries to compel sympathy for fellow man; it makes him a burden whereas love makes him a joy. When love takes over, the new man brings forth works. By these works God recreates the world. This includes virtual recreation of the whole universe. In other words, the church of Christ is responsible for continuous renewal of the social order.

Luther, however, is rather niggardly in his suggestions concerning universal social reform. He draws up no program. This is no accident; it reflects his view of faith. He knows that the devil is always at hand, even in the momentarily improved social order, and that there are no structures of life which are not tainted with man's sin. All specific programs of ethical reform are incompatible with spontaneous good works done to others. Good works can neither be planned nor predicted nor thought out in advance, for love discovers on the spur of the moment what best meets the needs of others. The good works which can be regularly predicted defeat their purpose. Thus the man who seeks to establish his own holiness and assurance of salvation by means of certain specified works, suffers a double loss: in the first place his sacrifices never succeed, for they lack faith and hence also the assurance of the Holy Spirit; and in the second place they have nothing to do with love since in the final analysis they are not focused on another's need but on one's own salvation. Where there is love there is no formal law, for the works of love are at times quite ordinary and at other times quite unusual. According to Luther's view of vocation man and wife, parents and children, masters and servants, rulers and citizens can expect to find themselves constantly in situations in which they cannot predict what they will do. If all the works of the new life could be programmed and planned in advance, the resultant ethical system might well replace man's relationship to God, jeopardizing that indefatigable and inventive spirit of love which God now uses to recreate his world.[7]

## VOCATION AND IMITATION

Because works of the new life cannot and must not be legislated, it follows that imitation has to be rejected as a pattern of behavior. The only proper way to do God's will is by fulfilling and practicing one's vocation. To do God's will I cannot imitate some other person, for no other person has the life environment God has given me. St. Francis, for example, cannot be my model, regardless of how spiritual and holy he may have been. When vocation is substituted for imitation it becomes necessary for each person to discover God's way for him personally in his own situation. Difficult and important decisions entail risk, but faith never shies away from taking a risk. He who would pattern his activity after someone else must free himself from his own temporal and spatial bonds, while he who seeks to fulfill his vocation accepts the total context of his life as God's gift. God has hidden himself in

our environment; all creation around us is God's mask. All creation includes the total environment: family, occupation, fellow
workers, neighbors, health, and wealth, as Luther lists them in explaining the fourth petition of the Lord's Prayer in his *Small Catechism.* In all these things we are to love our fellow man and to
concentrate our ethical activity on him. The Christian is not in
this world for himself or for his own salvation; he has been placed
here to serve others. The sole controlling principle in this service
is love; the program for implementing love, however, is not placed
in his hands, for that is something that must be determined by
the situation itself. This means that Christian faith must never be
made into an ideology. It also means that it would be inconsistent
with the principle and program of love to establish Christian
parties with specific platforms. Here we are at the crossroads
where the greatest difficulty and the highest ideal of the Lutheran
concept of faith come together: no laws or rules, only a passionate
love in action under God's blue sky in the service of others. If love
is lacking, the fault is in faith. The Christian is not compelled by
a morality but is grasped in his innermost being—his God-relationship, his need of salvation, his knowledge of sin—and freed by
Christ, who makes him alive and active as never before.

The same activity is not appropriate everywhere, with the result that diversity in professions and vocations is necessary. This
diversity is characteristic of life as such, and at least Luther found
it a cause for joy. We must say that in this he was clearly in harmony with the Creator himself, whose works bespeak his love of
variety. The cornerstone of Luther's social ethics might well have
the inscription: "Let each one concentrate on his own task." "This
is God's sure decision," Luther writes in his treatise *On Monastic
Vows,* "that all saints are to live in the same faith and to be compelled and led by the same Spirit, while in their outward lives
they carry out different tasks."[8] The reason is that "God does not
produce the same works in all of them, for, while leading them by
the same Spirit and faith, he brings his power to bear upon various
times, places, people, and activities." Thus the ways of God are

hidden. God has his saints perform, in their time and place, works they have not seen elsewhere. God's people must work without models; they must find their own way.

## FAITH MAINTAINS UNITY

To understand what has been said we must view it in the light of the idea of the two realms. In faith all Christians are alike. In their relationship to God and salvation there is no difference, for faith alone is important here; in the world of works the difference is great, for here we find a variety of professions, stations, and offices. Luther points out that while the sun shines in the same way upon peasant and king, weed and rose, the pig in the backyard and beautiful girls, the works that these perform in the light of the same sun are necessarily different. The fact that human talents and interests, skills and tasks are never identical is reflected in the rich variety we find in the world of works. Yet before God, in the matter of salvation, all men are alike.

Once we grasp this truth we appreciate Luther's strong emphasis upon faith. Faith is openness to God, receiving from him and living in dependence upon him. He who lives by faith will not be concerned about his lack of conformity with others. To him the only really vital thing is grace, which he receives as a gift and by which he lives.

In earthly tasks differences remain. We shall continue to have differences of position and status; there will be those who lead and those who are led. But since these differences of position and status have no value before God, the Christian can cheerfully submit to them in earthly matters. He will not be induced into false and idolatrous admiration of power and riches. Nor will he be compelled to admire the outward holiness of monks and the spirituality of the visionaries. Luther states his own position as follows:

> Whether, please God, I see a married person or a single person, a master or a servant, a learned man or a layman, gray clothes or red, fasting or eating, a sour face or a smiling one, what do I care about that? In other words, the differences that I see among them are all identical to me. For I have come to the insight that a girl in her red

coat or a prince in his golden spangles can be no less a Christian than a beggar in his gray coat or a monk in his shirt of wool or hair. With this insight I am safe against all kinds of outward masks.[9]

Both the absolute equality and the significant distinctions are of God, equality in salvation and distinctions in earthly tasks.

But if salvation is sought in the area of good works, complete chaos results. God's order is disrupted. If the foundation of faith is removed, then salvation has to be sought through works. But we do different things, so each must look upon his own way as the only way in which one can be saved. This is the fate of the heathen: each has his own way of salvation. But everyone who bases his salvation on what he does falls into the same error. With the introduction of changes in the sphere of works and customs the number of ways of salvation is increased and the chaos grows.[10] Luther illustrates this point in his *Church Postil* by explaining the fact that Judas Iscariot is mentioned by name while John is simply referred to as "the disciple whom Jesus loved."

> Notice now why St. John does not give his name; faith makes no sects, no differences, as works do. For that reason there is required of faith no specific work, which can be pointed out by name; for faith does all sorts of works best suited to the situation. To faith one good work is as acceptable as another. But it is the nature of Judas Iscariot to split up in works without faith. One is called bishop, by reason of his miter and staff, not because of his faith. Another is recognized as a barefooted friar, because of his gown and wooden shoes. Another is known as an Augustinian monk by his black robe, and so forth. One gets his name from this, another from something else. But faith is not recognized by external actions or stations; and for that very reason it is faith that produces disciples whom Jesus loves.[11]

When man believes that salvation depends upon works and outward conduct, he will demand similar works and outward conduct of everyone. This gives rise to endless groups and parties. And all because that which is outward has been made a way or condition of salvation.

The gospel changes all this. In the matter of salvation the decisive factor is not some holy work or another that we have performed. No form of outward conduct can be singled out as holy.

The law can indeed produce a formal similarity but in so doing it destroys true unity. The gospel, while permitting outward differences, builds true unity, for among hearts and consciences, in the matter of salvation, Christ is the only foundation and the only way. Outward differences remain, and must remain, for such differences are an aspect of Christian freedom and spontaneous ethical activity. Such differences are also necessary, for love seeks to serve the fellow man wherever and whenever it finds him in need. Differentiations are from God and point to his richness as the giver of gifts.

In the eyes of the world the manifold tasks vary in glory and importance. "But the eyes of God," says Luther, "regard not works but our obedience in them."[12] In this connection Luther refers to I Corinthians 7:20. Attention to the responsibilities of one's vocation makes a person a useful member of the whole body. Members have different functions. Were a member in its quest for holiness to break away from the body, it would destroy its own life and bring injury to other members. It is an important fact for Luther that no member of the body performs its functions in order to become a member of the body. I am already a member! My membership has been effected by Christ. I can therefore direct all my efforts to the welfare of the body and its members. The Christian need not select certain works for himself; he is no originator of sects. He is satisfied with his vocation, no matter how insignificant it may be. Since in faith all are alike he belongs to the body as much as any other member. For this reason dissimilarities in earthly matters need not cause division, for all stations and vocations are bound together from above. They are one in Christ, from whom they originate and whose masks they are. Luther knows about man's cooperation with God; however, the direction of this cooperation is never upward toward God, but always outward toward our fellow men. The Christian act has its origin in the love of God, and so the function of the Christian is that of a middleman, a mask of God. In elaborating on this thought Wingren states that "Luther's judgment of *imitatio* is negative; one is not to put confidence in anything external, but to act impartially before all human appearances.[13] Faith is not a temporal thing; it has to do with salvation. It cannot therefore reckon with differences among men. Peace of conscience before God, mediated by the gospel, robs human differences of their significance.

This is the reason for Luther's attack on imitation. Imitation stems from deficient ethical earnestness, since its purpose is not the service of others but the service of self. The goal of imitation is the holiness demonstrated by a familiar figure; its concern is the development of one's own personality, hence the self. Here salvation is not the source but the goal of one's action.[14]

Considering the present state of affairs, one must ask: Does not much of our Christianity, patterned as it is after the social club, fall under the same judgment as imitation? Is not conformity also our goal? How do we interpret Jesus' statement about losing and finding one's life? Does not imitation (conformity) represent a manner of viewing things in which man wants to save his soul but loses it by becoming—contrary to God's purpose—like everyone else?

## HOLINESS AND VOCATION

The focal point of the ethics of vocation is one's fellow man, not sanctification of self. This is the reason for the rejection of all forms of imitation. The only saint whom I could imitate would be the one who had the same neighbor as I and who was related to him in the same way as I. But where I stand no saint has ever stood before. The saints are our examples only in the sense that we are called to resemble them in their faithfulness to their tasks. This we cannot do by simply making their tasks our own.

Though the focal point of the ethics of vocation is one's fellow man and not one's sanctification of self, sanctification nevertheless does take place in vocation. By means of our vocation God puts to death the old man in us and awakens to life the new. The cross of one's vocation is God's strange work. It is burdensome to flesh and blood but wholesome for the Christian. Our faithfulness is tested as we bear the trials and sufferings that come our way. The trials are mine and to that extent no one can share them. Conversely, I cannot really know the life and trials of those around me. Thus I can never pose as their judge. Sanctification is always hidden from the world. It takes place in the many and different vocations of man. We have no way of measuring people and differentiating between them. We must say, "I believe in the holy Christian church." Faith clings to the fact that there are Christians, sanctified people, who fulfill their vocation in this world.

Because one cannot fulfill his vocation by imitation of someone else, man finds himself alone, without a model. But God the Creator continues to create that which is new, and to renew that which is, by means of the vocations he has assigned to men. For the time being the resultant holiness is hidden from the eyes of the world, but on the Last Day it will be revealed, and then all men will marvel at the judgment of God.[15]

## Chapter 17

# The State

God carries out his rule of the world by spiritual and earthly means. Man therefore confronts God in all things. The social order and the state are directly involved in God's program.

Initially Luther paid little attention to social and political issues. He was satisfied to accept Augustine's observation that the kingdom of God and the kingdom of darkness have been opposed to each other from the very beginning. The world was by and large the kingdom of darkness, so there was little reason to be concerned about it. But as the Reformation progressed social questions began to demand greater attention. People came to Wittenberg for advice and guidance in all sorts of life situations. Usually the advice had to do with problems of conscience, but the renewal of the life of the church touched public life at so many points that political questions could not be ignored very long.

Perhaps the most important of Luther's insights in the area of politics was the rather simple one that the gospel cannot be applied directly to political life. The spiritual and temporal government must be kept distinct. The gospel provides no direct guidance in matters of state and society, even though it influences corporate life in various ways.

The state in the modern sense did not exist in Luther's time. The small territorial divisions of late medieval Germany can hardly be compared to modern nations. They had no significance in the area of international politics; they provided relatively little opportunity for men to know the true character of the demon of power and the fateful meaning of political alternatives. The chief political agents were the princes and their subjects. Political life was largely a matter of personal relationships. The responsibilities of the state were limited largely to dispensing justice and maintaining order. The state had no need to concern itself with the welfare of its citizens in the modern sense of the welfare state. The theory of "social contract" was still a long way off.

To Luther a wise prince was better than all the laws and all the lawyers in the world. The true art of living was of much higher value than formal education; the admiration of systematic thought which has characterized the German spirit of later centuries was foreign to Luther.

### THE TASK OF THE STATE

The political order, *weltlich regiment,* existed because of sin. This must not be understood to mean that political life as such is sin. "Because of sin" means that the use of force on the part of the state is the only way in which order can be preserved in this world of sin. The Anabaptists and some pietistic movements of later periods have taken the opposite view, that the state as such represents sin. To Luther this is impossible.

The state must maintain a system of justice. For purposes of peace and order it has been given the sword. Its use of that sword assures a state of affairs in which the preaching of the gospel is possible.[1] In this sense temporal authorities are responsible also for the eternal welfare or salvation of their subjects. On this account the tasks of theologians and lawyers are intimately related. Theologians and lawyers are the pillars that support the cause of peace. Luther writes:

> We theologians and lawyers must stand or fall together. In this I am not wrong. When the theologians vanish the Word of God vanishes with them, leaving only heathen people, in fact, pure devils. When the lawyers vanish justice and peace disappear with them, leaving behind thievery, murder, vandalism, and violence, in fact, only wild beasts.[2]

The home, the courthouse, and the church provide the framework of life. They constitute what might be called the hierarchy of well-ordered life.[3]

Luther's thoughts about the state and society were occasional, prompted by pastoral concern. As guidance to those who were troubled in conscience, he wrote in 1523 the treatise on *Temporal Authority*. So violent was the stream of events associated with the Reformation that, beyond what was demanded of him as a university professor, Luther could write only what was absolutely necessary. For this reason his views especially on social ethics must be culled from writings that were produced out of necessity in connection with particular situations. This presents for the interpreter of Luther certain understandable difficulties. To be accurate the interpretation must on the one hand not place too much stress on the particular positions Luther took in the given situations, but it must on the other hand recognize that Luther may have stated in passing and without special emphasis things that are of central importance.

Since the task of the state as an agent of order and justice in this world involves it in the use of police methods, we turn our attention first to the questions of war and the use of force.

## FORCE AND WAR

The "Resist not evil" passage in the Sermon on the Mount has given theologians of all times considerable difficulty. At no other point do the views of state and church impinge upon one another as sharply as here. The state must under all circumstances preserve order and protect its subjects from violence. Against stubborn evildoers it must be able to use force when necessary to realize these purposes, at the same time limiting the freedom of its subjects as little as possible. The church on the other hand must under all conditions preach and promote peace and love.

Luther expressed his thoughts about war in his treatise *Whether Soldiers, too, Can Be Saved* (1526). He views the question of war largely from the legal standpoint. War is an event in the realm of justice. Either it destroys the divinely decreed peaceful order, or it serves to restore peace. To the extent that it destroys the order of justice, it must be classed with robbery, plunder, mur-

der, and adultery. To the extent that it serves the cause of peace
it is a punitive and protective function granted by God to the
state, in which case war serves the cause of love. Luther asks,
"What is proper war if not the punishment of evildoers and the
preservation of peace? When a thief, murderer or adulterer is
punished, an individual criminal is punished, but when proper war
is waged, punishment is meted out to a whole group of criminals,
whose crimes are in proportion to its size."[4]

To Luther the justification of war was no problem, since in
principle the same sword was in operation in the courthouse and
on the battlefield. War is punitive action. The character of war
as "right" or "wrong" depends on the status of the group that initiates it. In the medieval territorial system the lowest authority was
the lower nobility. Above them were the princes and rulers up to
the emperor. Highest in this hierarchy of power was God himself.

Even here Luther does not attempt to create a theory for the
justification of war. His purpose was to enlighten men's consciences and to make it possible for them to engage in military
activity according to God's will. For this reason he found no great
difficulty in justifying war under certain circumstances. In his
book *Against Latomus* Luther writes:

> So, if the Turks start a war against us—which, of course, they are
> not permitted to do—and will not be restrained, let us send the Lou-
> vainian theologians to them as ambassadors, for they will say, "You
> are not allowed to fight, for if you do we shall condemn you." Then
> we shall let them ravage, and vaunt ourselves as victors.[5]

This is the counsel of his opponents, Luther suggests. As to his
own position in regard to war, he writes elsewhere:

> When men write about war, then, and say that it is a great plague,
> that is all true; but they should also see how great the plague is that
> it prevents. If people were good, and glad to keep peace, war would
> be the greatest plague on earth; but what are you going to do with the
> fact that people will not keep peace, but rob, steal, kill, outrage women
> and children, and take away property and honor? The small lack of
> peace, called war, or the sword, must set a check upon this universal,
> world-wide lack of peace, before which no one could stand. Therefore

God honors the sword so highly that he calls it his own ordinance, and will not have men say or imagine that they have invented it or instituted it. For the hand that wields this sword and slays with it is then no more man's hand, but God's, and it is not man, but God who hangs, tortures, beheads, slays, and fights. All these are his works and his judgments.[6]

Luther therefore does not question the propriety of war when it is a matter of restoring a violated order of justice. As the servant of the just God, the state has the right to use even the sword, but only to the point where justice is again established.

Never idealizing violence or war, Luther saw the preservation of order as the task of the state. Without this order the gospel could not be preached and people could not live as Christians. In speaking of Christian freedom Luther makes it very clear that the state has nothing whatsoever to do with the individual's conscience. In matters of conscience the Christian is free. Totalitarian states cannot therefore appeal to Luther in defense of their aims.

## THE PEASANTS' WAR

Luther's enemies have always felt that his attitude toward the peasants during the Peasants' War was a serious lapse. He betrayed the cause of the peasants, they say, and took his stand with the lords. What are we to say about this?

Just prior to 1517 a general unrest settled over most of Germany. In the country as well as in the cities there were signs of dangerous tensions. The appearance of Luther and Zwingli undermined the position of the temporal and ecclesiastical authorities. Tracts were distributed demanding that the "common man" must make his stand known. It seemed that a time of liberation had arrived, a time when all injustices would be rectified. At the heart of this proclamation was the gospel and the message of Christian freedom. But how else could the common people understand this message of freedom except in material terms? The church and the nobility were the great landowners, and among them arbitrary action and actual oppression were not uncommon.

Already in his treatise on *Temporal Authority,* but especially in his *Admonition to Peace* (1525), Luther directed sharp words against the lords. The peasants were justified in their complaints against princes and bishops alike. Luther writes:

> In your temporal government, you do nothing but flay and rob your subjects, in order that you may lead a life of splendor and pride, until the poor common people can bear it no longer. The sword is at your throats, but you think yourselves so firm in the saddle that no one can unhorse you. This false security and stubborn perversity will break your necks, as you will discover.[7]

Luther notes that if the lords do not change their ways amicably and willingly, they will be compelled to it by force and destruction. If the peasants do not do it, others will. The lords must check the splendor of their living, so that the poor man too can keep something.[8]

Luther had something to say to the peasants too. He begins with admitting that their demands were in large measure moderate and just, and the crimes of the lords were evident. But then he continues:

> The fact that the rulers are wicked and unjust does not excuse tumult and rebellion, for to punish wickedness does not belong to everybody, but to the worldly rulers who bear the sword. Thus Paul says in Romans 13, and Peter, in I Peter 3, that they are ordained of God for the punishment of the wicked. Then, too, there is the natural law of all the world, which says that no one may be judge in his own cause or take his own revenge.[9]

Pointing to the existing situation, Luther asks the rebellious peasants:

> I make you the judges, and leave it to you to decide who is the worse robber, the man who takes a large part of another's goods, but leaves him something, or the man who takes everything that he has, and his living besides. The rulers unjustly take your property; that is the one side. On the other hand, you take from them the authority, in which their whole property and life and being consist. Therefore, you are far greater robbers than they, and intend to do worse things than they have done. [10]

In addition to arbitrary action in regard to the possessions of their subjects, the lords were guilty of withholding the gospel from them. But Luther felt that the peasants also were guilty of trampling the name of God underfoot. Unwilling to suffer wrong, they were taking the matter of defending their rights into their own hands. This in the face of the fact that Christ says, "Do not resist evil." Luther tells the peasants that if they are unwilling to heed this word, they should put off the name of Christian, and boast of another name that accords with their actions.[11] He points out:

> Now see how far the false prophets have led you away from them [Christian laws], and yet they call you Christians, though they have made you worse than heathen. For from these sayings, a child easily grasps that it is Christian law not to strive against wrongs, not to grasp after the sword, not to protect oneself, not to avenge oneself, but to give up life and property, and let who takes it take it; we have enough in our Lord, who will not leave us, as he has promised. Suffering, suffering; cross, cross! This and nothing else, is the Christian law![12]

Such Christian counsel could no longer stem the insurgent movement. Rather than appreciating Luther's warnings, the leaders of the revolt felt that Luther had betrayed them. And Luther's treatise came into their hands too late, when matters were already in full swing.

At first the peasants had been of one mind with Luther: they must not resort to violence. A protest must be made against the injustices but otherwise God's Word must be permitted to do its work. After all, the Word had been strong enough to empty many of the monasteries. Only when actually threatened were the peasants to take up arms. Such a situation soon developed. In 1524 Roman Catholic princes began an armed oppression of the adherents of the new faith. Evangelical ministers were expelled and their books burned. Under these circumstances the revolt burst into flame from one end of Germany to the other. Violent spirits, like Thomas Münzer, gained leadership of the movement, and soon things were beyond control. All of Germany was in danger of perishing in fire and blood. Plundered monasteries, burning castles and villages, and murdered nobles and priests were a glaring witness to a carnal interpretation of the freedom of the gospel. Had all this been permitted to continue unhindered, all of Germany would have been destroyed and the whole cause of the Reformation lost.

Faced by the critical circumstances, the princes turned cowards. Their hesitancy and inaction allowed whatever happened. A stronger grasp on things was needed; the rulers must take their responsibility seriously. To this end Luther wrote his famous treatise *Against the Robbing and Murdering Hordes of Peasants* (1525). The sharp statements of this treatise, such as that the killing of the peasants was a meritorious act before God, have been used since their publication to smear Luther's reputation. He supposedly betrayed the cause of the peasants, after siding with them in the beginning, thereby ruining the whole cause of the Reformation and demonstrating its deafness and blindness in social matters.

An unprejudiced analysis of the facts, however, shows an unfortunate intertwining of events. The demands of the peasants were largely just, but necessary reforms were not undertaken immediately, with the result that dissatisfaction burst into open violence that had to be stopped. The sword of the rulers represented God's own order. Unless this fact could be maintained, Luther felt, the gospel would have no room anywhere.

The writings that came out during the Peasants' War do not bear up the contention that Luther was socially unenlightened. They point to the fact that the situation called for restoration of order as something absolutely necessary. The alternative was utter chaos. Throughout the Peasants' War Luther never wavered in his stand that justice must be maintained. In speaking of the crushing of the revolt and of the shedding of blood which was inevitable, he was turning to Christian authorities. He had not undertaken to teach violent, senseless tyrants, who even after the battle cannot get their fill of blood and who never ask about Christ. "To these bloody dogs it is all one whether they slay the

guilty or the innocent, whether it pleases God or the devil. They
have the sword, but only that they may vent their lust and self-
will. I leave them to the guidance of their master, the devil, who
is, indeed, leading them," says Luther.[13]

The unfortunate course of events of the Peasants' War was determined largely by false spiritualistic teachers such as Münzer.
But perhaps more fateful was the failure of the authorities to take
action in time to correct evident injustices. And Luther's writings
apparently appeared too late. Some may want to lay this to his
charge. But who are we to judge him at this point, we who live
in an era that is making amazing advances in the area of transpor-
tation and mass communication. In regard to the sincerity of Luther's motives, however, we need have no doubt. The testimony
of his writings is sufficient for us.[14]

### SOCIAL REFORM

Luther's fundamental insight was that the social order rests primarily upon natural reason and is not to be derived from the law
of God. Further, the spiritual and earthly governments must be
kept distinct. Under the circumstances, then, we might ask if human society has not been left entirely outside the pale of God's
Word, dependent upon its own light.

In answering this question we must recall what has been said.
The modern welfare state was unknown in Luther's time. His state
was no association based on social contract and concerned about the
total welfare and fortune of the citizenry. And Luther did not feel
that the area of activity for love of fellow man must be enlarged
as much as possible by means of legislation. These ideas, inherent
in the modern view, were not self-evident in Luther's day. On the
contrary, Luther felt that good works produced under compulsion
of the law were neither good nor desirable, for they would be in
conflict with the principle of the righteousness of faith. The new
obedience must be spontaneous in order to be pleasing to God.

But if from all this we conclude that in Luther's theology the
influence of God's Word does not extend into the social realm, we

simply draw the wrong conclusion. Luther took for granted that the prince, the mayor, and the executioner heard the preaching of the gospel every week. They could not function in their offices except by God's will and as men who were accountable to him. This was pointed out to them repeatedly, making it one of the self-evident matters of that day.

Under the circumstances Luther did not direct his efforts toward renewal of society but toward renewal of the church. What he said about the dynamic character of God's Word, however, was applicable not only in the area of private masses but in the outward order in general. He felt that no man should be pulled out of the old order by the hair. Matters must be left with God. His Word must be permitted to function alone without our work or interference. Why? Luther answers:

> Because it is not in my power or hand to fashion the hearts of men as the potter molds the clay and fashion them at my pleasure (Ecclus. 33:13). I can get no farther than their ears; their hearts I cannot reach. And since I cannot pour faith into their hearts, I cannot, nor should I, force any one to have faith. That is God's work alone, who causes faith to live in the heart. Therefore we should give free course to the Word and not add our works to it. We have the *jus verbi* (right to speak) but not the *executio* (power to accomplish). We should preach the Word, but the results must be left solely to God's good pleasure.[15]

Social reform belongs in Luther's theology as a matter of principle. Its program, however, cannot be worked out by selecting certain Bible passages and making them into social legislation. Translated into a program of social reform, the gospel would cease to be the gospel. The gospel is and must be the work and gift of God alone. It must not be made into a program of human activity, for then it is brought down from its high place and changed into a law. This would be the greatest possible error; in the confusion of gospel and law the gospel would disappear completely.

Social reform is the establishment of new and better orders of justice. The earthly government is God's instrument for this specific purpose. But it remains an open question how far a perfect order of justice can be established under the conditions of this world. The spiritual righteousness, however, is something else again; it was in order to establish this righteousness that Jesus Christ was made Savior and Lord. If the earthly government is made a means for achieving this spiritual righteousness, the two governments are confused, something which Luther sought to avoid.

Luther knew that conditions could change radically in a moment. God could send a "hero" or "miracle man" *(vir heroicus),* a man especially called and prepared for a unique task.[16] Ordinary people on their part have the responsibility of their vocations, even when these provide few opportunities for social reform in the direct sense. God wants to create faith in every baptized Christian, and the works of faith are always new works, following no previous pattern or precedent. In this way God is active in renewing society, even though he does not ask men to write his program. All he asks is that Christians be faithful in their vocations, open to whatever he through his Holy Spirit wants to work in and through them.

Notes, Bibliography,
and Index

# Notes

## INTRODUCTION

[1]On "system" in Luther's theology cf. Jaroslav Pelikan, *Luther's Works* (Philadelphia: Muhlenberg), Companion Volume, *Luther the Expositor*, pp. 42 f.

[2]*Luther-Jahrbuch,* ed. Franz Lau (Berlin, 1933-1961).

[3]*Lutherforschung heute,* ed. Vilmos Vajta (Berlin, 1958).

[4]*Luther and Melanchthon,* ed. Vilmos Vajta (Philadelphia: Muhlenberg, 1961).

[5]Heinrich Bornkamm, "Luthers Bericht über seine Entdeckung der iustitia Dei," *Archiv für Reformationsgeschichte* (1940); and "Iustitia Dei in der Scholastik und bei Luther," *Archiv für Reformationsgeschichte* (1942).

[6]Wilhelm Link, *Das Ringen Luthers um die Freiheit der Theologie von der Philosophie* (1955).

[7]Axel Gyllenkrok, "Rechtfertigung und Heiligung in der frühen evangelischen Theologie Luthers," *Uppsala universitets årsskrift* (1952). Hereafter referred to as UUA.

[8]Uuras Saarnivaara, *Luther Discovers the Gospel* (1951).

[9]Carl Stange, *Die Anfänge der Theologie Luthers* (1957).

[10]Ernst Bizer, *Fides ex auditu* (1961).

[11]Hans Pohlmann *Hat Luther Paulus entdeckt?* (1959).

[12]Regin Prenter, *Der barmherzige Richter,* "Acta Jutlandica" (1961).

[13]Reinhard Schwarz, *Fides, spes und caritas beim jungen Luther,* "Arbeiten zur Kirchengeschichte" (1962).

[14]Bengt Hägglund, *De homine,* "Studia Theologica Lundensia" (1959); and *Theologie und Philosophie bei Luther und in der occamistischen Tradition,* LUA (1955).

[15]David Löfgren, *Die Theologie der Schöpfung bei Luther* (Göttingen, 1960).

[16]Aarne Siirala, *Gottes Gebot bei Martin Luther* (Helsinki, 1956).

[17]Bernhard Lohse, *Ratio und fides. Eine Untersuchung über die ratio in der Theologie Luthers* (Göttingen, 1958).

[18]Wilhelm Maurer, *Von der Freiheit eines Christenmenschen. Zwei Untersuchungen zu Luthers Reformationsschriften 1520/21* (Göttingen, 1949).

[19]Wilfried Joest, *Gesetz und Freiheit. Das Problem der tertius usus legis bei Luther und die neutestamentliche Parainäse* (Göttingen, 1951).

[20]Lauri Haikola, *Studien zu Luther und zum Luthertum,* UUA (1958); and *Usus legis,* UUA (1958).

[21]F. Edward Cranz, *An Essay on the Development of Luther's Thought on Justice, Law and Society,* "Harvard Theological Studies" (London, 1959).

[22]Martin Schloemann, *Natürliches und gepredigtes Gesetz bei Luther,* "Theologische Bibliothek Töpelmann" (1961).

[23]Werner Jetter, *Die Taufe beim jungen Luther* (1954).

[24]Wilfried Joest, *Die Taufe von Augustin bis zum jungen Luther* (1951).

[25]Hans Grass, *Die Abendmahlslehre bei Luther und Calvin* (1954).

[26]Erwin Metzke, *Sakrament und Metaphysik* (1948).

[27]Ragnar Bring, *Kristendomstolkningar* (1950).

[28]Carl Fr. Wisløf, *Nattverd og Messe. En studie i Luthers teologi* (1957).

[29]Rudolf Hermann, *Luthers These Gerecht und Sünder zugleich* (1930); and *Gesammelte Studien zur Theologie Luthers und der Reformation* (1960).

[30]Regin Prenter, *Spiritus Creator* (1953); and "Luthers Lehre von der Heiligung," *Lutherforschung heute* (1958).

[31]Svend Lerfeldt, *Den kristnes kamp. Mortificatio carnis* (1949).

[32]See note 7.

[33]Paul Althaus, "Die beiden Regimente bei Luther," *Theologische Literatur-Zeitung* (1956); and "Luthers Lehre von den beiden Reichen im Feuer der Kritik," *Luther-Jahrbuch* (1957).

[34]Ernst Kinder, *Geistliches und weltliches Regiment Gottes nach Luther* (1940); and *Luther und die politische Frage* (1950).

[35]Gustaf Törnvall, *Andligt och världsligt regemente hos Luther* (1940); in German trans., *Geistliches und weltliches Regiment bei Luther* (1947).

[36]Gerhard Pfeiffer, *Totaler Staat — und Luthers?* (1951).

[37]Johann Heckel, *Lex charitatis* (1953); and *Im Irrgarten der Zwei-Reiche-Lehre* (1957).

[38]Gunnar Hillerdal, *Gehorsam gegen Gott und Menschen* (1954).

[39]Philip S. Watson, *The State as a Servant of God* (1946).

[40]Franz Lau, *"Ausserlich ordnung" und "weltlich Ding" in Luthers Theologie* (1933); and *Luthers Lehre von den beiden Reichen* (1953).

[41]Heinrich Bornkamm, *Luther und das Alte Testament* (1948).

[42]Gerhard Ebeling, *Evangelische Evangelienauslegung* (1942).

[43]Walter von Loewenich, *Luther als Ausleger der Synoptiker* (1954).

[44]Walter von Loewenich, *Luthers theologia crucis* (1954).

[45]Nathan Söderblom, *Humor och melankoli och andra Lutherstudier* (1919).

[46]Ragnar Bring, *Dualismen hos Luther* (1959).

[47]Eric Vogelsang, *Der angefochtene Christus bei Luther* (1932).

[48]Paul Theophil Buehler, *Die Anfechtung bei Martin Luther* (1942).

[49]Horst Beintker, *Die Überwindung der Anfechtung bei Luther* (1954).

[50]Roland H. Bainton, *Here I Stand* (1950).

[51]E. G. Schwiebert, *Luther and His Times* (1950).

[52]Horst Stephan, *Luther in den Wandlungen seiner Kirche* (1951); Ernst Wolf, "Über neuere Lutherliteratur und den Gang der Lutherforschung," *Christentum und Wissenschaft* (1934); Otto Wolff, *Die Haupttypen der neueren Lutherdeutung* (1938); Walter von Loewenich, "Zehn Jahre Luther-forschung," *Theologie und Liturgie* (1952).

[53]Ragnar Bring, "Einige Blätter aus der schwedischen Lutherforschung," *Zeitschrift für systematische Theologie* (1931); Hjalmar Lindroth, *Luther-renässansen i nyare svensk teologi* (1941); Eino Sormunen, "Luther in Finn-land," *Finnland und Deutschland* (1944).

## CHAPTER 1

[1]*D. Martin Luthers Werke,* Kritische Gesamtausgabe (Weimar, 1883-), 1, 354(1518). Hereafter referred to as *WA.* American Edition of *Luther's Works* (Philadelphia and St. Louis, 1955-), 31,52. Hereafter referred to as *LW.*

[2]Walter von Loewenich, *Luthers theologia crucis* (Munich, 1954), p. 13.

[3]*Invisibilia* in Thesis 19 is contrasted with *visibilia et posteriora Dei* in Thesis 20, and *per ea, quae facta sunt* in Thesis 19 is contrasted with *per passiones et crucem* in Thesis 20.

[4]*WA* 1,362 (1518); *LW* 31, 52.

[5]*WA* 3, 463 (1514).
[6]*WA* 1, 357 (1518).
[7]*WA* 40$^I$, 76 (1531). Cf. Karl Holl, "Was verstand Luther unter die Religion," *Gesammelte Aufsätze* (Tübingen, 1932).
[8]*WA, Tischreden* 1, 644 (1533). Hereafter referred to as *WA TR.*
[9]Gustaf Wingren, *Man and the Incarnation* (Philadelphia: Muhlenberg, 1959), p. 33.
[10]*WA* 1, 563 (1518).
[11]*WA* 24, 37 (1527).
[12]*WA* 23, 117 (1527).
[13]*WA* 30 $^I$, 204 (1529).
[14]*WA* 3, 35 (1513-15).
[15]*WA* 7, 585 (1521)
[16]*WA* 7, 588 (1521).
[17]*WA* 18, 711 (1525). *The Bondage of the Will,* trans. J. I. Packer and O. R. Johnston, (London; Clarke, 1957), p. 207.
[18]*WA* 40$^{III}$, 221 (1523-33); cf. *WA* 6, 554 (1520).
[19]*WA* 16, 353, 512 (1524-27); 51, 242 (1534-35); 47, 242 (1537-40); 49, 137 (1540); 40$^{III}$, 689, (1544).
[20]John 1:1-3. Cf. G. Wingren, *op. cit.,* pp. 5, 20, 116. *WA* 1, 20 f., and 3, 200 (1514).
[21]*WA* 40$^I$, 348 (1531).
[22]*WA* 40$^{III}$, 221 (1523-33).
[23]*WA* 50, 42 (1536).
[24]*The Bondage of the Will,* p. 206 *(WA* 18, 710).
[25]*WA* 39$^I$, 50 f. (1535).
[26]*The Bondage of the Will,* pp. 208 f. *(WA* 18, 712).
[27]*WA* 16, 447 (1524-27).
[28]*The Bondage of the Will,* pp. 316 f. *(WA* 18, 785).

## CHAPTER 2

[1]Emanuel Hirsch, *Luthers Gottesanschauung* (1918), p. 3.
[2]*Ibid.,* p. 5.
[3]Lennart Pinomaa, *Der Zorn Gottes* (Helsinki, 1938), p. 166. Cf. Aarne Siirala, *Gottes Gebot bei Martin Luther* (Helsinki, 1956), pp. 53 ff. On the subject of *Anfechtung,* see also, chapter 9, pp. 89-100, in this volume.
[4]L. Pinomaa, *op. cit.,* p. 115.
[5]*WA* 2, 98 (1518).
[6]E. Hirsch, *op. cit.,* pp. 8 ff.

## CHAPTER 3

[1]*WA,* Briefwechsel 8, 99 (1537). Hereafter referred to as *WA Br.*
[2]*Assertio omnium articulorum (WA* 7, 142 ff. [1520]).
[3]Cf. R. Bring, *Kristendomstolkningar* (1950), p. 208.
[4]*Ibid.,* p. 174.
[5]*Ibid.,* pp. 176 ff.
[6]*Ibid.,* pp. 205 ff.
[7]*The Bondage of the Will,* p. 203 *(WA* 18, 708).
[8]*Ibid.,* p. 204 *(WA* 18, 709).
[9]*Ibid.,* p. 208 *(WA* 18, 712).

[10]A. Runestam, "Inledning," *Martin Luther, Den trälbundna viljan* (Uppsala, 1925); and Torsten Bohlin, *Gudstro och Kristustro hos Luther* (Uppsala, 1927), p. 277.

[11]A. Nygren, *Agape and Eros* (London, 1939), II, 463 ff.

[12]*The Bondage of the Will*, p. 203 *(WA* 18, 708).

[13]*Ibid.*, p. 204 *(WA* 18, 709).

[14]*Ibid.*, p. 207 *(WA* 18, 712).

[15] R. Bring, *Dualismen hos Luther* (Stockholm, 1929), p. 291.

[16]*The Bondage of the Will*, p. 93 *(WA* 18, 626).

[17]*Ibid.*, pp. 103 f. *(WA* 18, 635).

[18]Lammers, *Luthers Anschauung vom Willen* (1935), p. 15.

[19]G. Aulén, *Den kristna gudsbilden* (Uppsala, 1927), p. 216.

[20]L. Pinomaa, *Der Zorn Gottes* (Helsinki, 1938), pp. 138-143.

## CHAPTER 4

[1]*WA* 7, 143 (1520).

[2]*The Bondage of the Will*, p. 137 *(WA* 18, 661).

[3]*Ibid.*, p. 140 *(WA* 18, 664).

[4]*Ibid.*, p. 201 *(WA* 18, 707).

[5]*Ibid.*, p. 278 *(WA* 18, 760).

[6]Cf. L. Pinomaa, "Järjen Jumala-kuva ja uskon Jumala-kuva," *Luther-tutkielmia* (Helsinki, 1939), p. 120.

[7]*The Bondage of the Will*, pp. 286 f. *(WA* 18, 766).

[8]*Ibid.*, p. 151 *(WA* 18, 672).

[9]*Ibid.*, p. 159 *(WA* 18, 677).

[10]*Ibid.*, p. 162 *(WA* 18, 679).

[11]*Ibid.*, p. 164 *(WA* 18, 681).

[12]*Ibid.*, p. 165 *(WA* 18, 681).

[13]*Ibid.*, p. 237 *(WA* 18, 733).

[14]*Ibid.*, p. 184 *(WA* 18, 695).

[15]*Ibid.*, p. 234 *(WA* 18, 731).

[16]*Ibid.*, p. 217 *(WA* 18, 719).

[17]*Ibid.*, p. 216 *(WA* 18, 718).

[18]*Ibid.*, p. 258 *(WA* 18, 747).

[19]*Ibid.*, p. 256 *(WA* 18, 746).

[20]*WA* Br. 8, 99 (1537).

[21]*The Bondage of the Will*, p. 317 *(WA* 18, 785).

## CHAPTER 5

[1]Gerhard Ritter, "Luthertum, katholisches und humanistisches Weltbild," *Zeitwende* (1946-47), pp. 67 f. Quoted by H. Zahrnt, *Luther deutet Geschichte* (Munich, 1952), p. 11.

[2]L. Pinomaa, *Der Zorn Gottes* (Helsinki, 1938), pp. 104 ff.

[3]*WA* 6, 261 (1520). *Works of Martin Luther,* (Philadelphia, 1943), II, 265-266. Hereafter referred to as *Works.*

[4]*WA* 50, 383 ff. (1538).

[5]*WA* 44, 467-472 (1545).

[6]L. Pinomaa, *op. cit.,* pp. 81 ff.

[7]The formulation is by H. Zahrnt, *(op. cit.,* pp. 20 f.), who makes reference to *WA* 19, 626; 42, 507; 18, 710.

[8]Zahrnt, pp. 23 ff.

[9]*WA* 19, 206 (1526).
[10]Zahrnt, *op. cit.,* pp. 25 ff.
[11]*Ibid.,* pp. 29 ff.
[12]*WA* 19, 154 (1526).
[13]L. Pinomaa, *op. cit.,* p. 115.
[14]L. Pinomaa, "Luomakunnan asema Lutherin teologiassa," *Talenta quinque* (Helsinki, 1953), pp. 228 ff.
[15]*WA* 10^I, ^2, 26 (1522).
[16]Cf. *supra,* chapter 1, pp. 1-11.
[17]E. Vogelsang, "Der Confessio-Begriff des jungen Luther," *Luther-Jahrbuch* (1930), p. 94.
[18]G. Wingren, *Luther on Vocation* (Philadelphia: Muhlenberg, 1957), p. 39.
[19]Cf. George W. Forell, *Faith Active in Love* (New York: American Press, 1954), pp. 136-139.
[20] G. Wingren, *op. cit.,* pp. 156 ff.
[21]*WA* 51, 212 (1535).
[22]Zahrnt, *op. cit.,* pp. 192 ff.

## CHAPTER 6

[1]E. Vogelsang, *Die Anfänge von Luthers Christologie* (Berlin, 1929), pp. 11 ff.
[2]*Ibid.,* pp. 16 ff.
[3]*Ibid.,* pp. 63 ff.
[4]*Ibid.,* pp. 88 ff.
[5]*Ibid.,* pp. 96 ff.
[6]*Ibid.,* pp. 105 ff.
[7]H. Bornkamm, *Luther's World of Thought* (St. Louis: Concordia, 1958), pp. 182 ff.
[8]E. Vogelsang, *op. cit.,* pp. 109 ff.
[9]H. Bornkamm, *op. cit.,* pp. 166 ff.
[10]*Ibid.,* p. 166.
[11]*Ibid.,* p. 148.
[12]*WA* 3, 542 (1513-15). Cf. E. Vogelsang, *op. cit.,* pp. 111 ff.
[13]*The Book of Concord,* ed. T. G. Tappert (Philadelphia: Muhlenberg, 1959), p. 414.
[14]R. Bring, *Dualismen hos Luther* (Stockholm, 1929), pp. 104 ff.
[15]*WA* 40^I, 438 (1531).
[16]E. Vogelsang, *Der angefochtene Christus bei Luther* (Berlin, 1932), p. 99.
[17]*WA* 10^{I,1}, 13-14. *LW* 35, 121.
[18]E. Vogelsang, *op. cit.,* pp. 100 ff.
[19]*WA* 40^I, 229 (1531).
[20]*WA* 50^I, 546 (1531).
[21]*WA* 12, 546 (1523). Cf. E. Vogelsang, *Christusglaube und Christusbekenntnis bei Luther* (Leipzig, 1935), p. 14.

## CHAPTER 7

[1]Anders Nygren, "Simul iustus et peccator hos Augustinus och Luther," *Filosofi och motivforskning* (1940), pp. 140, 147.
[2]Cf. R. Hermann, *Gerecht und Sünder zugleich* (Gütersloh, 1930); W. Joest, *Gesetz und Freiheit* (Göttingen, 1951); A. Gyllenkrok, *Rechtfertigung und Heiligung in der frühen evangelischen Theologie Luthers* (Uppsala, 1952).

[3]*WA* 56, 226 (1515).

[4]*WA* 56, 62 (1515).

[5]*WA* 40[II], 331 (1532).

[6]*WA* 5, 35 (1519); cf. *WA* 16, 296 (1525).

[7]*WA* 28, 173, 175 (1528).

[8]*WA* 40[I], 312 (1531).

[9]*WA* 56, 258 (1515).

[10]R. Hermann, "Luthers These 'Gerecht und Sünder zugleich,' " *Zeitschrift für systematische Theologie* (1928), p. 310.

[11]*WA* 40[II], 352, 354 f. (1532).

[12]*WA* 40[II], 353 (1532).

[13]*WA* 56, 350 (1515-16). Cf. *WA* 56, 346; R. Hermann, *Luthers These,* p. 282, and the same author's *Gerecht und Sünder zugleich* (Gütersloh, 1930), pp. 22 f.

[14]*WA* 56, 343 (1515-16).

[15]*WA* 50, 599 (1539). *Works,* 234.

[16]*WA* 47, 671-673 (1539).

[17]R. Prenter, *Spiritus Creator* (Philadelphia: Muhlenberg, 1953), p. 59.

[18]A. Siirala, *Gottes Gebot bei Martin Luther* (Helsinki, 1956), pp. 137, 330.

[19]E. Vogelsang, *Der angefochtene Christus bei Luther* (Berlin, 1932), p. 4. On the subject of *Anfechtung* see also chapter 9, pp. 89-100, in this volume.

[20]*WA* 3, 46 (1513-15). Cf. L. Pinomaa, "Die profectio bei Luther," *Werner Elert-Gedenkschrift* (1955), pp. 119-127 and *Die Heiligung in Luthers Frühtheologie* (Helsinki, 1959).

[21]*WA* 4, 400 (1513-15).

[22]*WA* 4, 320 (1513-15).

[23]R. Prenter, *op. cit.,* p. 39.

[24]*WA* 40[I], 293 (1531).

[25]*WA* 40[I], 230 (1531).

[26]R. Prenter, *op. cit.,* pp. 69 f. and *Der barmherzige Richter* (Copenhagen, 1961), pp. 140-148.

[27]*WA* 40[I], 368 (1531).

[28]*WA* 50, 599 (1539).

[29]*WA* 40[II], 351 (1531).

[30]*WA* 40[II], 351 (1531).

[31]*WA* 45, 615 (1538).

[32]A. Siirala, *op. cit.,* pp. 82 ff., 304 ff.

[33]*WA* 40[I], 69 (1531).

[34]L. Fendt, *Luthers Schule der Heiligung* (Leipzig, 1929), pp. 14 f.

[35]Cf. R. Bring, *Gesetz und Evangelium und der dritte Gebrauch des Gesetzes in der Theologie Luthers* (Helsinki, 1943), pp. 48 ff. and R. Prenter, *Spiritus Creator* (Philadelphia: Muhlenberg, 1953), p. 83.

[36]Cf. L. Pinomaa, *Der Zorn Gottes* (Helsinki, 1938), pp. 30 ff.

[37]A. Siirala, *op. cit.,* pp. 272 ff.

[38]*WA* 56, 408 (1516).

[39]Cf. A. Siirala, *op. cit.,* p. 92; and L. Haikola, *Usus legis* (Helsinki, 1958).

[40]R. Bring, *Dualismen hos Luther* (Stockholm, 1929), pp. 154 ff.; by the same author, *Gesetz und Evangelium* (1943); and L.Pinomaa, *Der existenzielle Charakter der Theologie Luthers* (Helsinki, 1940), pp. 155. ff.

[41]*WA* 5, 408 (1520).

[42]*WA* 8, 355 (1521). Cf. *WA* 10[I,1], 99 (1522).

[43]*WA* 39[I], 46 (1535).

[44]Cf. *supra,* chapter 3, pp. 20-26.

[45]*WA* 10[I,1], 107 (1522).

[46]*WA* 10^{III}, 5 (1522).
[47]Cf. Matt. 25:31-46; Rom. 2:6; 15:18; I Cor. 3:12 f.; Gal. 6:4; I John 3:17 f.; and James 2:17.


## CHAPTER 8

[1]*WA* 4, 95 (1514-15). Cf. L. Pinomaa, *Der existenzielle Charakter der Theologie Luthers* (Helsinki, 1940), p. 85.
[2]R. Prenter, *Spiritus Creator* (Philadelphia: Muhlenberg, 1953), p. 44.
[3]*Ibid.*, pp. 47 ff. Cf. A. Siirala, *Gottes Gebot bei Martin Luther* (Helsinki, 1956), pp. 53-61.
[4]R. Prenter, *op. cit.*, pp. 247 ff.
[5]*Ibid.*, pp. 251 ff.
[6]*Ibid.*, pp. 255 ff.
[7]*Ibid.*, p. 262.
[8]*Ibid.*, pp. 266 ff.
[9]*Ibid.*, pp. 273 ff.
[10]*Ibid.*, pp. 277 ff.
[11]*Ibid.*, pp. 282 ff.


## CHAPTER 9

[1]Hausrath, *Luthers Leben* (Berlin, 1913), I, 2. Cf. *WA* 10^{I,1}, 372 (1522).
[2]N. Söderblom, *Humor och melankoli* (1919), pp. 129 ff; Hausrath, *op. cit.*, pp. 31 ff.; K. Holl, *Gesammelte Aufsätze* (Tübingen, 1932), I, 68.
[3]K. Holl, *op. cit.*, p. 67. E. Vogelsang, *Der angefochtene Christus* (Berlin, 1932), pp. 10 ff.
[4]*Ibid.*, p. 4.
[5]*WA* 30^{I}, 49 (1528).
[6]K. Holl, *op. cit.*, p. 34. *WA* 22, 168. *WA* TR. 2, 1351 (1532), 5, 5897. E. Wolf, *Staupitz und Luther* (Leipzig, 1927), pp. 152 ff. E. Vogelsang, *op. cit.*, pp. 15, 17, 31.
[7]E. Vogelsang, *op. cit.*, p. 14. *WA* 40^{III}, 541 (1534).
[8]E. Vogelsang, *op. cit.*, pp. 18, 25 ff. Cf. *WA* 40^{I}, 558 (1531).
[9]*WA* 1, 557 (1518). Cf. L. Pinomaa, *Der Zorn Gottes* (Helsinki, 1938), pp. 8 f.
[10]*WA* 10^{I,2}, 27 (1522).
[11]G. Jacob, *Der Gewissensbegriff in der Theologie Luthers* (Tübingen, 1929), pp. 23 ff.
[12]*WA* 5, 209 (1520).
[13]*Ibid.*
[14]WA 10^{I,2}, 105 (1522).
[15]K. Holl, *op. cit.*, pp. 68 ff. Cf. E. Vogelsang, *op. cit.*, pp. 26 ff.
[16]*WA* 44, 99 (1544).
[17]*WA* 1, 557 (1518); 16, 459 (1525); 25, 232 (1528).
[18]*WA* TR, 1, No. 141 (1531).
[19]*WA* 44, 100 (1544).
[20]*WA* 1, 75 (1516).
[21]*WA* 1, 159 (1517).
[22]*WA* 5, 204 (1520).
[23]*WA* 5, 204 (1520). Cf. E. Vogelsang, *op. cit.*, p. 62.
[24]*WA* 5, 204 (1520).
[25]*WA* 5, 166 (1520).

[26]*WA* 5, 346 (1520).
[27]*WA* 5, 171 (1520).
[28]*WA* 2, 693 (1519).
[29]*WA* 2, 694 (1519). The "sign" has reference to the elements of the Lord's Supper.
[30]Especially Luther's larger *Commentary on Galatians.*
[31]E. Vogelsang, *op. cit.,* pp. 52 ff.
[32]*WA* 5, 86 (1519).
[33]*Ibid.*
[34]*WA* 5, 606 (1521).
[35]E. Vogelsang, *op. cit.,* pp. 53 ff.
[36]*Ibid.,* p. 56.
[37]*Ibid.,* p. 54.
[38]*Ibid.,* p. 82.
[39]*WA* 40$^I$, 439 (1531). Cf. *supra,* pp. 55-57.
[40]*WA* 40$^I$, 282, 235, 585 (1531).
[41]*WA* 40$^{II}$, 31 (1531).
[42]E. Vogelsang, *op. cit.,* pp. 31 ff.
[43]*WA* 56, 382 (1516).
[44]*WA* 2, 688 (1519).
[45]*WA* 56, 386 (1516).
[46]*WA* 56, 402 (1516).
[47]*WA* 5, 619 (1521).
[48]*WA* 44, 97 (1535-45).
[49]*The Bondage of the Will,* p. 217 *(WA* 18, 719). Cf. *WA* 5, 172 (1519).
[50]*WA* 5, 622 (1521).
[51]See note 46.
[52]*WA* 56, 387 (1516).
[53]*WA* 2, 690 (1519).
[54]*WA* 5, 387 (1520-21).
[55]*WA* 5, 172 (1519).
[56]*Ibid.*
[57]*WA* 5, 173 (1519).
[58]*WA* 5, 622 (1521). Cf. *WA* Br. 4, 590 (1528).
[59]Cf. L. Pinomaa, *op. cit.,* pp. 153-182.

## CHAPTER 10

[1]*WA* 10$^{III}$, 15 (1522). *LW* 51, 76.
[2]*Ibid.*
[3]*WA* 10$^{III}$, 16 (1522). *LW* 51, 77.
[4]*WA* 10$^{III}$, 18 (1522). *LW* 51, 77.
[5]Cf. G. Ljunggren, "Paradoxen som teologiskt uttrycksmedel," *Svensk Teologisk Kvartalskrift* (1928), pp. 333 ff.
[6]R. Prenter, *Spiritus Creator* (Philadelphia: Muhlenberg, 1953), p. 106.
[7]R. Prenter, *op. cit.,* pp. 106-114.
[8]*WA* 10$^{I,1}$, 626 (1522).
[9]R. Prenter, *op. cit.,* p. 116.
[10]E. Wolf, "Die Christus Verkündigung bei Luther," *Jesus Christus im Zeugnis der Heiligen Schrift und der Kirche* (Munich, 1936), pp. 182 ff. Quoted in R. Prenter, *Spiritus Creator* (Copenhagen, 1946), p. 130.
[11]R. Prenter, *op. cit.,* pp. 115-122.

## CHAPTER 11

[1]H. Bornkamm, *Luther's World of Thought* (St. Louis: Concordia, 1958), pp. 134-140.
[2]*Ibid.*, pp. 141 f.
[3]Fr. Heiler, *Der Katholizismus* (Munich, 1933).
[4]H. Fagerberg, "Die Kirche in Luthers Psalmenvorlesungen 1513-1515," *Elert-Gedenkschrift* (1955), pp. 109 f.
[5]P. Althaus, *Communio sanctorum* (Munich, 1929), I, 27 ff.
[6]*The Book of Concord,* ed. T. G. Tappert (Philadelphia: Muhlenberg, 1959), p. 305.
[7]*Ibid.*, p. 309.
[8]*Ibid.*
[9]*Ibid.*, p. 298.
[10]*WA* 40$^I$, 584, 194 (1531).
[11]*WA* 40$^{II}$, 96 (1531).
[12]*WA* 40$^{II}$, 101 (1531).
[13]*The Bondage of the Will,* p. 123 *(WA* 18, 652).
[14]*WA* 10$^{III}$, 408 (1522).
[15]*Large Catechism,* Third Article.
[16]*Ibid.*
[17]*Works* V, pp. 131-300.
[18]A. Nygren, "Corpus Christi," *This Is the Church* (1952), p. 13. R. Bring, "The Subjective and the Objective in the Concept of the Church," *This Is the Church* (1952), p. 211.
[19]L. P. Tapaninen, *Lutherin kirkkonäkemys* (Helsinki, 1942), pp. 24 f. G. Aulén, *Till belysning av den lutherska kyrkoidén* (Stockholm, 1912), p. 24.
[20]*WA* 10$^{I,1}$, 140 (1522).
[21]*WA* 7, 721 (1521).
[22]H. Bornkamm, *op. cit.,* pp. 95 f.
[23]*WA* 50, 647 (1539).
[24]*WA* 50, 628. *Works of Martin Luther* (Philadelphia, 1915-1943), V, pp. 269 f. Hereafter referred to as *Works.*
[25]*WA* 40$^I$, 69 (1531).
[26]*WA* 40$^I$, 197 (1531).
[27]*WA* 40$^{II}$, 88, 107 (1531).
[28]*WA* 2, 756 (1519). *LW* 35,70.
[29]P. Althaus, *op. cit.,* pp. 39 ff.

## CHAPTER 12

[1]*Supra,* pp. 111-112.
[2]V. Vajta, *Luther on Worship* (Philadelphia: Muhlenberg, 1958), pp. 109 ff.
[3]*WA* 6, 407 (1520). *Works,* II, p. 66.
[4]*Ibid.*
[5]*WA* 2, 454 (1519).
[6]*WA* 6, 408 (1520). *Works,* II, p. 68. Cf. *WA* 6, 566 (1520); *LW* 36, 116.
[7]*WA* 6, 409 (1520). *Works,* II, p. 69.
[8]*WA* 6, 441 (1520). *Works,* II, p. 120.
[9]See note 2. Also G. Hök, "Luther's Doctrine of the Ministry," *Scottish Journal of Theology* (1954), pp. 16 ff.
[10]H. Brunotte, *Das geistliche Amt bei Luther* (Göttingen, 1959), p. 10.
[11]*Ibid.*, p. 13.
[12]*Ibid.*, p. 21.

[13]Hök, *op. cit.,* p. 21.
[14]*Ibid.*
[15]*WA* 6, 507 (1520). *LW* 36, 21.
[16]*WA* 6, 546 (1520). *LW* 36, 87.
[17]*WA* 6, 566 (1520). *LW* 36, 116.
[18]Brunotte, *op. cit.,* p. 51.
[19]*Ibid.,* p. 56.
[20]*Ibid.,* p. 68.
[21]*Ibid.,* pp. 112-116.
[22]*WA* 30[I], 498 (1530). *LW* 40, 365 f.
[23]*WA* 30[II], 472 (1530). *LW* 40, 333.
[24]*WA* 30[II], 472 (1530). *LW* 40, 334.
[25]Hök, *op. cit.,* p. 26.

# CHAPTER 13

[1]W. Jetter, *Die Taufe beim jungen Luther* (Tübingen, 1954), pp. 1 ff.
[2]*Ibid.,* pp. 58 ff.
[3]*Ibid.,* pp. 109 ff.
[4]*Ibid.,* p. 127.
[5]Cf. L. Pinomaa, *Der existenzielle Charakter der Theologie Luthers* (Helsinki, 1940), pp. 143 ff.
[6]W. Jetter, *op. cit.,* pp. 175 ff.
[7]*Ibid.,* pp. 258 ff.
[8]*WA* 2, 728 (1519). *LW* 35, 30.
[9]*Ibid.*
[10]*WA* 2, 729 (1519). *LW* 35, 32.
[11]*WA* 2, 730 (1519). *LW* 35, 33 f.
[12]*WA* 2, 731 (1519). *LW* 35, 34.
[13]*WA* 6, 518 (1520). *LW* 36, 44.
[14]*WA* 6, 526 (1520). *LW* 36, 57.
[15]*WA* 6, 530 (1520). *LW* 36, 62.
[16]*WA* 6, 530 (1520). *LW* 36, 62.
[17]R. Josefson, *Luthers lära om dopet* (Stockholm, 1943), pp. 14 ff.
[18]*WA* 57[III], 232 (1518).
[19]*WA* 6, 533 (1520). *LW* 36, 67.
[20]*WA* 6, 534 (1520). *LW* 36, 68.
[21]*WA* 36, 98 (1532).
[22]*WA* 6, 354 (1520). *LW* 35, 81.
[23]*WA* 6, 359 (1520). *LW* 35, 86.
[24]*WA* 6, 359 (1520). *LW* 35, 87.
[25]*WA* 6, 359 (1520). *LW* 35, 86.
[26]*WA* 6, 365 (1520). *LW* 35, 94.
[27]*WA* 6, 366 (1520). *LW* 35, 96.
[28]Cf. *supra,* p. 83.
[29]V. Vajta, *op. cit.,* pp. 112 f.

# CHAPTER 14

[1]H. Gerdes, *Luthers Streit mit den Schwärmern um das rechte Verständnis des Gesetzes Mose* (Göttingen, 1955), pp. 24 ff.
[2]Cf. *supra,* chapter 1, pp. 1-11.
[3]H. Steinlein, "Luther und das Alte Testament," *Luthertum* (1937), pp. 178 f.

[4]A. Siirala, *Gottes Gebot bei Martin Luther* (Helsinki, 1956), pp. 75, **131 f.**
[5]*Ibid.*, pp. 136 ff.
[6]R. Bring, *Förhållandet mellan tro och gärningar inom luthersk teologi* (Åbo, 1933), pp. 3 ff.
[7]*WA* 19, 629 (1526). *Works,* V, p. 39.
[8]*WA* 47, 853 (1539).
[9]F. Lau, *Luthers Lehre von den beiden Reichen* (Berlin, 1953), pp. 21 ff.
[10]G. Törnvall, *Andligt och Världsligt regemente hos Luther* (1940), p. 39.
[11]*WA* 11, 265 (1523). *Works,* III, p. 255.
[12]*WA* 11, 263, (1523). *Works,* III, p. 252.
[13]*WA* 11, 271 (1523). *Works,* III, p. 262.
[14]J. Heckel, *Im Irrgarten der Zwei-Reiche-Lehre* (Munich, 1957), pp. 5 ff.
[15]L. Pinomaa, *Jumalan valtakunta ja maallinen yhteisö* (1941), pp. 41 ff.
[16]J. Heckel, *Lex charitatis* (Munich, 1953), pp. 31 ff.; and *Im Irrgarten der Zwei-Reiche-Lehre,* pp. 6 ff. Cf. Althaus, "Die beiden Regimente bei Luther," *Theologische Literatur-Zeitung* (1956), pp. 129 ff. and "Luthers Lehre von den beiden Reichen im Feuer der Kritik," *Luther-Jahrbuch* (1957), pp. 40 ff. Cf. also E. Kinder, "Gottesreich und Weltreich bei Augustin und Luther," *Elert-Gedenkschrift* (1955), p. 32.
[17]*WA* 20, 555 (1526). Cf. H. Jordan, *Luthers Staatsauffassung* (Munich, 1917), p. 34.
[18]*WA* 36, 385 (1532). Cf. *WA* 20, 530.
[19]G. Törnvall, *op. cit.,* pp. 28 ff. Cf. Lau, *op. cit.,* p. 34.
[20]Lau, pp. 34 ff., 38.
[21]*WA* 11, 251 (1523). *Works,* III, pp. 236 f.
[22]A. Nygren, "The State and the Church," *This Is the Church* (Philadelphia: Muhlenberg, 1952), p. 299.
[23]H. Jordan, *op. cit.,* pp. 28 f.
[24]*Infra,* chapter 17, pp. 179-189.
[25]R. Bring, "Der Glaube und das Recht nach Luther," *Elert-Gedenkschrift* (1955).
[26]*Ibid.,* p. 152.

## CHAPTER 15

[1]O. Lähteenmäki, *Sexus und Ehe bei Luther* (Turku, 1955), pp. 25 ff.
[2]*Ibid.,* pp. 30 f.
[3]*WA* 30[I], 163 (1529).
[4]O. Castren, "Naimattomuuden ja avioliiton ongelmasta katolisessa ja evankelisessa etiikassa," *Teologinen Aikakauskirja* (1957), pp. 246 f.
[5]O. Lähteenmäki, *op. cit.,* pp. 32 ff.
[6]*Ibid.,* pp. 43 f.
[7]*WA* DB. 7, 12 (1522).
[8]L. Pinomaa, *Der Zorn Gottes* (Helsinki, 1938), pp. 66 ff. and *Der existenzielle Charakter der Theologie Luthers* (Helsinki, 1940), pp. 37 f. Cf. O. Lähteenmäki, *op. cit.,* pp. 46 ff.
[9]Cf. *LW* 1, 116 f.
[10]O. Lähteenmäki, *op. cit.,* pp. 48 ff.
[11]*WA* 10[1,1], 707 (1522).
[12]O. Lähteenmäki, *op. cit.,* pp. 51 ff.
[13]*WA* 2, 167.
[14]O. Lähteenmäki, pp. 54 ff. Cf. L. Pinomaa, "Luomakunnan asema Lutherin teologiassa," *Talenta quinque* (Helsinki, 1953), p. 229.

## CHAPTER 16

[1]G. Törnvall, *Andligt och världsligt regemente hos Luther* (1940), p. 73.
[2]G. Wingren, *Luther on Vocation* (Philadelphia: Muhlenberg, 1957), p. 27.
[3]*Ibid.,* p. 31.
[4]*Ibid.,* pp. 37 ff.
[5]*Ibid.,* p. 154.
[6]L. Pinomaa, "Luomakunnan asema Lutherin teologiassa," *Talenta quinque* (Helsinki, 1953), p. 229.
[7]G. Wingren, *op. cit.,* pp. 48 ff.
[8]*WA* 8, 588 (1521).
[9]*WA* 32, 510 (1532). *LW* 21, 255.
[10]G. Wingren, *op. cit.,* pp. 172 ff.
[11]*WA* 10[I,1], 322 (1522). Quoted by G. Wingren, *op. cit.,* pp. 176 ff.
[12]Quoted by G. Wingren, *op. cit.,* p. 178.
[13]Wingren, p. 180.
[14]*Ibid.,* p. 177.
[15]*Ibid.,* pp. 181 ff.

## CHAPTER 17

[1]*WA* 23, 514 (1527). Cf. *WA* 23, 9 (1527).
[2]*WA* 30[II], 578 (1530).
[3]*WA* 50, 652 (1539).
[4]*WA* 19, 628 (1525). *Works,* V, p. 38.
[5]*WA* 8, 51 (1521). *LW* 32, 149.
[6]*WA* 19, 626 (1525). *Works,* V, p. 36.
[7]*WA* 18, 293 (1525). *Works,* IV, pp. 220 f.
[8]*WA* 18, 294, 299 (1525). *Works,* IV, pp. 221, 224.
[9]*WA* 18, 303 (1525). *Works,* IV, pp. 226 f.
[10]*WA* 18, 305 (1525). *Works,* IV, pp. 227 f.
[11]*WA* 18, 308 (1525). *Works,* IV, p. 230.
[12]*WA* 18, 310 (1525). *Works,* IV, pp. 230 f.
[13]*WA* 18, 400 (1525). *Works,* IV, p. 280.
[14]Niels Nojgaard, *Martin Luther* (Copenhagen, 1945), pp. 173 ff. Cf. H. Zahrnt, *Luther deutet Geschichte* (Munich, 1952), pp. 68 ff.
[15]*WA* 10[III], 15 (1522). *LW* 51, 76.
[16]Cf. *supra,* pp. 41 f.

# Translator's Bibliography

(Additional books and articles on Luther's life and thought.)

Bainton, Roland H. *Here I Stand: A Life of Martin Luther.* Nashville: Abingdon-Cokesbury, 1950.

———. "Luther and the *Via Media* at the Marburg Colloquy," *Lutheran Quarterly,* I (November, 1949), 394.

———. "Luther's Simple Faith," *Luther Today.* Martin Luther Lectures, Vol. 1. Decorah, Iowa: Luther College Press, 1956.

———. "Luther's Struggle for Faith," *Church History, XVII* (September, 1948), 193.

Baughman, Harry. "Martin Luther the Preacher," *Lutheran Church Quarterly,* XXI (January, 1948), 21.

Bergendoff, Conrad. "Christian Love and Public Policy in Luther," *Lutheran Quarterly,* XIII (August, 1961), 218.

———. "Church and State in the Reformation Period," *Lutheran Church Quarterly,* III (January, 1930), 36.

Berner, Carl W. "The Word Principle in Martin Luther," *Concordia Theological Monthly,* XIX (January, 1948), 13.

Boehmer, Heinrich. *Road to Reformation.* Translated by John W. Doberstein and Theodore G. Tappert. Philadelphia: Muhlenberg Press. 1946.

Brunner, Peter. "Luther and the World of the Twentieth Century," *Luther in the Twentieth Century.* Martin Luther Lectures, Vol. 5. Decorah, Iowa: Luther College Press, 1960.

Carlson, Edgar M. "Luther's Conception of Government," *Church History,* XV (December, 1946), 257.

———. *The Reinterpretation of Luther.* Philadelphia: Westminster Press, 1948.

Carlson, Oscar. "Luther's Conception of Government," *Church History,* XV (December, 1946), 261.

Cranz, Ferdinand E. *An Essay on the Development of Luther's Thought on Justice, Law, and Society.* Cambridge: Harvard University Press, 1959.

Dallmann, William. "Henry the Eighth's Divorce and Luther," *Concordia Theological Monthly,* XVIII (February, 1947), 81; (March), 161.

———. *Martin Luther, His Life and His Labor.* St. Louis: Concordia Publishing House, 1951.

Dillenberger, John. *God Hidden and Revealed: The Interpretation of Luther's Deus Absconditus and its Significance for Religious Thought.* Philadelphia: Muhlenberg Press, 1953.

Evjen, John O. "Luther's Ideas Concerning Church Polity," *Lutheran Church Review,* XLV (July, 1926), 207; (October), 339.

Fife, Robert H. *Young Luther: The Intellectual and Religious Development of Martin Luther to 1518.* New York: Macmillan Co., 1928.

Forell, George W. *Faith Active in Love.* Minneapolis: Augsburg Publishing House, 1960.

———. "Luther and Politics," *Luther and Culture.* Martin Luther Lectures, Vol. 4. Decorah, Iowa: Luther College Press, 1959.

———. "Luther and the War Against the Turks," *Church History,* XIV (December, 1945), 256.

———. "Luther's Conception of 'Natural Orders,'" *Lutheran Church Quarterly,* XVIII (April, 1945), 160.

———. "Luther's View Concerning Imperial Foreign Policy," *Lutheran Quarterly,* IV (May, 1952), 153.

Green, Lowell C. "Luther and Melanchthon," *The Mature Luther*. Martin Luther Lectures, Vol. 3. Decorah, Iowa: Luther College Press, 1958.

———. "Resistance to Authority and Luther," *Lutheran Quarterly*, VI (November, 1954), 338.

Grimm, Harold J. "Luther and Education," *Luther and Culture*. Martin Luther Lectures, Vol. 4. Decorah, Iowa: Luther College Press, 1959.

———. "Luther, Luther's Critics, and the Peasant Revolt," *Lutheran Church Quarterly*, XIX (April, 1946), 115.

———. "Luther's Conception of Territorial and National Loyalty," *Church History*, XVII (June, 1948), 79.

———. *The Reformation Era*. New York: Macmillan Co., 1954.

Hall, George F. "Luther's Eschatology," *Augustana Quarterly*, XXIII (January, 1944), 13.

———. "Luther's Preface to the Old Testament Apocryphal Books," *Augustana Quarterly*, XIII (July, 1934), 195.

———. "Luther's Standards of Canonicity," *Augustana Quarterly*, XV (October, 1936), 299.

Heick, Otto W. "Luther on War," *Augustana Quarterly*, XXVII (October, 1948), 323.

Heinecken, Martin J. "Luther and the 'Orders of Creation' in Relation to a Doctrine of Works and Vocation," *Lutheran Quarterly*, IV (November, 1952), 393.

Hoelty-Nickel, Theo. "Luther and Music," *Luther and Culture*. Martin Luther Lectures, Vol. 4. Decorah, Iowa: Luther College Press, 1959.

Holm, Bernard J. "The American Image of Luther," *Luther in the Twentieth Century*. Martin Luther Lectures, Vol. 5. Decorah, Iowa: Luther College Press, 1960.

Holmio, Armas K. "Luther and War," *Lutheran Quarterly*, IV (August, 1952), 261.

Kooiman, Willem J. *By Faith Alone: The Life of Martin Luther*. New York: Philosophical Library, 1955.

———. "Luther's Later Years," *The Mature Luther*. Martin Luther Lectures, Vol. 3. Decorah, Iowa: Luther College Press, 1958.

Kramm, H. H. W. *The Theology of Martin Luther*. London: J. Clarke, 1947.

Krodel, Gottfried G. "The Lord's Supper in the Theology of the Young Luther," *Lutheran Quarterly*, XIII (February, 1961), 19.

Kukkonen, Walter J. "The Problem of Sin in the Light of Finnish Luther Research," *Augustana Quarterly*, XXV (April, 1946), 121.

Lazareth, William H. *Luther on the Christian Home*. Philadelphia: Muhlenberg Press, 1960.

Lilje, Hans. *Luther Now*. Translated by Carl J. Schindler. Philadelphia: Muhlenberg Press, 1952.

McNeill, John T. "Natural Law in the Thought of Luther," *Church History*, X (December, 1941).

Mattes, John C. "Luther's Views Concerning Continence: A Correction of Some Current Misrepresentations," *Lutheran Church Quarterly*, IV (October, 1931), 409.

Mayer, F. E. "The *Una Sancta* in Luther's Theology," *Concordia Theological Monthly*, XVIII (November, 1947), 801.

Mueller, John T. "Notes on Luther's Conception of the Word of God as the Means of Grace," *Concordia Theological Monthly*, XX (August, 1949), 580.

Mueller, William A. *Church and State in Luther and Calvin*. Nashville: Broadman Press, 1954.

Nettl, Paul. *Luther and Music.* Translated by Frida Best and Ralph Wood. Philadelphia: Muhlenberg Press, 1948.

Pauck, Wilhelm. "Luther and the Reformation," *Theology Today,* III (October, 1946), 314.

―――. "Martin Luther's Faith," *Religion in Life,* XVI (Winter, 1946-47), 3.

Pelikan, Jaroslav J. *From Luther to Kierkegaard.* St. Louis: Concordia Publishing House, 1950.

―――. "Luther and the Liturgy," *More About Luther.* Martin Luther Lectures, Vol. 2. Decorah, Iowa: Luther College Press, 1957.

―――. *Luther the Expositor.* St. Louis: Concordia Publishing House, 1959.

―――. "Luther's Attitude Toward John Huss," *Concordia Theological Monthly,* (1948).

Plass, E. M. *This Is Luther.* St. Louis: Concordia Publishing House, 1948.

Prenter, Regin. "Luther on Word and Sacrament," *More About Luther.* Martin Luther Lectures, Vol. 2. Decorah, Iowa: Luther College Press, 1957.

Preus, Herman A. "The Christian and the Church," *More About Luther.* Martin Luther Lectures, Vol. 2. Decorah, Iowa: Luther College Press, 1957.

―――. *The Communion of Saints.* Minneapolis: Augsburg Publishing House, 1948.

Quanbeck, Warren A. "Biblical Interpretation in Luther's Early Studies," *Lutheran Quarterly,* I (August, 1949), 287.

―――. "Luther's Early Exegesis," *Luther Today.* Martin Luther Lectures, Vol. 1. Decorah, Iowa: Luther College Press, 1956.

Reu, J. M. *Luther and the Scriptures.* Columbus: Wartburg Press, 1944.

Rohr, John von. "The Sources of Luther's Self-Despair in the Monastery," *Journal of Bible and Religion* (1951).

Rupp, E. Gordon. "Luther and the Puritans," *Luther Today.* Martin Luther Lectures, Vol. 1. Decorah, Iowa; Luther College Press, 1956.

―――. *The Righteousness of God.* New York: Philosophical Library, 1953.

Saarnivaara, Uuras. "The Church of Christ According to Luther," *Lutheran Quarterly,* V (May, 1953), 134.

―――. *Luther Discovers the Gospel.* St. Louis: Concordia Publishing House, 1951.

Sasse, Hermann. *This Is My Body.* Minneapolis: Augsburg Publishing House, 1959.

Schwiebert, Ernest G. *Luther and His Times.* St. Louis: Concordia Publishing House, 1950.

―――. "The Medieval Pattern in Luther's Views of the State," *Church History,* XII (June, 1943), 98.

Smend, Friedrich. "Luther and Bach," *Lutheran Quarterly,* I (November, 1949), 399.

Spitz, Lewis W. "Luther's Ecclesiology and His Concept of the Prince as *Notbischof,*" *Church History,* XXII (June, 1953), 113.

Stevenson, R. "Luther's Musical Achievement," *Lutheran Quarterly,* III (August, 1951), 255.

Tappert, Theodore G. "Luther in His Academic Role," *The Mature Luther.* Martin Luther Lectures, Vol. 3. Decorah, Iowa: Luther College Press, 1958.

Tillmann, W. G. *The World and Men Around Luther.* Minneapolis: Augsburg Publishing House, 1960.

Vajta, Vilmos. *Luther on Worship.* Philadelphia: Muhlenberg Press, 1958.

―――. (ed.) *Luther and Melanchthon.* Philadelphia: Muhlenberg Press, 1961.

Watson, Philip S. *Let God Be God.* Philadelphia: Muhlenberg Press, 1949.

―――. *The State as a Servant of God.* London: Society for Promoting Christian Knowledge, 1946.

Wentz, Abdel Ross. "Luther and Modern Business," *Lutheran Church Quarterly,* VII (January, 1934), 41.

Wentz, Frederick K. "The Development of Luther's Views on Church Organization," *Lutheran Quarterly,* VII (August, 1955), 217.

# Index of Names and Subjects

*Type used in this book*

Body, 11 on 13 and 9 on 10 Garamond.
Display, Bodoni Modern.
Paper: "R" Standard White Antique.